P95.8 COM

Communicating Pol...

KU-573-804

Communicating Politics

Mass communications and the political process

edited by
PETER GOLDING
GRAHAM MURDOCK
and
PHILIP SCHLESINGER

1986
Leicester University Press

First published in 1986 by Leicester University Press
First published in the United States of America 1986 by
Holmes & Meier Publishers, Inc.
Copyright © Leicester University Press 1986

Designed by Geoffrey Wadsley
Photoset in Linotron 101 Palatino
Printed and bound in Great Britain at the Bath Press, Avon

British Library Cataloguing in Publication Data

Communicating politics: mass communications
and the political process.
1. Mass media – Political aspects
I. Golding, Peter   II. Murdock, Graham
III. Schlesinger, Philip
302.2'34   P95.8

ISBN 0–7185–1253–7
ISBN 0–7185–1301–0 Pbk

To the memory of
Philip Ross Courtney Elliott, 1943–1983
Friend, colleague, scholar

Contents

Part Three   Reporting the State and the State of Reporting

Introduction

This book has been produced as a tribute to Philip Elliott who died in 1983, aged 40, after a distinguished but tragically foreshortened career in mass communication research. The contributors all either worked with him or in fields to which he made a notable contribution.

Philip Elliott spent his entire professional life at the Centre for Mass Communication Research at Leicester University. He joined the Research Unit of the Television Research Committee, the embryo which became the Centre, as a Research Officer in 1966. Typically of his lifelong love of boats, his application came from his then postal address, a houseboat on a canal south of Manchester.

After taking his degree in Politics, Philosophy and Economics at Oxford, Philip had gone to the sociology department at Manchester. It was there that he added a sociological imagination to his fascination with political institutions and processes. It was at Manchester, too, that he came across two bodies of work that he was later to apply so inventively to the analysis of mass media: social anthropology, and more especially the concepts of ritual and symbol; and the sociology of occupations. His postgraduate thesis on professional education became the basis for his first solo book, *The Sociology of the Professions*.

At Leicester Philip developed his interest in the ideologies and practices of the professions by focusing on the esoteric and culturally complex world of the 'communicators'. It was while he was visiting Nigeria in 1971 for the preparatory stages of a comparative study of broadcast journalism that the first signs of severe illness became apparent. In a labelling process, the irony of which did not escape him in later days,

1

Philip endured fruitless searches for tropical infection, but the devastating truth, that he had a rare and unpredictable form of leukaemia, emerged only slowly.

In the ensuing 12 years he worked with quite extraordinary courage and commitment despite recurrent hospitalization, punitive medication and much pain. He remained a stimulating and generous colleague, and a patient and much-respected teacher. Against appalling odds he continued to produce a range of original, lucid and penetrating papers which cumulatively performed a major creative role in establishing mass communication research in Britain. As a member of the Communication and Cultural Studies Board of the Council for National Academic Awards from 1974 to 1982, and its chair in 1981 to 1982, he also made a substantial administrative contribution to the development of communication studies outside the universities.

But Philip will probably be best remembered for his pioneering work in the sociology of journalistic production. At the very outset of his professional research career, in his monograph *The Making of a Television Series* he developed an analysis which has since exercised a profound influence on others in the field. Combining his sociological interest in occupations with a broader anthropological sensitivity to how culture is produced and maintained, Elliott focused on the way a current affairs series on prejudice was put together. His study uncovered the shared assumptions at work in television's relatively closed world, its rules of thumb in production, the mechanisms of control and information flow, and how television producers deal with their audiences. He explored these themes further the following year in the collaborative study *Demonstrations and Communication*, producing an acute sketch of the workings of the television newsroom.

Elliott used television journalism as a way of analysing the more general question of how mass culture is produced, and the consequent problem of meaningful communication. Although his work in those two early studies was mainly concerned with the transfer of meaning as a purely cognitive process, he was well aware of its necessarily symbolic, non-cognitive aspects. The construction of social meanings, he argued, cannot be adequately assessed in terms of some pure correspondence with 'the facts', or otherwise understood merely as a distortion of 'the real'. Rather, in a term which he first introduced to the field, the mass media should be conceived of as constructing and continually modifying a 'media culture', a complex set of shared significances, which are crucially shaped by the dominant political, economic and cultural forces, in society mediated through professional routines. In retrospect, the themes of *The Making of a Television Series* may be judged to inform much of the rest of Elliott's work. Indeed, one way of interpreting it is to see what followed as an elaboration of *The Making's* conclusions. In these, Elliott noted a secular shift in the media towards 'showing more mass characteristics in content and organisation'; that 'although the professional communicator has gradually emerged as a new-style intellectual in society, the tendency is for him to be preoccupied with the form rather than the content of communication'; and that 'the unplanned product of following accepted production routines within established organisational systems' means that 'what is said will in the main be fundamentally supportive of the socio-economic structure of the society in which those organisations are set' (Elliott 1972: 165–6). Elliott's critique of journalism – both print and broadcast – was developed in a number of seminal essays and monographs. A reading of these shows that it was a considered and consistent analysis, never prone to conspiracy theories, and disciplined by both historical awareness and succession of empirical investigations of contemporary practice.

In one long review of writings on media organizations and occupations, Elliott argued that the analysis of the organization of work practices and structures in the media offered a key to understanding the production of media culture in democratic capitalism: 'the peculiarities of media organisations and occupations set in the context of British history and social structure have real consequences for the production of media culture' (Elliott 1977: 143). That culture he saw as 'restricted, consensual and anodyne'. While the structure of the British media offered some space for variation and innovation he judged this to be 'relatively rare, unstable and grounded in the margins of the cultural production process in democratic, capitalist society' (*ibid.*: 165). The scope for dissent, he thought, was conditioned by the tensions between the bourgeois and aristocratic traditions as embodied in the 'mixture of elites which dominate British society'. This was his view in the mid-1970s. By the early 1980s, as we shall see, his views on the possibility of operating in the margins had become much bleaker.

In a historical sketch of journalism as a profession, Elliott argued that changes in the occupation and its practices were 'a result of changes in the organisation and market of the press' (Boyce *et al.* 1978: 186). The long-term effect of capitalist media production was to limit variation, and the market could simply not act as the guarantor of truth. Against these constraints of the system one could weigh the claims of the self-styled professionals with an anthropologically sceptical eye. Myths abounded: of the reporter as investigator, the editor as independent hero, the great story as personal discovery, objectivity as inherent in the production process. Against the myths were set the inherent limitations of organizational routines. In many ways 'journalism is more analogous to settled agriculture than hunting and gathering' (*ibid.*: 187).

This sociological critique of professionalism's self-delusions also carried a political edge. Elliott was profoundly committed to an ideal of public enlightenment and popular involvement in political debate and decision-making. In his view, the press in Britain functioned as the 'self-appointed script-writer to the national morale', and its overarching style was to go for easy, recognizable plots, with clear-cut heroes and villains, to lack a real commitment to a norm of objectivity and to conceal from the public the shaky credibility of official sources (Elliott 1978). Coupled with the growth of information management and official secrecy, British journalism needs a transformation of organization and training, for its present deficiences block off the public's access to relevant analysis and information.

Elliott's indignation was most aroused by what he saw as the scandalously poor reporting of Northern Ireland. He wrote the first thorough sociological study of this failure, building upon his own original research into media content and practice and what could be pieced together from the disclosures of disenchanted journalists (Elliott 1977). He also popularized his criticisms and the example frequently reappeared in his various essays. His work on the propaganda war offered a model of committed and exact scholarship which others have followed. At one level, Elliott provided sufficient evidence of how routine press and television reporting failed to explain the political and historical roots of the crisis, and resulted in the standard privileging of the authorities' version of events.

But there was a sense, too, in which the limitations of, especially, broadcast news could not be laid purely at the door of what Elliott so effectively disparaged as the British style. Secrecy, parochialism, incorporation all played their part to be sure. However, the findings of his collaborative cross-national study of television news in Ireland, Sweden and Nigeria obviously suggested something much more profound (Golding and Elliott 1979). What this study disclosed was the broad similarity of news production practices and of the news values embodied in the output of these three quite diverse societies, despite the distinctive relationships of broadcasting to the state in each case. The study presented broadcast news as an 'international genre' with significant national variations, and argued for an understanding of news as ideology, in its emphasis upon consensus, its alignment with the assumptions and preoccupations of the powerful, and in its inherent inability to provide 'a portrayal of social change' or to reveal 'the operation of power in and between societies' (*ibid.*: 211). On the view of this study, broadcast news was largely beyond meaningful reform, and this raised basic questions about 'the complex of relationships between broadcasting and society' (*ibid.*: 218).

Other projects on journalism were begun, but were to remain incomplete, due to the decline of Elliott's health. He did a great deal of work on the British end of a comparative study of journalists in Britain and West Germany, but this was never written up. He also did substantial preliminary work on the role of the news media in the Falklands/ Malvinas propaganda war, which, again, sadly never saw the light of day.

That war, with its massive symbolic mobilization against a clear-cut enemy, and with its simplistic celebrations of a bellicose British national identity, fascinated Elliott. He would undoubtedly have produced an analysis which went well beyond merely looking at the mechanics of producing propaganda. How it might have developed may be seen from his work on media performances as ritual processes. This brings us to another level of Elliott's work on Northern Ireland and how this preoccupation opened up a seminal line of theoretical inquiry into the role of the media's activities understood as part of a ritual process. In this connection, he drew upon recent attempts to reconceptualize ritual *not* so much as a Durkheimian exercise in consensus-building, but as 'a structured performance in which not all the participants are equal' (Elliott 1980: 145). Media ritual was defined as 'rule-governed activity of a symbolic character involving mystical notions which draws the attention of its participants to objects of thought or feeling which the leadership of the society or group hold to be of especial significance' (*ibid.*: 147).

The media coverage of Northern Ireland interested Elliott because in mainland Britain the nature of media mobilization against the 'terrorist threat' during assassinations of prominant figures, bombing outrages, sieges and the like has brought into play exceptional forms of coverage. According to Elliott's analysis, the media were engaged in a multiplex political ritual which in part 'cauterised' the wounds of the society, and also reaffirmed its positive characteristics, by retailing the views of a stage army drawn from the dominant institutions. Such rites, he argued, were irreducible to a rational or cognitive dimension alone, contrary to what exponents of the dominant ideology thesis believe.

Rather, they invited subordinate groups to participate emotionally in the reaffirmation of national identity, and the 'nature of the British media system is such that the invitation is difficult to refuse' (*ibid.*: 173).

The question of meaning and interpretation involved in ritual processes was also central to the series of collaborative studies of political discourse which Elliott undertook. One of these centred on the handling of the category 'communism' in Western cultures. The central thesis pursued was that the interpretation of communism in a capitalist society such as Britain, whilst at one level propagandistic and instrumental, at another was revealing of some of the fundamental cultural patterns of the society. The study showed how communism, both in the popular media and in social theories, was commonly interpreted in terms of difference, threat and irrationality – here sharing a great deal with the war against terrorism (Elliott and Schlesinger 1979c).

A further development of this work (which Elliott's worsening illness brought to a halt) lay in analysing the international ideological conflict over how to interpret the rise of 'Eurocommunism'. The focus on this occasion lay with the role of elite media (such as foreign policy journals) and political intellectuals, and their supporting institutions (such as think-tanks and political parties). The study charted the ways in which 'Eurocommunism' as a category became a contested figure in elite foreign policy circles as the communist parties in Italy, France and Spain appeared to be edging nearer to exerting some political power in the mid to late 1970s. However, the foreign policy analysts were divided between fundamental cold warriors and containment theorists – the former seeing communism as essentially unchanging, the latter being prepared to acknowledge the possibility of reform. The totalitarian theory views of the former, however, were found to predominate at the more popular level of media output, thus revealing the stratified nature of political knowledge very clearly. The study also analysed the process whereby the leaderships of the Western communist parties tried to appropriate the figure 'Eurocommunism' and use it with a positive, liberal meaning, thus causing their ideological enemies to engage in a campaign of conceptual delegitimation on a grand scale (Elliott and Schlesinger 1979a, 1979b, 1980).

The study of contested meaning was also central to Elliott's collaborative work on the television coverage of terrorism (Elliott *et al.* 1983; Schlesinger *et al.* 1983). Written during the last few months of his life, *Televising 'Terrorism'* was, he felt, the most important study he had been associated with. Here, a number of distinctive ways of interpreting terrorism were analysed – the official, alternative, populist and oppositional – together with their institutional sources of support. The way in which these frameworks were employed in television coverage and the extent to which this coverage was conditioned by censorship were the central themes of the book. This obviously picked up the work on Northern Ireland, and also the methodology employed in the Euro-communism study. It also made links between factual and fictional forms of representation, once again emphasizing the connectedness of . culture (with due weight to its discontinuities).

Televising 'Terrorism' was a conscious intervention both against the pro-censorship lobby and against the simplistic nostrums of much current media theory fashionable on the Left. Elliott always rejected a purely instrumentalist view of broadcasting's relationship to the state, whilst, of course, recognizing that it was open to such uses in given circumstances. In this, his last major contribution to the field, he felt strongly that the public service character of British broadcasting still offered some slight openings for critical journalism and creative drama, and this was a view supported by the evidence cited. As much as anything, *Televising 'Terrorism'* was an argument about the *potentialities* of broadcasting and an intended spur to the Left to reorganize its thinking and recognize media opportunities where they existed. The margins, then, were not yet closed off.

However, Elliott's longer-term view was undoubtedly a bleak one, and well reflected in his last substantial essay, written for the journal *Media, Culture and Society* on whose editorial board he sat. Concerned with the intellectual, and the 'information society', it drew upon the half-articulated fears of his generation. For Elliott, the proliferation of highly commercialized distribution technologies, the growth of the strong state and the assault upon the 'public sphere' were between them going to have a devastating effect upon the wider culture. Far from the intellectuals taking the lead in inheriting the earth, as envisaged in the more fanciful writings of Alvin Gouldner, they 'are about to be robbed of those public forums in which they could engage in their "culture of critical discourse". Their toe-hold on power is crumbling under their feet' (Elliott 1982: 243). It was a far-sighted piece, which, well in advance of current debate, grasped and synthesized the crucial issues concerning new media technologies and their likely impact on public sector broadcasting and democracy generally. The prophets of the information society, said Elliott, were peddling a lie: the consumption of products from the alleged cornucopia of media abundance was in no measure the same as equal participation in deciding one's fate democratically. Elliott was, therefore, amongst the first to make a positive revaluation of the role of public service broadcasting in the context of the accelerating privatization of the national economy. He was also intensely aware of the internationalization of the information economy and the threatened erosion of national cultural identity.

Dan Schiller's piece, which opens Part One, pursues Elliott's concern with the new information market-place's deleterious effect on public debate in the context of their shared interest in the changing organization of the news industry. Schiller argues that the distinction between elite and mass-commercial forms is increasingly being emphasized as government and big business more successfully manage available images and information. In fact, his argument goes further, to suggest that the traditional category of 'news' is in the process of disintegrating, as new technological developments tend to produce a new information commodity. As newspaper chains in the USA become increasingly linked into satellites and computer-based data banks, an electronic 'news and information market-place' is emerging in which the traditional product is repackaged for other uses. A further point concerns the ways in which the price of commercialized information closes off access to non-corporate subscribers, which, together with the privatization and limitation of government information, is reshaping the potentialities of rational public debate.

It is precisely this point which is Nicholas Garnham's starting-point. Agreeing with Schiller about current trends, he observes that the political import of transforming public information into a private good is considerable. He is critical of the lack of theoretical grasp of media developments on the Left. As a move to remedy this, he proposes a position derived from a critique of Habermas's analysis of the 'public sphere'. The rational core of this, he considers, is that it concerns itself with the issue of universal involvement in public debate and reasoning. Historically, the public sphere has best been realized not in the commercial press but in public service broadcasting which has addressed individuals as citizens rather than as consumers. Garnham sees public service broadcasting as the only possible site for preserving the moment of communicative universality in the nation-state, at a time when the economy is internationalizing. Indeed, an *international* public sphere is required, he argues, to counter the free flow of multinational capital. At a more practical level, he criticizes the limitations of journalistic professionalism in its knowledge-broking role, and argues for wider access – on their own terms – for both communities of expertise and political parties.

Some of the difficulties in defending public broadcasting at the present time are highlighted in Stuart Hood's contribution. He points to the contradictory nature of the original concept. On the one hand, it assumed that since broadcasting operated with a scarce public resource (the usable part of the radio spectrum) it needed to be carefully regulated to ensure that it operated as a utility or service in the public interest. On the other hand, there were equally strong justifications for regulation stemming from fears of the subversive potential of a more open system of transmission and reception. Hood argues that the first of these rationales is now under concerted attack from the libertarians of the new Right as cable and other new distribution technologies undermine the traditional arguments from scarcity. However, as Hood points out, these demands that broadcasting be deregulated and subjected to the disciplines of the market-place are at odds with the equally strong moral impetus within the new conservatism which seeks to retain and extend controls on the flow of imagery and argument. Faced with this two-pronged attack from supporters of the free market and the strong state, Hood argues, the left finds itself in disarray and he ends with a plea for a concerted debate directed to providing a new rationale for public broadcasting.

The next two contributions move away from the analysis of general trends in the relations between communications systems and political institutions, to consider how the professional beliefs and practices of broadcasters and their relations to political actors and organizations shape the daily flow of political communication. Drawing on their study of the introduction of the sound broadcasting of Parliament in Britain in 1978, Jay Blumler and Michael Gurevitch set out to show that the interactions between journalists and political institutions are more complex and multi-layered than many previous analysts have allowed for. The coverage of Parliament, they argue, was the product of two sets of intersecting criteria: 'pragmatic' judgements based on professional notions of newsworthiness and audience appeal, and a 'sacerdotal' orientation rooted in more general social values concerning the symbolic role and legitimacy of the institution. These two dimensions, they suggest, generated permanent tensions which were resolved in various ways by different groups of broadcasters depending on their role within the broadcasting system. They go on to argue that far from being unique to the reporting of Parliament this interplay between 'pragmatic' and 'sacerdotal' judgements characterizes the coverage of all political groups and institutions, and that recognizing this raises a series of important new questions for research.

Drawing on his long experience of working in BBC Current Affairs, Roger Bolton offers a practitioner's view of the internal and external pressures facing the political journalist in broadcasting. He points out that government constraints on decision-making are a permanent possibility, and describes the tensions that arose in the summer of 1985 following the decision by the BBC governors not to broadcast a scheduled documentary on politics in Northern Ireland, featuring Martin McGuiness, an elected Sinn Fein member of the Ulster Assembly and the alleged Chief of Staff of the IRA, following a strongly worded letter from the then Home Secretary. In Bolton's view, however, journalists' over-reliance on official sources and their self-censorship can be just as important as external political pressures, though the critical incidents he describes clearly sent shock waves among many supporters of BBC independence both inside and outside the organization. Bolton also draws attention to the 'limitations of the medium' by pointing to its 'massness', its weakness in explaining political ideas and its tendency to simplify the complex. In Bolton's view the explosion of daily news coverage has led to an overemphasis on foreground, and he draws attention to the skewed nature of foreign reporting (with its undue concentration on the USA) and the customary dependence on national stereotypes. Bolton is certainly one media practitioner for whom the findings of media sociology have come home. Aside from the problems already outlined, he acknowledges the role of subjective judgement in reporting and argues for a programme of political education for television producers in which media analysis and analysts should play a role.

The contributions which comprise Part Two approach the question of political communication by exploring the ways that audiences participate in the process. David Chaney offers an exposition and application of Philip Elliott's views on ritual, which he also updates by relating them to some recent writings on national identity and the cultural role of tradition and ceremony in society. His approach raises important questions about the role of ritual in maintaining the political order of an ostensibly secular society. Chaney takes as his case Mass Observation's study of the 1937 Coronation of George VI. He develops his analysis into the more general argument that media rituals function for the individual as a means of participation in the public sphere. This raises issues about the concept from a quite different angle from that discussed by Garnham and Schiller. In Chaney's view, ceremonial events address us and are interpreted in ways that differ according to our vantage-points in the wider society. In presenting this perspective,

Chaney develops Elliott's suggestion that the analysis of rituals offers a means of exploring private responses to public events, and makes a break with mechanistic notions of effects.

Where Chaney deals with the way participation in the rituals promoted by the established media reaffirm existing political arrangements, Denis McQuail explores the conditions for satisfactory political communication in an era when the electronic media are undergoing rapid change. His argument centres around the need to increase the choices open to the citizen as audience member by expanding the diversity of political interests and issues that are represented within the communications system. He distinguishes two main types of diversity within the present system: the 'external' variety represented by the party political press where sharply differentiated world views are carried by mutually exclusive media to audiences of like-minded persons; and the 'internal' form promoted by public broadcasting, where a variety of views is available in a range of presentational forms which all command a mixed audience. This latter system, argues McQuail, works on the principle of 'reflective' diversity which publicizes views in proportion to the strength of their popular support and thereby privileges established political organizations. In contrast, the ideal of 'open' diversity offers more or less equal access to all serious and legitimate viewpoints.

Where Elliott saw the rise of the new media as inexorably reducing the diversity of political communication and consigning audiences ever more to the role of spectators, McQuail rejects this pessimistic conclusion as premature. It is at least possible that the new media may promote more 'open' forms of diversity which break with the consensualism and ritualism of the established media, allow more space to emerging interest groups and issues and offer audiences more opportunities for choice and participation. At the very least, argues McQuail, the future of diversity remains an open question which merits more attention and research.

The four essays in Part Three explore the problematic relations between journalists, governments and state agencies, from a variety of perspectives and vantage-points. The section opens with John Downing's overview of the ways that the governments of Britain and the United States attempt to control the flow of information about their activities. He suggests that the difference in openness between the two systems is most plausibly explained by variations in the mobilizing potential of oppositional groups. In Britain, he argues, the fact that knowledge is potentially convertible into power through the national mobilizing capacity of the Labour Party has been a key factor in buttressing the defence of secrecy. Conversely, the dispersal of opposition in the United States among separate interest groups and single-issue campaigns means that that degree of openness is less likely to threaten the prevailing power-structure, and is thus allowable. However, he concludes by noting that America, like Britain, retains a strong apparatus of secrecy and news management in areas defined as relevant to 'national security' and the 'national interest'.

This observation provides the starting-point for Edward Herman's essay. In contrast to studies of news which focus on the internal constraints arising from the organization of journalism, Herman highlights the ability of the United States 'government to mobilize a mostly compliant media around its preferred definitions of events and issues'. He suggests that this is especially prevalent in the area of foreign policy, where the behaviour and performance of the media frequently conform to the characteristics of a propaganda system in which official versions of events gain widespread publicity, while subsequent repudiations and challenges are either suppressed, given muted and episodic attention, or confined to marginal media. Herman argues that the dynamics of this system emerge particularly clearly in the contrasted handling of similar events with different political implications for America's international interests. He develops this argument through an analysis of the way the American news media treated the shooting down of a South Korean commercial airliner by the Soviet Union in 1983 and the shooting down of a Libyan commercial airliner by Israel in 1973. In the former case, he argues, the United States government successfully organized a worldwide campaign of denunciation, while in the Israeli case, similar facts led to much less coverage and no significant outcry in the West.

In contrast to Downing's emphasis on the strength of secrecy and to Herman's stress on the government's ability to mobilize the media behind official versions of events, David Paletz and John Ayanian point to the relative leakiness of the present system and the 'internal' blocks to better coverage of defence issues which arise from the current organization of journalism. They develop their argument through a case study of the coverage given to the malfunction of the North American Air Defense Command's computer, which erroneously registered Soviet missiles heading towards the United States and led to nuclear bomber crews being put on full alert on 3 June 1980. They show how the apparatus of secrecy broke down when the story was unofficially leaked to a local reporter, and how the Pentagon responded by releasing its version of events, but was unable to uniformly enforce it on the news media. Although some reporters acted as simple conduits for the official view, others were very perturbed by the alert and produced sensational stories stressing the country's closeness to accidental nuclear war. At the same time, they show that comparatively few reports explored the wider implications of the incident and that most gave scant coverage to the international ramifications. However, they attribute these failings to the internal deficiencies of the news system and end by urging journalists to reflect more critically on the assumptions and routines that guide their work.

Like Roger Bolton's earlier contribution, the final essay, written by Peter Taylor, a British journalist with considerable experience of reporting Northern Ireland, exemplifies the kind of critical reflection on the handling of contentious issues that Paletz and Ayanian call for. Taylor takes up the vexed question of political terminology in reporting. 'Terrorist', 'guerrilla', 'freedom fighter': what you are called, he argues, is conditioned by the political context within which journalism works. In an original survey of Fleet Street and television editors' thinking on the semantics of political violence, Taylor shows that political discourse is inherently contested and that this takes the form of disputes over key categorizations. Despite the qualified nature of the response of many of the journalists, the identification of the IRA as 'terrorists' stands out, as does the easing of the problem of which label to use when reporting from outside the national territory. Taylor, incidentally, tells us how his own terminology was adjusted on one occasion.

All our contributors, whether academics or working journalists, view arguments about communicating politics as debates about real problems in the real world. For Philip Elliott, tackling these issues required constant dialogue, and the need for researchers to speak to practitioners was always at the forefront of his mind. A natural stylist, he took great pains to make his own work as accessible as possible, and the clarity of his writing, combined with its integrity and insight, gained him widespread respect among media professionals. As Roger Bolton notes at the end of his piece, Philip's work was:

> full of sympathy, understanding and good sense, even when it hurt. He eschewed the easy gibe and the easy answer and he was never deflected from the central questions. He underlined our limitations without self-righteousness. He knew that broadcasters and media academics have a responsibility to educate each other, as well as to educate themselves.

This commitment to constructive dialogue is by no means universal within either group, however. Some researchers continue to conceal their arguments behind a dense thicket of jargon and concept-spinning, to be met by practitioners with summary dismissal. The result is a mutual antipathy and a widening gap. As the BBC's Assistant Director General, Alan Protheroe, told Peter Taylor while he was researching his contribution to this book:

> They use code. There is no communality of language [between us and them]. I genuinely believe that media sociology is a pseudo science whose practitioners are looking for a gravitas they do not possess. There's a mutual targeting of objectives because each wants to reinforce the other's strategy. They all want to be each other's footnotes.

Dismantling this mutual mistrust requires more than a shared language, however. It also entails active co-operation between professionals and researchers in the practice of research.

Here, Philip's patient and sympathetic manner gave him access where the more abrasive style of later, less successful, researchers would meet with rebuff. His ethnographic studies of production were only possible because of these personal skills allied to his ability to see in situations what most others, including many of the participants, missed. It was therefore somewhat ironic that his path-breaking study, *The Making of a Television Series*, should have elicited such a hostile review from the doyenne of television current affairs, Grace Wyndham Goldie, in the *Listener* (a journal to which Elliott later contributed, for a period, a witty and perceptive broadcasting review column).

Mrs Wyndham Goldie's point was that generalization from a single television series is impossible since each production is unique. Furthermore, since television producers operate with shared professional understandings, which do not require articulating, their working premises and values are imperceptible to even the most careful of eavesdroppers. Sourly lashing at the Leicester Centre, and the entire enterprise of mass communication research, it was the cry of a closed professional culture defending its practices from outside scrutiny. Elliott, typically, did not rise to the bait, but two colleagues supplied the necessary corrective to Mrs Wyndham Goldie's acerbic misreading in a letter to the *Listener* of 26 October 1972. As they pointed out, she seemed to assume:

> that research is about what people say, not what they do, and that the covert intimacy of a production team is impervious to the naive outsider unaware of the implications of argot, gesture, and understanding. . . . Yet if she is right, her belief that generalisation from case studies of production is impossible is surely absurd, since only if there are recurrent problems met and resolved in similar ways can these common understandings she be-

lieves so mysterious be workable, or even exist . . . And if she is wrong, and
the activities of people in the media are no more or less obscure than those
in other industries, then the search for regularities and routines is a perfectly valid procedure.

But the methodology of research in sensitive settings remained an
abiding concern of Elliott's. The appendix to *The Making of a Television
Series* deals with the problems both of generalization and of inference.
His comments start from the fundamental observation that 'all social
research can be said to depend on the participant observations made by
the researcher through his ordinary life experience' (Elliott 1972: 170).
Generalization is indeed hazardous but 'can be established not only by
doing frequency research but by doing more comparative participant
observation studies in a variety of settings', an injunction he was to
obey in much of his later work. As he went on, 'The important test to
apply to the analysis of participant observation data seems to me not to
be simply how many other cases is this likely to be true for – a question
which cannot be answered within the terms of the method; but how
plausible is the posited relationship between belief, behaviour, and
situation in the light of possible alternative explanations?' (*ibid.*: 174).

In a later succinct and thoughtful conference paper Elliott enlarged
on these reflections. It is a masterly summary of the virtues and pitfalls
of observational studies. Here he identifies the 'three "Cs"' of cre-
ativity, confidence and chance which form the kernel of debate in
broadcaster/researcher understanding, a particular instance of a general
problem where 'one group's role is defined by the practical problems of
processing an output, while the other group, the researcher, has the
more diffuse responsibility of producing new knowledge' (Elliott 1971:
105). His conclusions were profound and comprehensive. 'The important point to establish is that the basic aims of the research are to try and
develop knowledge and understanding. These are better weapons with
which to fight off criticisms of politicians and interested parties than the
suspicions which grow from ignorance. Trying to batten down the
hatches will only make the suspicions grow a little bit larger' (*ibid.*:
112–13).

It was a credo which was to inspire Philip Elliott's career and to
inform his entire contribution to mass communication research. It provided a standard to which his colleagues and successors might aspire,
yet at the same time was a salutary reminder that imagination, per-
spicacity and personal skills, in all of which Philip was so richly
endowed, can alone provide a guarantee of effective research into
cultural production. These themes in his work cohered into a passionate

conviction that a better world was possible, and that communications were at once a means to create it and an obstacle to its achievement. It is a conviction which his many friends and colleagues continue to share, from however varied a range of perspectives. It is to the memory of Philip Elliott's work, and to the beliefs and objectives which provided his inspiration and towards which his work was such a powerful contribution, that this book is dedicated.

Peter Golding   August 1985
Graham Murdock
Philip Schlesinger

Part One

Media Organizations and Political Institutions

1
Transformations of News in the US Information Market

Dan Schiller

*I*n the classical theory of liberal democracy, the news system occupies a key role as the major source of the information that citizens need to arrive at rational political judgements and choices.

To achieve this, two conditions have to be fulfilled. First, the whole range of relevant information needs to be equally available to everyone. Secondly, news organizations need to be independent of both government and big business so that they can deliver disinterested accounts of the key sources of power affecting people's daily lives. More than that, according to liberal theory, they have a positive duty to act as a Fourth Estate, a public watchdog, checking for abuses of corporate and governmental power on behalf of the wider public interest.

From the beginning of the modern news system in the last century, however, these ideals have been steadily eroded and undermined by the political and economic realities of the environment in which newspapers operate.

In the first place, both governments and corporations made increasingly vigorous efforts to restrict the public reporting of potentially embarrassing information, while offering news organizations convenient packages of positive publicity about their activities in the form of press releases and briefings, orchestrated by the burgeoning public relations industry. This trend has deepened with the growth of the business corporation's political and economic interests and social role.

In the second place, news organizations themselves became major businesses, subject to the same tendencies towards economic concentration characteristic of the business system as a whole. Very formidable barriers to entry as well as extensive interlocks between news media and other businesses have sharply reduced the potential for the press to play a truly independent role.

In the third place, the free market system, far from giving all citizens equal access to the most important information in public circulation, created systematic inequalities in access by tying access to ability to pay.

The result has been a highly stratified information system in which much of the important information required for considered political judgement and choice was confined to elite newspapers and magazines – if it was available at all. The mainstream commercial press, in contrast, sought to appeal to mass readerships by elevating entertainment over information and emphasizing crimes, scandals, sports and human oddities.

Under current conditions, these historic features of the news system are being massively intensified. The gap between information-rich elite consumers and information-impoverished citizens is widening dramatically. At the same time both government and big business are intensifying their efforts to manage the imagery and information available to the general public to engineer a favourable impression of their actions in a time of political and economic uncertainty.

The big picture

In a context of mounting commercialism and political manipulation, the news commodity is being broken down and reconstituted. Backed by sophisticated communications technology, news media and other non-media businesses together are accomplishing a massive redefinition of news content, industry structure and markets. Far from engendering democratic enlightenment, however, the new technology is being harnessed to those very sources of social power that have sought to prevent it.

Distinct since the commercialization of the press in the mid-nineteenth century (see Elliott 1982), elite and mass news today are diverging on entirely disparate paths. Elite news is increasingly no longer even intended for a public comprised of individual citizens. Rather, it is focused on the needs and deep pockets of transnational corporations. Available are ever more timely, authoritative and costly accounts of specialized economic, political, scientific and technical developments. Such news travels increasingly over high-speed computer networks. In this way better access to better information can sometimes be had by non-news organizations than by newspapers – or their readers.

For the public of individual citizens the philosophy of private enter-prise in information bequeaths only the empty husk of the news. As one-time Knight-Ridder executive Derek Daniels explains, 'If [news-papers] are to meet the new challenges, they must, above all, recognize that reading is work . . . that newspapers should devote more space to things that are helpful, enjoyable, exciting and fun as opposed to undue emphasis on "responsible information"' (quoted in Bogart 1982).

New technology, including satellites, cable television, electronic newsgathering and computer data bases are playing a special role in grooming the citizenry for yet another dismal shift 'downmarket'. Global trivialization, round-the-clock happy talk, total commercialism and downright manipulation are its strange fruit. Mass news, in Jan Eckekrantz's apt phrase, now engenders systemic ignorance.

As new alloys are forged in the crucible of commercial culture, news as a discrete form is disappearing or, rather, past forms of news are being subjected to radical change. Boundaries between news, enter-tainment, public relations and advertising, always fluid historically, are now becoming almost invisible.

The effect of these arrangements is that real information becomes available more broadly and easily than ever before – for an elite group of fee-paying corporations. News produced for the mass audience, however, is subjected to the same market-place logic that is responsible for the Hollywood blockbuster *The Empire Strikes Back*. And public information availability is eroded not just at the distribution end but also at the collection end, where events first become grist for the news media mill.

The new information industries

Already a $3 billion annual business, computerized information delivery still pales in size when placed beside the three other major publishing markets: newspapers, magazines and books. Yet while these print businesses are growing at best by 11 per cent each year, electronic products are racing ahead at over 25 per cent a year, as more and more companies receive growing quantities of information over computer networks.

Proliferation of corporate news and information services is occurring even when traditional news media retain their legendary profitability. Publicly held newspapers enjoy a profit rate *double* the average for all US corporations (see Bogart 1982: 69; Gomery 1984). To position themselves for future profits, and to ward off turf attacks, however, newspapers *must* enter unfamiliar electronic information markets. As they do so, they can capitalize on several existing assets. Newspapers have printing and distribution facilities. They have intimate knowledge of local advertisers and their needs. They have large investments in information-gathering and -processing staff and organizational resources. Finally, newspapers have a decade-long commitment to front-end systems – computerized editorial systems which permit direct linkages between the paper and outside electronic networks. (There were only 23 video display terminals in US newsrooms in 1970, but at the end of 1981 there were 41,000.) Once information is *in* newspaper computers it can be easily and inexpensively transformed into new products.

News media are systematically repackaging information resources for sale in many markets, in the process subordinating long-standing distinctions between news, advertising and entertainment. One pioneer in moving content across media boundaries is Harte-Hanks Communications. With 27 daily and 25 weekly newspapers, four television and nine radio stations, a cable TV operation and a large direct marketing subsidiary, Harte-Hanks is well placed to initiate creative new product development. 'No other newspaper company I know has gone as far as Harte-Hanks in managing from a strictly business point of view', asserts one newspaper analyst. The company can supply market research for an advertiser's campaign, design the advertising, print it, deliver it (by mail or independent carrier) and then measure its impact. Using its own mailing lists and others, the company can now reach 96 per cent of the nation's households.

The Harte-Hanks strategy is not just to produce newspapers, but to offer advertisers and readers (whom it terms 'information consumers') a choice from an ever-expanding series of products. The newspaper is only one option. Others include magazines, newsletters, free-sheets and speciality publications aimed at specific demographic groupings. The company calls this concept the 'community information center', but it may be more appropriately thought of as multimedia information management. Harte-Hanks's drive to capitalize on current assets, including a distribution system, an advertising sales force, a writing staff and printing presses, explicitly subordinates news – and newspapers – to a larger, encompassing product mix (Jones 1984a).

In its Annual Report for 1983 another conglomerate, Media General, reveals the overall corporate priority between editorial and commercial matter in devising such new products: 'Our daily newspapers ... can

use computers to identify non-subscribers so that a newspaper adver-
tisement can be mailed to this group and thus provide total market
coverage. This can be further tailored to include on the zip code areas of
special interest to the advertiser.'

Many multimedia firms are following suit, hawking news and related
products across several markets. CBS News produces for American
Airlines a Magazine of the air – whose concern is 'to inform – and we
hope to amuse' – to profit a second time from recycled news. The *Los
Angeles Times* operates 'Business Pulse', a 60-second news report dialled
over the telephone; diverse other 'dial-it' services are planned for 26 US
cities. The Gannett chain's *USA Today*, hailed 'MacPaper' by irreverent
journalists, relies on existing staff at papers round the country to
produce a daily national journal.

Computers and satellites further hasten development of new kinds of
national and transnational information networks. Newspapers are
undertaking commercial-access data bases, growing first from their
own in-house electronic libraries ('morgues'), to provide a broad array
of local news to organizational customers. Other marketable information then may be added, such as profiles of major in-state companies
and state legislative tracking services. Smaller papers can piggyback
their own offerings on larger firms' computer systems and national
marketing capabilities. New relations thus are forged between giant
newspaper chains, data base publishers, libraries and the local press.
Building initially on holdings around the country, but then opening out
to independent papers and other organizations as well, companies like
Times-Mirror and Knight-Ridder are laying the groundwork for a new
variant of the television network-affiliate tie. With its vast marketing
and distribution capabilities and computer resources, the large newspaper chain provides a ready means to market information of many
kinds.

Knight-Ridder's *Journal of Commerce* unit thus inaugurated an electronic data base in 1984 which lets subscribers determine instantly the
most economical way of shipping cargo between any two cities in the
world. The data base updates 900,000 pages of ocean shipping tariffs
to reflect an estimated 1,500 changes each day. In addition, Knight-
Ridder's Commodity News Services embrace 26 options accessible via a
network of 2,400 satellite dishes; 17,500 subscribers worldwide can
receive economic news, agribusiness news, market prices, economic
statistics, commodity futures quotations and other news. In this market
Knight-Ridder faces stiff global competition from Reuters, the British
news agency founded in 1851. Reuters furnishes trading information

on equities, currency transactions and other financial matters to 15,000 clients, mainly brokerage houses, banks, governments and news organizations. Sales of such data now dwarf Reuters' news business by nine to one. In 1984 the firm held a public offering of about 30 per cent of its stock, partly to finance further expansion of its already mammoth electronic distribution network (see Feder 1984; Jones 1984b; Tully 1983).

Other news media are equally keen. *US News and World Report* is enlarging its computer-based publishing services and its satellite transmission network. United Press International will utilize a private satellite network to market agricultural forecasts, regional economic news and detailed political analyses to local governments and companies, including the news media. Dun and Bradstreet, the credit-reporting agency that owns 19 business and trade publications, now sells more than half of its credit information electronically. D&B also has acquired a major British financial data supplier, Datastream, and the US-based ratings and market research giant, A. C. Nielsen, raising prospects for aggressive growth in electronic services. Times-Mirror operates Grassroots California with two other newspaper publishers, to furnish information on the state's agribusinesses. Local weather reports, news, stock and commodity prices, chemical, seed and livestock information, and specialized farm management programs will be available through terminals.

Participation in the electronic news and information market-place is open, however, to a very wide range of companies. Personal computer manufacturers are looking to new information services of varied kinds to sell more hardware. Nine million personal computers already installed in the USA, on the other hand, comprise a ready market for electronic software. To tap into it, IBM's joint venture with Merrill Lynch ('International Marketnet') will deliver stock quotes, financial data and news to IBM PCs – first of all, to 10,000 Merrill Lynch account executives.

The 1984 break-up of a long vertically integrated national telephone company, AT&T, leaves the entire telephone industry groping for new profit sources. Like their parent, the seven new Regional Bell Operating Companies are casting about for information services to induce subscribers to make heavier use of their telephone lines, and thus to stimulate traffic for their under-utilized transmission networks (see Drucker 1984; Koenig 1984; Pollack 1984b).

The electronic information market-place is broader still. Citicorp, whose electronic network connects with thousands of corporate offices worldwide, will be a major force in electronic data base access and retrieval. A professional grouping, The American Chemical Society, makes research papers and patents available in computerized form to the technical community. Mead Corporation, whose main business remains paper and forest products, also operates Lexis, for lawyers researching court decisions, and Nexis, which brings on-line information published by magazines and newspapers, including *Time* and the *New York Times*.

Prices and rights

In the emerging information market-place, right of access to strategic information is conditional upon ability to pay. Current prices are already often far beyond the pockets of most private citizens, and of many public information providers, such as libraries, as well. The main market is the corporate sector.

For corporate consumers specialized information services, hard information predominates. Advertising is relegated to the margins: subscriptions or usage charges carry these media. Of 70-odd periodicals, newsletters and electronic data bases aimed at the telecommunications industry *alone*, most have price-tags starting at a couple of hundred dollars a year. An example is *Communications Daily*, now a staple of business executives and government officials, available (since 1981) for $950 a year. *Telecommunications Reports*, a dense weekly whose 40 to 50 packed pages are consumed by industry insiders, can be had for $294. Telecommunications manufacturers especially can benefit from an electronic data base offering strategic news about world equipment markets, access to which is sold by the consulting company Arthur D. Little. Its sliding price scale starts at about $10,000 a year.

A more encompassing elite information service is 'Newsnet'. With a data base of business information embracing 200 specialized newsletters, Newsnet adds 2,000 stories each day for immediate access through computers and telephone lines. An electronic clipping service permits subscribers to obtain listings of all new articles in the data base that mention pre-specified companies, names, or subjects. Their advertising makes it clear that this coverage of a wide range of industries and professions is intended for 'business executives – and reporters, investors, librarians, lawyers and doctors'. Fees are based on a minimum monthly charge of $15, to which additional usage is tacked on at a rate between $24 and $48 *per hour*.

Specialized business periodicals were initiated in the mid-nineteenth century as one of many innovations called forth by the railroads; scientific and technical journals can trace a longer pedigree. Both grew to maturity with big business. Today such publications are produced increasingly in computer-accessible form, for every industry sector, every professional and technical field: energy, aerospace, microelectronics, medicine, engineering, and so forth. They inform and empower an emerging corporate 'public'. Such a private public is, of course, a contradiction in terms. As the major wielders of political and economic power, none the less, business corporations today comprise the vital audience for authentic news and information.

Corporate control of public information

Corporations are also obtaining greatly enhanced control over the flow and presentation of news and information for general public consumption. Increasing restrictions on circulation of key corporate intelligence, accomplished both through pricing and important changes in the law, are being accompanied by more concerted, sophisticated attempts to massage the mass news system in the interests of business image-making.

Corporate rights to privacy have been amplified by recent legal decisions. In 1984 a federal appeals court ruled that corporations have a constitutional right to keep certain documents private even after they have been filed in court. As a result, 'control over vast quantities of evidence pried out of corporations during pretrial manoeuvering may shift from the courtroom to the boardroom' (Glaberson 1984: 144). Such litigation is the current cutting edge of a more general controversy, as more and more companies find ways of fighting press coverage they dislike. Mobil Oil Corporation now provides its executives with insurance to cover the cost of such court battles, while the conservative American Legal Foundation maintains a Libel Prosecution Resource Center *to assist plaintiffs.* Major rulings by higher courts continue to usurp the privileged position of news media, by proving hostile to traditional press claims of a special 'Fourth Estate' status. They have been simultaneously supportive, however, of broader corporate rights of free speech (see Schiller 1981: 79–97).

Business has not been slow to exercise these new prerogatives. At scores of major companies, in-house public affairs staffs routinely practice 'issues management', by circulating 'the company side' of stories like Love Canal, Three Mile Island, Rely Tampons, Tylenol and other 'unscheduled events' (Close 1983). They are active also on more everyday, but equally vital, matters.

26

The growing scale and sophistication of public relations has been matched by an increasing willingness to experiment with new technology to carry out corporate objectives. Long skilful at insinuating private messages into the public press, public relations agencies rely on communications technology to achieve a wholly new level of penetration. Over the last 30 years a half-dozen private wire services, which charge clients to distribute press releases, have sprung up in the United States (others now operate in a dozen nations, mainly in Western Europe). Stories are often rewritten to resemble AP and UPI reports. They are then sent out over the wire, to teletypewriters installed without charge in the newsrooms of subscribing organizations. PR Newswire today reaches 300 media in 85 cities. PR Newswire is also available on the Newsnet services, which declares in its advertising that: 'There is one source of official business and other news that often has more detail than even the most frequently published business newspapers and magazines: PR Newswire. The up-to-date PR Newswire contains the full, unreduced text of press releases from more than 7,000 sources.' The general manager of another such service, Business Wire, estimates that one newspaper – the *San Francisco Chronicle* – uses about a fifth of the stories it receives. Publicity reports are also sometimes picked up by the AP or the UPI themselves, and accorded further treatment as news (see Sandman *et al*. 1982: 154).

To take full account of newsroom computerization, however, public relations wires themselves 'must become computer-compatible with the press'. Business Wire and PR Newswire now move client company messages *directly* into newsroom computers. Once they are there, editors can call up stories and conveniently commit them to print without labour-intensive rekeying – without translation from hard copy into computer memory banks (Weiner 1980: 206–12). Communications technology once again is employed not to reinvigorate the independence of the press, but to subvert it.

Newspapers are not entirely innocent victims. The major aim of computerization is to cut production costs (especially labour costs), so direct inputting by public relations agencies is a logical extension. Computerization, however, also has significant implications for the future of journalists' work – reducing the scope for critical and investigative reporting and favouring industrialized production. A story written half – but only half – in jest, in the trade journal *Editor and Publisher* for 12 November 1983, chronicles the introduction by the Spokane *Spokesman-Review* of 'robotic writing' programs for local basketball stories and wedding announcements. The programs contained over 50 variations for basketball stories. One version was created for upsets, another for the high-point man being on the winning team, one for when the high scorer was on the losing team, and so on. For weddings, the writing program furnished 12 variations. The director of electronic publishing for Cowles Publishing, who conceived the idea when he was managing editor, said it came to him during the basketball season when 'the sports staff was stretched too thin'. Though the robotic writing experiment ended quickly ('It gave the impression that we were cold'), E&P affirmed: 'Reporters who think their jobs are immune from automation should think again.'

Extensions of pre-packaged information may provide news media with nothing less than a complete presentational format. Electronic press kits pervading television newscasts furnish an example. Video equivalents of written press releases now routinely appear on hundreds of local television broadcasts, report the film studio executives who helped initiate the practice. Such material is often neither labelled nor described as publicity. The kits are created, in this case, as interviews with film stars or directors, and are designed especially to permit local reporters to inject themselves into the tape – to make the interview appear to be original. Each meticulously organized kit contains a videocassette, written transcripts with suggested introductions for newscasters and texts of feature stories, including narrations and interviews. Each videotape usually has two soundtracks, one with the film studio's narrator and one blank, for use by the newscaster. By early 1984 Universal Pictures had produced 13 electronic press kits, MGM/UA had made 20 and Columbia Pictures, 40. Average cost of production and distribution to 200 stations is over $100,000 for a single kit; but the promotion created for the movie E.T. gained $700,000 worth of free air time. The *War Games* kit, running 34 minutes, was used at least in part by 139 of the 200 stations which received it, for a total of 16 hours of free advertising. A producer at one of the dozen-odd companies which have sprung up to execute these promotions reveals their editorial limitations: 'The questions are designed by us but we clear all of them in advance with the studios' (S. B. Smith 1984b: 28).

In yet another instance, CBS purchased rights to broadcast 90 minutes of conversations between former president Richard M. Nixon and a one-time aide, for $500,000. There have been previous instances where such payments were made for news material, but in the past CBS bought the right to have its own correspondents ask the questions and retained full editorial control. With the Nixon interviews the network bought a package of questions and answers already conducted *outside* the news organization (S. B. Smith 1984a: 28).

Originating outside the orbit of the established news media, the new forms for distributing news and information to the general public dissolve the line between informational programming and corporate promotion. A service called videotex furnishes vivid illustrations. Videotex utilizes computerized data bases, home television monitors equipped with special keypads, and telephone or cable television lines, to provide two-way banking, shopping and merchandise ordering, hotel and airline reservations and other services.

Nationally videotex is being developed by industry groups often combining both news and non-media interests. Knight-Ridder, for example, has been closely involved with AT&T as it experimented with a videotex system in South Florida. Field Enterprises has entered into partnership with a telecommunications company, Centel, and a computer firm, Honeywell. Times-Mirror, with its own papers sprinkled across the nation, has teamed up with Infomart, the data base and videotex subsidiary of Southam, which in turn is the largest Canadian newspaper chain. Major fanfare has been reserved for still another joint venture, that between IBM, Sears and CBS. IBM brings not only its millions of installed personal computers, which can act as terminals, but also unrivalled technical experience with sophisticated networking. Sears provides the huge customer base and the ability to handle complicated billing and marketing, as well as financial services that will employ videotex for real estate, stock brokerage and insurance transactions. CBS, finally, furnishes skills needed to cultivate, develop and exploit information and entertainment programming.

Program format changes reflect this expanded participation in videotex by non-media interests. As Vincent Mosco has shown, with videotex 'the division between program and commercial, never a rigid one, is now completely obliterated' (Mosco 1982: 106). 'Informercials' of varying length integrate instantaneous audience and market research (achieved by polling viewers on-line) into program content. A book review program sponsored by a book retailing chain, for example, incorporates results of questions about reading habits directly into the show. At no time is the show identified as a commercial. A variant is produced by Procter and Gamble for the USA cable network. A daily half-hour magazine called 'The Great American Homemaker' includes a five-minute informercial which uses the show's resident cooking personality, Beverly Nye, 'to demonstrate a recipe featuring P.&G.'s Butter Flavor Crisco'. Such sponsored cable shows are reportedly the fastest-growing segment of the entire television programming industry (McFadden 1984: 15). In still another context, Harte-Hanks is airing videotex informercials produced by its own Consumer Cable Corporation unit in Texas shopping malls (Pollack 1984a: E9).

The new technologies also allow corporations and other interest groups to bypass conventional mass distribution systems – old and new – altogether, and to address citizens directly in their own home with material controlled completely by them. The entire range of communications technologies, including satellites, private video and computer networks, and direct mail, according to one analyst, 'are providing corporations whose main economic activities are not in media production with remarkable opportunities to reach mass audiences directly with their messages' (Schiller 1981: 80).

On 26 March 1984, for instance, a top American Express Company executive, James F. Calvano, sent a special mailing to 8 million credit card holders. 'By the time this letter reaches your home, Congress could be dangerously close to restricting your right to use your own charge or credit cards where and when you please', the missive warned. It went on to lobby against legislation which would permit merchants to levy special surcharges on credit card purchases, to shift paperwork costs directly to the credit card holders who instigate them.

American Express reportedly spent more than a million dollars on *postage* for the mailing. Enclosed with the four-page appeal were three fill-in-the-blank postcards to be sent to the cardholder's local congressperson and senators. 'Just complete the enclosed return cards and mail them', urged Calvano (a stamp was also needed): 'Personally fill in your members' names and add your signature so they'll know of your sincere concern. I assure you, they'll be impressed by your commitment.'

Assuredly, they were. As a result of this direct mail campaign, 3 million postcards flooded into Washington (Fuerbringer 1984: 20).

Such direct marketing is both enhancing and shifting the power of the editorial, which is no longer confined to the news media proper. Relying on computerized listings to pinpoint 'most-needed audiences' with unsurpassed precision, direct mail and telephone advertising expenditures totalled an astounding $12 billion in 1983, while outlays for all forms of television advertising amounted to $16 billion. From early on direct marketing was intimately linked to the political rise of the authoritarian Right. Richard Viguerie, the far right-winger who has been a key innovator of direct mail technology, contends: 'For a number of reasons we had trouble getting our messages to people through the general newspapers and the networks. But direct marketing has given conservatives a national voice, direct marketing has increased the power of conservatives in Congress, and direct marketing helped Ronald Reagan, at best a fifth-ranked candidate, take the White House' (Burnham 1984a: 20).

What we are witnessing, then, is a double movement whereby corporations are able to restrict access to strategic information about their activities while at the same time gaining unparelleled control over the flow of positive images to the public at large. The result is to intensify still further the imbalance in the information system. An avalanche of managed material flows from the boardrooms to the citizen, but it is increasingly difficult for citizens (or the journalists who claim to act on their behalf) to gain access to the information on which an independent assessment could be made. The news media are therefore less and less able to fulfill the historic liberal ideal of acting as a Fourth Estate.

Moreover, their willingness to do so is under increasing pressure from critics on the Right. As a central part of what, in England, Stuart Hall terms 'the great moving right show', the media are increasingly chastised when they do not carry off an impeccably right-wing performance on their own. A prominent example of a pressure group created specifically to perform this function is Accuracy In Media (AIM). With close ties to the Reverend Moon, the Teamsters and high Reagan administration figures, and with a host of major corporate backers, AIM now regularly excoriates media coverage of the nuclear freeze movement, environmental and energy issues, and Agent Orange victims. More influential groups, such as the National Conservative Political Action Committee, endorse similar means. In the run-up to the 1984 election, for example, NCPAC spent 2 million dollars to expose the 'liberal record' of presidential candidate Walter F. Mondale, because it wants the public to believe that the journalists' union – which endorsed Mondale – would order reporters to bias news in his favour (Wolf 1984: 24–38). The Heritage foundation, a right-wing think-tank, runs a features syndicate that sends condensed versions of its views on topical issues to nearly 95 per cent of the nation's daily and weekly newspapers, between 200 and 500 of which buy them. Then the foundation's clipping service sends copies to home-town congresspersons, as 'a reminder' (Mayer 1984a: 64).

Secrecy and selling: the two faces of government

Right-wing criticisms of news are part of a general climate of political authoritarianism. At the heart of this is the government's pursuit of policies based on the combination of market forces and a strong state.

This at once rolls back state intervention in the economic sphere to permit enhanced scope for market forces and the pursuit of profits, whilst in the political sphere underwriting increased secrecy and manipulation both at home and abroad.

The free market side of this combination can be seen in the varied moves to privatize official information by converting it from a publicly available resource to a privately purchasable commodity. There has been a critical shift in the official attitude towards public information. Continuous efforts are under way to introduce market criteria into production and distribution of all sorts of government information products. Under the banner of reducing red tape and spending, about one out of every four Government Printing Office publications has been discontinued. 'The termination or consolidation of redundant and superfluous publications and unnecessary printing facilities will reduce costs to the taxpayer by $85 million annually and eliminate 150 million copies of publications', states Edwin Mees (*New York Times*, 7 January 1984: 6). A bill before Congress would require federal departments and agencies, which must now submit some 2,600 reports periodically to each of the 535 members of Congress, to obtain a written request for each report before forwarding it (Hunter 1984: 12). Untold government information collection and distribution activities, from the Census to remote sensing satellites, are being handed over to private companies for profitable exploitation, with dire consequences for public information availability (see Schiller and Schiller 1982: 461–3; United States General Accounting Office 1984).

Often the technical shift towards computer networks expedites an institutional shift towards information as a commodity. The US Securities and Exchange Commission plans to introduce an electronic filing and retrieval system to permit companies to send information to it via electronic means. Currently the agency receives some 6 million pages of documents each year, including stock prospectuses, quarterly and annual reports, tender offers, proxy statements and registration forms for public offerings of securities. After testing, however, the SEC will allow a private contractor to make this information available instantaneously to investors and analysts, on computer screens – and for a fee. To gain access, news media themselves will have to pay. Even before computerization this crucial change is already under way. Disclosure, Incorporated, already sells copies of SEC documents to the public at 50 cents a page, and with a $25 minimum order.

Alongside this push to commercialize governmental information, compiled originally at the taxpayers' expense, we are also witnessing the growth of an authoritarian state. The basic processes at work here are identical to those already outlined for the corporate sector, with the same attempt to restrict public access to information that might be embarrassing or problematic, coupled with aggressive promotion of positive imagery through a whole battery of news management techniques. The result combines intensified selling with escalating secrecy.

In Grenada reporters were simply barred from covering military invasion activities. (The best case US media executives make in response is to insist that 'the press [can] be trusted to keep military secrets' (Friendly 1984: A3). The clampdown on access to government information, however, is occurring across a sweeping vista. Reporters are told they may not name publicly even known CIA agents. Attempts to eviscerate the Freedom of Information Act are continuous from the first days of the Reagan administration. The classification system is refurbished to ensure that more rather than less information will be kept secret. Potential news sources are simply being shut up; a shocking 120,000 government employees are forced to acquiesce to lifetime censorship. In a measure aimed ostensibly at news leaks, key decisions about CIA covert operations – never public – are now made by a clique of top executive branch administrators. A move to forestall circulation of *un*classified Defense Department-sponsored research is pressuring universities to join the campaign to diminish and subjugate what can be publicly known. Pentagon officials insist on briefings with unnamed sources, to ensure that military versions of events are reported without accountability or rebuttal. 'This practice has become routine in Washington', *The New York Times* concedes, 'largely because news organizations, in most instances, have been unwilling to decline invitations to briefings and have only infrequently protested the ground rules' (see Abrams 1983; Burnham 1984b; Halloran 1984a).

Yet it is not only by diminishing access that government is introducing a new scale of news management. Equally vital is a grossly inflated apparatus for injecting preferred messages *into* the public press. Government attempts to smuggle messages into the public realm, true, have a long history. Both the systematic use of news manipulation and the explosive growth of executive branch press and publicity operations, however, are unprecedented. In the Kennedy era, according to long-time veteran of the White House press corps James Deakin, there was but one press secretary, an assistant and a few stenographers. 'Today it is estimated that the White House press staff numbers in the hundreds ... The press operation is very large, very powerful' (Gamarekian 1984: 8).

During the 1984 election year the US population became the target of global news management. President Reagan launched his 1984 re-election bid from Beijing. With more than 300 US journalists on hand to cover his visit (each television network fielded about 50), saturation coverage blanketed the United States. The arrival scene, choreographed by the White House and complete with stage directions, dominated each network's morning news show. 'The smallest details – from the tape marking where the president should stand in the Great Hall of the People to his plans to reciprocally serve his Chinese hosts with chopsticks – have been arranged at the highest levels', the *Wall Street Journal* reported. When queried to see if there was any room left in the schedule for spontaneity, presidential adviser Michael Deaver – who is called 'the Toscanini of political orchestration' – simply answered, 'No' (Mayer 1984b: 54).

Then, at the June 1984 economic summit conference between leaders of the USA, France, Canada, West Germany, Italy, Japan and Britain, held in London, the White House excluded an American reporter to make room for a cameraman hired to film re-election campaign commercials. A staggering 3,300 journalists from around the world were kept at bay in meeting rooms 2 miles from the conference site. A camera crew from Reagan's campaign, however, was with him throughout a ten-day European trip and was given greater access to events than (was) permitted for news organizations. Another election year extravaganza celebrating the anniversary of the Allied landings in France featured Reagan leading a new invasion of Normandy for an international audience – courtesy CBS, NBC, ABC *and* the BBC and other overseas broadcasters (Jaroslavsky 1984: 60).

Amid savage cutbacks in most non-military programmes, the Reagan Administration increased the 1983 budget for foreign information activities by 23 per cent, with similar increases in 1984 and 1985. The chief goal of these expenditures is to influence foreign public opinion, for example in Western Europe, where the peace movement has helped weaken a uniform anti-détente posture among NATO countries (Seib 1983: 1, 43).

Administration officials are also relying upon new satellite technology to enhance global propaganda capabilities. Directed by the United States Information Agency (USIA), 'Worldnet' is a carefully planned attempt to penetrate foreign media with the US administration's live messages. Signals are made available to local television stations and, sometimes, to American embassies – to which local journalists can be invited and, always in predetermined cases, permitted to question a televised speaker. The global network consists of several components. A 'Euronet' subsystem provides a direct relay from Washington to London, Bonn, Rome, The Hague, Paris, Geneva, Stockholm, Brussels, Vienna, Madrid, Copenhagen and Oslo. Other segments serve capitals in the Middle East, the western Pacific and the Indian subcontinent. A Latin American subsystem was utilized to relay a news conference called by Henry Kissinger in January 1984 on the enthusiastically militaristic report of his Central American Commission. Simultaneous translation into Spanish facilitated maximum impact in Buenos Aires, Caracas and San Jose (Costa Rica); Portuguese expedited the Brazilian transmission.

Worldnet manifests the growing extra-territorial power of the US state. Present plans call for the system to expand to three hours of two-way television conferences each day. Not only will new satellite technology be used to allow US administrators to field questions wherever around the world they happen to be. More important, it will permit Washington to influence global public opinion *directly*. Special newscasts, for example, are scheduled so as to achieve maximum television exposure in overseas evening news shows and morning newspaper editions (Farrell 1984: 6).

USIA officials laud Worldnet as 'the most important advance in the way this agency tells America's story since the Voice of America went on the air'. Foreign journalists are sometimes less enthusiastic. Jon Snow, of the British Independent Television Network, complains that because the system 'makes follow-up questions virtually impossible, the format is designed to assure that no depth is reached' (Burnham 1984c: 3).

After recent congressional review, American media were permitted to offer *printed* accounts of Worldnet satellite broadcasts. No questions were raised about whether news reports generated by a satellite conference and subsequently published in the United States 'might place the agency in the position of indirectly violating the prohibition against directing propaganda at the United States'.

Conclusion

An epochal change in news is taking place. The essential benefits of hard information continue to be gained, but only by an emerging corporate 'public' which can pay handsomely for up-to-the-minute electronic news in dozens of specialized areas. The *citizenry*, however, is being buried in an avalanche of misinformation, as it encounters cruel new hybrids of news, advertising and entertainment, with a hefty dash of government manipulation thrown in. As media and non-media businesses race to deploy communications technology as a competitive weapon, the news available to the average inhabitant of a society threatened by war, unemployment and environmental catastrophe is being rapidly transformed into a social hallucinogen.

2

The Media and the Public Sphere

Nicholas Garnham

I want to argue in this essay that a shift in focus is required in research and debate on the relationship between the media and politics. In recent years that research and debate has largely taken for granted the existing structure of both the media and politics, the one articulated around the relationship between a privately-owned commercial press and a state-regulated broadcasting system, the other around political parties and some form of representative parliamentary or congressional government.

The overwhelming focus of concern has been the problem of representation in the mediatic sense of that word: that is to say, the question posed has been how well or badly do the various media reflect the existing balance of political forces and the existing political agenda and with what effect upon political action, in particular on voting patterns.

It seems to me that, important as these questions are, they miss the central and most urgent question now raised by the developing relationship between the media and politics, because they fail to start from the position that the institutions and processes of public communication are themselves a central part of the political structure and process.

It is a commonplace to assert that public communication lies at the heart of the democratic process; that citizens require, if their equal access to the vote is to have any substantive meaning, equal access also to sources of information and equal opportunities to participate in the debates from which political decisions rightly flow. I want to argue that it follows that changes in media structure and media policy, whether these stem from economic developments or from public intervention, are properly political questions of as much importance as the question of whether or not to introduce proportional representation, of relations between local and national government, of subsidies to political parties; that the policy of Western European governments towards cable TV and satellite broadcasting is as important as their attitude towards the development of a United Europe; that the FCC's policy towards broadcast regulation is as important as the question of states' rights and that politicians, political scientists and citizens concerned with the health and future of democracy neglect these issues at their peril.

However, political theory has largely neglected the implications of such a position and, in particular, has neglected the problem of how, materially, the institutions and processes of public communication are sustained and of the political effects of the specific ways in which a given social formation may choose to provide those resources.

Changes in the structure of public communication

I have argued elsewhere, at greater length than is possible here, that our inherited structures of public communication, those institutions within which we construct, distribute and consume symbolic forms, are undergoing a profound change (Garnham 1983). This change is characterized by a reinforcement of the market and the progressive destruction of public service as the preferred mode for the allocation of cultural resources; by a focus upon the TV set as the locus for an increasingly privatized, domestic mode of consumption; by the creation of a two-tier market divided between the information rich, provided with high-cost specialized information and cultural services, and the information poor, provided with increasingly homogenized entertainment services on a mass scale; by a shift from largely national to largely international markets in the informational and cultural spheres. Symptoms of this shift are the expansion of new TV delivery services such as videocassette, cable and Direct Broadcasting Satellite, under market control and on an international basis; the progressive deregulation and privatization of national telecommunication monopolies; the shift of Reuters from a general news agency to being largely a provider of specialized commercial information services; the increased penetration of sponsorship into the financing of both sport and the arts; the move, under the pressure of public spending cuts, of educational and research institutes, such as universities, towards the private sector; proposals to make profitability the criterion for the provision of public information through such bodies as the Stationery Office, the Ordnance Survey and the US Government Printing Office; the shift in the library service, in the USA at least, away from the principle of free and open access towards access to proprietary data bases on a payment by usage basis. All these are examples of a trend to what has been dubbed, usually by those in favour of these developments, the Information Society or Information Economy. This trend represents an unholy alliance between Western governments, desperate for growth and in deadly competition with one another for that growth, and multinational corporations in search of new world markets in electronic technology and information goods and services. The result of this trend will be to shift the balance in the cultural sector between the market and public service decisively in favour of the market and to shift the dominant definition of public information from that of a public good to that of a privately appropriable commodity.

What are the implications of these developments if we accept the argument that channels and processes of public communication are integral to the democratic process?

The media and democracy

The debate about the political function and effect of modes of public communication has traditionally largely been carried on within the terms of the Hegelian state/civil society dichotomy. The dominant theory within that debate has been the liberal theory of the free press, which has either simply assumed that the market will provide appropriate institutions and processes of public communication to support a democratic polity, or in its stronger form argues that only the market can ensure the necessary freedom from state control and coercion. The critique of this position has been able to collect impressive evidence of the way in which market forces produce results, in terms of oligopoly control and depoliticization of content, that are far from the liberal ideal of a free market-place of ideas. But the strength of the hold that liberal theory still exercises can be judged by the inadequacy of proposals for press reform generated by the Left and the weakness with which such proposals have been pursued. For the Left itself remains trapped within a free press model inherited from the nineteenth century. The hold of this model is also illustrated by the way in which no equally legitimated theory has been developed to handle the dominant form of public communication, broadcasting. The public service, state-regulated model, whether publicly or privately funded, has in effect always been seen, not as a positive good but as an unfortunate necessity imposed by the technical limitations of frequency scarcity. Those on the Left who are opposed to market forces in the press none the less have in general given no more than mealy-mouthed support to public service broadcasting. They have concentrated their critique on the question of the coercive or hegemonic nature of state power. Seeing the public service form as either a smokescreen for such power or as occupied from within by commercial forces, they have concentrated on criticizing the inadequacy and repressive nature of the rules of balance and objectivity within which public service broadcasting is forced to operate. The Left has, therefore, tended to fall back either on idealist formulations of free communications given no organizational substance or material support, or on a technological utopianism which sees the expansion of channels of communication as inherently desirable because pluralistic. Both positions are linked to some version, both political and artistic, of free expression, for example, the long debate and campaigns around Channel 4, the touching faith in cable access, Left support for 'free' or 'community' radio, and so on. Alternatively, the problem has simply been postponed until after the take-over of state power.

In my view, the implications of current developments are better understood, and an escape from the bind of the state/market dichotomy and from the hold of free press theory and the necessary accompanying re-evaluation of public service is better provided, by looking at the problem from the perspective of the theory of the Public Sphere.

Habermas and the Public Sphere
The theory of the Public Sphere, as articulated in particular by Habermas, argues that, just as the participatory democracy of the Athenian agora depended upon the material base of slavery, so it was the development of competitive market capitalism that provided the conditions, initially in eighteenth-century Britain, for the development of both the theory and practice of liberal democracy. It did so by making available to a new political class, the bougeoisie, both the time and material resources to create a network of institutions within civil society, such as newspapers, learned and debating societies, publishing enterprises, libraries, universities and polytechnics and museums, within which a new political power, public opinion, could come into existence.

This Public Sphere possessed the following key characteristics. It was protected from the power of both church and state by its access to the sustaining resources of a wide range of private individuals with an alternative source of economic power. It was in principle open to all in the same way that access to the market was open to all, because the cost of entry for each individual was dramatically lowered by the growth in scale of the market. The Public Sphere thus took on the universalistic aspects of the Hegelian state, membership of the Public Sphere being conterminous with citizenship. All participants within the Public Sphere were, as with the competitive market, on terms of equal power because costs of participation were widely and evenly spread and because social wealth in general, within the bourgeoisie, was evenly distributed. It was distinct from the private interests that governed civil society, on the other hand, because, in the Enlightenment tradition, it obeyed the rules of rational discourse, political views and decisions being open, not to the play of power, but to that of argument based upon evidence, and because its concern was not private interest but the public good. It thus also took over the rationalist aspects of the Hegelian state.

Habermas went on to argue that the Public Sphere, this space for a rational and universalistic politics distinct from both the economy and the state, was destroyed historically by the very forces that had brought it into existence. The development of the capitalist economy in the direction of monopoly capitalism led to an uneven distribution of wealth, to rising entry costs to the Public Sphere and thus to unequal access to and control over that sphere. In particular, the rise of advertising and public relations has exemplified these trends since they represent the direct control by private or state interests of the flow of public information in the interest, not of rational discourse, but of manipulation. At the same time these developments in the economy led to related development by the state, which itself became an active and major participant in the economy, thus coming to share the private interests there pursued. At the same time the state was called in, by those class forces which wished to defend and expand the Public Sphere against the encroaching power of private capital, to itself provide its material support, through for instance the provision of public education, public libraries, systems of public cultural subsidy. In addition, the growth of the state's role as a co-ordinator and infrastructural provider for monopoly capitalism led to the massive development of state power as an independent administrative and bureaucratic interest, distinct from the rationalist determination of social ends and of the means to those ends in that political realm guaranteed by the existence of the Public Sphere. Thus the space between civil society and the state which had been opened up by the creation of the Public Sphere was squeezed shut between these two increasingly collaborative behemoths. In Habermas's words, 'The liberal model of the public sphere . . . cannot be applied to the actual conditions of an industrially advanced mass-democracy organized in the form of the social welfare state. In part the liberal model had always included ideological components, but it is also in part true that the social pre-conditions, to which the ideological elements could at one time at least be linked, had been fundamentally transformed' (Habermas 1979: 200).

However, Habermas wishes to distinguish between the set of principles upon which the bourgeois sphere was based and which, in the fight against feudalism, it brought into existence, on the one hand, and the set of specific historically concrete institutions which embodied those principles, on the other. For Habermas, while the specific forms in which they are embodied will vary, the principles are the indispensable basis of a free society. These principles are general accessibility, especially to information, the elimination of privilege and the search for general norms and their rational legitimation.

The set of concrete institutions within which public opinion is formed, which include the media of public communication, elections, publicly accessible courts, and so on, are distinguished from the state, although the legitimation of the democratic state lies in its role of guarantor of the Public Sphere through law.

Public opinion is to be distinguished from mere opinion as presupposing the existence of a reasoning public.

The centrality of these principles for Habermas derives from his more general concern with undistorted communication. Pursuing the tradition of critical theory, Habermas has sought concrete grounds for the validation of critical social judgement and for the claims to human emancipation. He has attempted to ground truth claims in the social sciences upon what he has called the Ideal Speech Situation. He argues that human interaction, the field of meanings and values, presupposes language and exists in language. He goes on to argue that we can therefore discover within the structure of speech itself the essential grounding presuppositions of all human interaction and thus of all social organization. He argues that every time we speak we are making four validity claims, to comprehensibility, truth, appropriateness and sincerity, which in their turn imply the possibility of justifying those claims. Thus the claim to truth implies a social context within which factual claims about external nature can be validated by evidence and logical argument, while claims to appropriateness, that is, to the social right to make the statement, implies a social context in which social norms can be rationally debated and consensual agreement arrived at. In real historical societies characterized by differential power relations and resource distribution such conditions do not hold and we are thus in the presence of 'distorted communication'. But, for Habermas, the essential human attribute of speech provides the ground for an ideal society against which existing societies can be judged and found wanting and to which we can aspire (see Held 1980: ch. 10; Habermas 1982).

Thus the concept of the Public Sphere and the principles it embodies represent an Ideal Type against which we can judge existing social arrangements and which we can attempt to embody in concrete institutions in the light of the reigning historical circumstances.

The strengths of the concept, to which we need to hang on, are that it identifies and stresses the importance for democratic politics of a sphere distinct from the economy and the state and thus helps us to escape from that dichotomy, to which I pointed earlier, as one of the major blocks to the formulation of a democratic response to current developments in the media. Secondly, it stresses the materiality of any Public Sphere and therefore the need to consider the future of democratic politics, and of the institutions and practices of public communication which are a necessary part of such a politics, in terms of the allocation of scarce social resources. From this point of view the concept is firmly anti-idealist.

Another strength is that the concept identifies the importance of rationality and universality as key moments in any democratic political practice and holds out the, in my view proper, aspiration to resist the reduction of politics to either simply the clash of power interest, in particular class forces, or to questions of state administration. It forces us to remember that in politics universal ends are always, or ought always, to be at issue, as are choices between incompatible public goods, which cannot be reduced to differences of material interest. Thus on the one hand the concept of the Public Sphere challenges the liberal free press tradition on the grounds of materiality, and on the other it challenges the Marxist critiques of that tradition on the grounds of the specificity of politics.

Criticism of the concept of the Public Sphere
At the same time the weaknesses of the concept are not difficult to see. First there is the problem of the relation of the concept to the historical reality of class division and class politics. As many critics have pointed out, in the period to which Habermas assigns the golden age of the Public Sphere, access to that sphere was in fact far from universal, but was restricted to bourgeois males. To the extent that it was able to operate on the basis of consensus as to the public good it was not because the Public Sphere had escaped determination by the private

interests that ruled civil society, but because the bourgeoisie who participated in this Public Sphere did so on the basis of a tacit prior acceptance of bourgeois class interests as conterminous with the public good and as not themselves open to the scrutiny of public rational argument that was supposed to rule within the Public Sphere. Indeed this observation is central to Marx's own development of the theory of ideology. Moreover, this bourgeois public sphere was actively involved in suppressing the development of an alternative and oppositional proletarian public sphere based upon the radical press, trade unions, and so on. While I think this criticism is correct it does not follow in my view that we need to give up on the universalistic possibility of a general Public Sphere and fall back upon the development of a number of clashing and sectionalized Public Spheres.

This indeed seems to me to be the main problem with Negt and Kluge's concept of the Proletarian Public Sphere. Its strength is that it recognizes the need to break out of factionalism and out of a vanguard party tradition that sees channels of proletarian communication as merely functional tools of political propaganda and organization. Its weakness is a mysticism that attempts to ground its universality, not in a consensus reached after rational debate between competing interests, but in a Lukácsian notion of an imputed class-consciousness which is inherently universal (Negt and Kluge 1979).

A further weakness of the Public Sphere model is that it is conceived by Habermas in individualistic terms. I do not believe this is a necessary attribute of it, but it does have certain consequences for how the concept might be used. For Habermas the Public Sphere, and the concept of a rational politics that goes with it, is based upon the assumption, which seems to me wholly unrealistic, that all participants possess complete information and engage in all debates. This is another version of the liberal economic argument that underpins free press theory, that all market participants possess full information and that the costs of searching for that information are nil. In complex societies characterized, as ours are, both nationally as well as internationally, by highly developed divisions of labour, both functionally and spatially, such a presupposition is simply idealistic. It means that the concept in its present form cannot deal with the political problem of mediation. There is no place in the theory for the social role and power of expertise and expert knowledge nor, and this is crucial, for the role and social interests associated with knowledge-broking. Thus it becomes difficult to handle the problem of the role of those who in fact manage the conduct of the information-gathering and debate which is the Public

Sphere's *raison d'être*, namely, in particular, journalists and politicians themselves. It is a further result of this weakness that the theory has no place for what I regard as an essential and central organizing institution within the Public Sphere, the political party.

The Public Sphere and public service broadcasting

I want now to return to my starting-point and look at the implications of the concept of the Public Sphere for the debate on the structure and function of the mass media. In doing so I want to focus upon broadcasting and upon the public service model of broadcasting as an embodiment of the principles of the Public Sphere. Such a focus is a conscious corrective to the more normal focus, in debates about the media and politics, upon the press and upon a free press model derived from the history of print communication. I have tried to clarify the strengths and weaknesses of the concept of the Public Sphere because the public service model of public communication, as actualized in broadcasting, shares these strengths and weaknesses and because confusions stemming from them have bedevilled the debates about the nature and validity of the public service model.

The great strength of the public service model, to which we need to hang on through all the twists and turns of the argument that has raged around it, is the way it (a) presupposes and then tries to develop in its practice a set of social relations which are distinctly political rather than economic, and (b) at the same time attempts to insulate itself from control by the state as opposed to, and this is often forgotten, political control. Reith's original vision was undoubtedly drawn from the tradition of the Scottish enlightenment and, within the very narrow limits within which the economic and political forces of the time allowed him to operate, the early practice of the BBC, as Scannel and Cardiff's recent research shows, made a noble effort to address their listeners as rational political beings rather than as consumers (Scannel 1980; Cardiff 1980). It is easy to argue that the agenda for debate and the range of information considered important was hopelessly linked to a narrow class-based definition of the public good and that it was doomed to failure, because public aspirations were already so moulded by the consumerist ideology secreted by the dominant set of social relations in society, that this alternative set, as the experience of Radio Luxemburg demonstrated, could only be imposed on listeners by the brute force of monopoly. But this is to miss the point of the enterprise and its continuing importance as both historical example and potential alternative. After all, one could use the same argument (indeed people are already using this argument in relation to the power of local government) that because of declining voter turn-out one should simply abolish elections.

The economic and the political
For the problem with liberal free press theory is not just that the market has produced conditions of oligopoly which undercut the liberal ideal nor that private ownership leads to direct manipulation of political communication, although it does, but that there is a fundamental contradiction between the economic and the political at the level of their value systems and of the social relations which those value systems require and support. Within the political realm the individual is defined as a citizen exercising public rights of debate, voting, and so on, within a communally agreed structure of rules and towards communally defined ends. The value system is essentially social and the legitimate end of social action is the public good. Within the economic realm, on the other hand, the individual is defined as producer and consumer exercising private rights through purchasing power on the market in the pursuit of private interests, his or her actions being co-ordinated by the invisible hand of the market.

This contradiction produces two clashing concepts of human freedom. On the one hand, as expressed for instance by Hayek and in some versions of Thatcherism and Reaganism, human freedom is defined in economic terms as the freedom to pursue private interest without political constraint. On the other hand, the socialist and Marxist traditions define freedom in political terms and advocate political intervention in the workings of the market in order to liberate the majority from its constraints. Both traditions assume that the contradiction is resolvable by suppressing either the political or the economic. These clashing concepts of freedom are reflected in debates about the media's political role. On one side the market is seen as a bulwark against the great enemy, state censorship. Thus private ownership of the means of communication is at best a positive good and at worst the lesser of two necessary evils. On the other side capitalist control of the media is seen as an obstacle to free political communication and as the explanation of the media's role in maintaining capitalist class hegemony. In both traditions politics is equated with state power.

I want to argue that this contradiction is irresolvable because in social formations characterized by an advanced division of labour, both functionally and spatially, only the market is capable of handling the necessary scale of allocative decision-making across wide sectors of human productive activity, while at the same time there is a range of social decisions which no democratic society will be prepared to leave to the market, or rather if it does leave them to the market, it forfeits all claims to democracy. These include the control of social violence, the provision of a basic level of health and material well-being and above all includes control over the development of the market itself, both in its internal structure, for example, the problem of monopoly, and its externalities, such as environmental questions.

Once we recognize this irresolvable contradiction then the analytical task becomes one of mapping the interactions between the two spheres and the political task, one of working out the historically appropriate balance between recognizing, on the one hand, that pursuit of political freedom may override the search for economic efficiency, while on the other the extent of possible political freedom is constrained by the level of material productivity.

The field of the mass media is a key focus for examining this contradiction because they operate simultaneously across the two realms. Thus a newspaper or a TV channel is at one and the same time a commercial operation and a political institution. The nature of the largely undiscussed problems this creates can be illustrated if one points to the elaborate structure of law and convention which attempts to insulate politicians, public servants and the political process from economic control – rules against bribery, laws controlling election expenditure, the socially validated view, however often it may actually take place, against the use of public office for private gain. And yet at the same time we allow what we recognize as central political institutions, such as the press and broadcasting, to be privately operated. We would find it strange now if we made voting rights dependent upon purchasing power or property rights and yet access to the mass media, as both channels of information and fora of debate, is largely controlled by just such power and rights.

But the incompatibility between the commercial and political functions of the media is not just a question of ownership and control, important as such questions are. It is even more a question of the value system and set of social relations within which commercial media must operate and which they serve to reinforce. For it is these that are inimical, not just to one political interest group or another, but to the very process of democratic politics itself. Thus political communication which is forced to channel itself via commercial media – and here I refer not just to the press but to public service broadcasting so far as it competes for audiences with commercial broadcasting and on its dominant terms – becomes the politics of consumerism. Politicians relate to potential voters not as rational beings concerned for the public good, but in the mode of advertising, as creatures of passing and largely irrational appetite, to whose self-interest they must appeal. Politics, as Reagan so strikingly demonstrates, becomes not a matter of confronting real issues and choices, but of image. Appeal to people's dreams and fantasies and reality will take care of itself. Politics becomes no longer a matter of balancing priorities or choosing between desirable but incompatible ends within a political programme, but of single issues which can be packaged in easily consumable and sellable form, like soap powder, and to which the response, like that of the decision to purchase, is a simple and immediate yes or no, not the 'just a moment' of debate. The contemporary prevalence of this model of politics among voters is well illustrated by H. Himmelweit *et al.*'s recent book *How Voters Decide* where what the authors identify as the consumer model of voting appears to best explain actual voting behaviour. Following this model, as the authors put it, 'what matters is that the act of voting, like the purchase of goods, is seen as simply one instance of decision making, no different in kind from the process whereby other decisions are reached' (Himmelweit *et al.* 1985). Unfortunately, however, there is no mechanism in the political realm like that of the invisible hand of the market, to ensure that individual responses to distinctly presented political issues result in coherent political action. It is a form of politics and political communication which enables both citizens and politicians to live in an essentially apolitical world where all our desires can be satisfied, where we can have higher welfare benefits, higher defence expenditure and lower taxes, where we can strengthen the rights of women without challenging the rights of men, where we can appeal to the majority but at the same time protect minorities. Such a politics is forced to take on the terms of address of the media it uses and to address its readers, viewers and listeners within the set of social relations that those media have created for other purposes. Thus the citizen is appealed to as a private individual rather than as a member of a public, within a privatized domestic sphere rather than within that of public life. For instance, think of the profound political difference between reading a newspaper in one's place of work or in a café and discussing it with those who share that concrete set of social relations on the one hand, and watching TV within the family circle or listening to radio or watching a video-cassette on an individual domestic basis on the other. Think of the Sony Walkman as a concrete embodiment of social isolation, as opposed to participation at a rock concert.

Public service and knowledge-broking

However, while I want to argue that the public service model of the media has at its heart a set of properly political values and that its operation both requires and fosters a set of social relations distinct from and opposed to the economic values and relations which are essential to an operating democracy, at the same time in its actual historical operation it has so far shared with the Habermasian concept of the Public Sphere a crucial failure to recognize the problem of mediation within the Public Sphere and thus the role of knowledge-brokers within the system. In particular the public service model has failed to come to terms with the proper and necessary social function of both journalists and politicians. In relation to both groups there is a failure sufficiently to distinguish between two communicative functions within the Public Sphere, on the one hand the collection and dissemination of information and on the other the provision of a forum for debate.

Journalists within public service broadcasting, under the banner of balance and objectivity, claim to carry out both functions and to do so in the name of the public. However, this produces a contradiction. On the one hand, the function of information search and exposition, that carried out at its best, for instance, by teachers, cannot simply be equated with political advocacy. Here Jay Blumler is right (Blumler *et al.* 1978). On the other hand, journalists are not in any way accountable to the public they claim to serve and themselves constitute a distinct interest. How then are we to ensure that this function is carried out responsibly? It clearly needs to be accompanied by a structure of Freedom of Information, and so on. It also needs much better trained journalists. It also, because of its expense, quite clearly depends upon a public service structure of provision, since otherwise high quality information will become not a public good but an expensive private asset. But it still remains that the function cannot simply be left to unaccountable journalists. It needs a public accountability structure of its own and a quite distinct code of professional values separate from the political debate function. Within such a structure much greater direct access needs to be given to independent fields of social expertise. It is a perennial and justifiable criticism of journalists by experts that journalists themselves decide the agenda of what is relevant and at the same time too often garble the information for presentational purposes. Perhaps bodies such as the Medical Research Council, the Economic and Social Research Council, Greenpeace, Social Audit, and one could list many others, should have regular access to broadcasting and print channels and employ their own journalists to clarify current issues for the general public as a background to more informed political debate.

On the other hand, the debate function needs to be more highly politicized, with political parties and other major organized social movements having access to the screen on their own terms rather as was the case until recently in Holland, although that model is itself in the process of being undermined by the very economic forces to which I pointed at the outset. Here one might envisage a situation where any group that could obtain a membership of over a certain size would be eligible for regular access to air time and national newspaper space. Indeed Habermas himself seems to envisage some such arrangement when he argues that the Public Sphere today requires that 'a public body of organized private individuals take the place of the now defunct public body of private individuals'. Such organizations would themselves, he argues, have to have democratic internal structures. The Public Sphere, he writes, 'could only be realized today, on an altered basis, as a rational reorganization of social and political power under the mutual control of rival organizations committed to the public sphere in their internal structure as well as in their relations with the State and each other' (Habermas 1979: 201).

Public service and the political party

To date, the operation of public service broadcasting has tended to reinforce the apoliticism of consumerism by pitting broadcasting, not just aganst the state, but against politicians. It is politicians that are seen as inherently untrustworthy, as having to be criticized, as trying to interfere in and control broadcasting. Furthermore, as it has operated within the confines of a tradition of critical journalism and of balance and objectivity, broadcasting has contributed to the observable decline of the political party. It has done so by pre-empting its role as a communicator of politically relevant information and as a structurer of political debate. As the press has become steadily more depoliticized, politicians and political parties have been forced to communicate to the electorate via TV on terms largely dictated by journalists. The parties are unable to expound a coherent position, but are forced to respond issue by issue. By concentrating on personalities TV has at the same time enhanced the position of political leaders at the expense of party organizations. This decline of the political party matters because, in societies split by conflicts of interest (in my view all conceivable societies), parties represent the rationalist and universalist moment of the Hegelian state. That is to say, they are the indispensable institutional form by which the views of individuals are shaped into that necessary hierarchy of interlocking, mutually interdependent ends and means that we call a political programme, without which rational political action in terms of some version of the public good is impossible. That is not to say that the present pattern of parties is optimal. But the current fashion for movement politics, CND, the women's movement, and so on, which is in itself in part a response to the decline of political parties induced by existing patterns of media dominance, in part a product of that very consumerist ideology I am concerned to critique, in part an expression of dissatisfaction with the programmes of existing parties, in no way provides an alternative to the political party, as indeed these movements are discovering. You cannot develop a realistic and realizable movement towards disarmament or women's rights unless it is integrated with other social and economic objectives into some structure and universal programme of political priorities.

A similar argument holds against the other alternative posed to the public service model, that of some version of pluralism, however the material base of that pluralism might be decided. But in general such visions, such yearnings for a return to a golden age of press freedom, are attempts precisely to avoid the crunch of political choice. Indeed, that is perhaps the main unconscious attraction of the free press model and indeed of the market model, that it removes the weight of conscious social choice.

Public service, universalism and an international public sphere

One of the strengths of the public sphere concept which I would want to stress and which I would want to link to any revitalized notion of public service is that of universalism. I mean by this the notion that the scope of a political decision structure must be conterminous with the scope of the powers it aims to control. In recent tradition this has in general meant within the boundaries of the nation-state, so that citizenship of such states is defined in terms of certain nationally universal rights and obligations. The principle of tying voting to property rights was an important expression of this because it recognized the importance of the relationship between the right to participate in decision-making and a not easily avoidable involvement in the consequences of those decisions. It is precisely for this reason that capital, so long as it can flow internationally with ease, should not be accorded such rights. Within this envelope of rights and obligations all citizens, whether they are on the winning or losing side of a political debate, are forced to live with its consequences. Thus proper democratic participation cannot be irresponsible by definition. In some countries this important truth is embodied in laws requiring all citizens to vote. Now, while it would clearly be both impossible and undesirable to require all citizens to participate in a minimum amount of political information consumption and debate or to make electoral participation dependent upon such participation, in principle it is a mere corollary of a requirement to vote. Indeed this is the principle which trade unions correctly mobilize against the institution of mandatory postal ballots. However, public policy should, if democracy is to be taken seriously, favour citizen participation in such debate. If that is the case debate must include as many of the existing views in a society on the relevant issues as possible. This cannot, by definition, be provided by sectionalized, ghettoized media talking only to a particular interest group or the party faithful. In terms of national issues it must take place at a national level and is undercut by a multiplication of simultaneous viewing and listening options. It is this that is the rational core of the argument mobilized in favour of the existing public service broadcasting duopoly in Britain: namely, that the existence of a national focus for political debate and information is important to the national political process. The problem of the relations of scale needed between communication channels and political power then takes on a different dimension when we consider the transnational aspect of current media developments.

If we see media structures as central to the democratic polity and if the universalism of the one must match that of the latter, clearly the current process by which national media control is being undercut is part of that process by which power is being transferred in the economy to the international level without the parallel development of adequate political or communication structures. This is already apparent from the problem facing European governments, in the face of satellite broadcasting, of trying to match their different systems of advertising control and indeed, although so far as I know this has not yet been discussed, systems of political access.

Let us be clear. It is in the interest of the controllers of multinational capital to keep nation-states and their citizens in a state of disunity and disfunctional ignorance unified only by market structures within which such capital can freely flow, while at the same time they develop their own private communication networks. The development of the *Financial Times* and the *Wall Street Journal* and of private, high-cost, proprietary data networks and services on an international scale to serve the corporate community and its agents is a clear sign of this trend. Thus not only do we face the challenge of sustaining and developing the public sphere at a national level. Such a development will simply be bypassed, if we do not, at the same time and perhaps with greater urgency, begin to develop a public sphere where at present one hardly exists, namely, at the international level. It is here that current threats, led by the US government, but supported and abetted by the UK, to UNESCO and the ITU, need to be seen for what they are, attempts to destroy what little public sphere actually exists at an international level. It is significant that the crime of which these institutions stand accused is 'politicization'.

In conclusion, I have tried to argue here that the necessary defence and expansion of the public sphere as an integral part of a democratic society requires us to re-evaluate the public service model of public communication and, while being necessarily critical of its concrete historical actualization, defend it and build upon the potential of its rational core in the face of the existing and growing threats to its continued existence.

3
Broadcasting and the Public Interest: from Consensus to Crisis

Stuart Hood

*T*he *last* few years have seen the end of a period during which the concept of public service in certain areas of control and management – not only in the field of broadcasting – has been an almost unquestioned element in a wide consensus. In Britain that period dates back to the 1920s when, on the basis of experiences gained in the management of scarce resources and essential services during the First World War, there was a generally accepted view that public corporations were the most effective and socially most acceptable instruments for managing certain sectors of the economy. The pattern was established in Britain by the Forestry Commission, set up in 1919, as a result of the dangerous shortage of timber experienced during the Great War. It was followed by the Central Electricity Board, legislation for which went through Parliament in 1926, its creation being almost simultaneous with that of the British Broadcasting Corporation. The latter was in that year transformed from the British Broadcasting Company, a cartel of radio manufacturers, into a public service institution. In the case of both the BBC and the Central Electricity Board it is significant that the evident confusion and the contradictory interests within the respective industries were factors which led to a governmental decision to place them under the control of public corporations. It is symptomatic, too, of the extent to which the consensual view of the appropriateness of such bodies prevailed that in neither case was there any party opposition to their creation. Both the BBC and the Central Electricity Board were set up by a Conservative government. The London Transport Bill, which created the London Transport Board in 1933, was introduced under a Labour government and passed into law under the right-wing coalition government which we know as the National Government. Its originator, Herbert Morrison, the Labour boss of the London County Council, saw in the kind of public corporation represented by the Transport Board a 'combination of public ownership, public accountability and business management for public ends' (Dalton 1935: 141). It is a formulation from which Sir John Reith as founder of the British Broadcasting Corporation would not have dissented, for it was in the same terms that he saw his own institution. Nor was such thinking unfamiliar in the United States where, in 1925, Herbert Hoover told a congressional hearing that radio communication was not to be seen merely as a business carried out for private gain but as a public concern 'impressed with the public trust and to be considered primarily from the standpoint of public interest to the same extent and upon the same principles as our other public utilities' (Head 1972: 420).

Although an essentially Fabian concept it was accepted beyond Fabian circles and belonged in fact to the political consensus. There were those, however, who saw in public corporations the foundation stones of a socialist economy. One such was Hugh Dalton, who was to become Chancellor of the Exchequer in the 1945 Labour government. Writing in the 1930s on the subject of public corporations he described the BBC as 'on its financial side a socialist model' (Dalton 1935: 97). Reflecting on the record of the British public corporations in the previous decade he formulated a definition of public corporations which was intended as a blueprint for the future. The service or industry for which they were responsible should be under a single control; should have neither private investors nor distributed profits; should work to a plan aiming at efficient public service; and should be ultimately controlled by Parliament and the minister responsible for the particular area of the economy. It was in the 1930s, too, that a study of the public corporation in Britain based on a doctorate, supervised appropriately by the Fabian don G. D. H. Cole, described transport, broadcasting and the supply of electrical energy (in that order) as sharing certain general characteristics that made them eminently appropriate for management by a public corporation. The enterprises they controlled, the author argued, were such that they could not be handed over to completely unregulated private enterprise. There were grave disadvantages in the operation of even a limited profit motive and equally grave disadvantages in state interference in the shape of civil service administration. The author then enunciated the view that what made these enterprises particularly suitable for control by public corporations was the combination of outstanding importance to the community with what he described as 'a natural monopoly' (Gordon 1938: 316).

Scarcity and trusteeship

The idea of broadcasting as 'a natural monopoly' because of the limited access (under prevailing technological conditions) to the radio spectrum was commonplace in both the United States and Britain. Thus in 1918 the US Secretary for the Navy said of radio that it was the profound conviction of every person in the United States and abroad who had studied the question that radio was a monopoly – 'a natural monopoly' (Barnouw 1966: 53). This view fitted naturally with the navy's desire to retain that control of radio which it had established during the war 'for all time' on the grounds that much would be lost by 'opening the use of radio communication again to rival companies' (*loc. cit.*). The need to protect what Herbert Hoover, speaking at the First Radio Conference in 1922, called 'a great national asset' found support among American conservationists who were to become engaged in a struggle with the National Electrical Light Association, representing the generating companies, to preserve another national asset – America's rivers. The twin concepts of natural monopoly and public service or public utility were to inform the Radio Act of 1927, the first American attempt to legislate on broadcasting. Eric Barnouw has described it as a law written for a world that no longer existed (Barnouw 1966: 200) for by the time it came on to the statute-book commercialism was too firmly established for its utopian principles to apply. They included the view that the radio waves belonged to the people, the electromagnetic spectrum being a natural resource of the nation which would be destroyed by uncontrolled commercial exploitation. From this it followed that broadcasting was an unique service which had to be equitably distributed; that not everyone was eligible to use a channel; and that the government had discretionary powers over broadcasting, although these powers were obviously not absolute since broadcasting was protected by the First Amendment. The Act was based, according to Wallace H. White, the senator who sponsored it, on the view that 'the right of our people to enjoy the means of communication can be preserved only by the repudiation of the idea . . . that anyone who will may transmit and by the assertion in its stead of the doctrine that the right of the public to service is superior to the right of any individual to use the ether' (Head 1972: 160). It was from the 1927 Act that the impetus came to set up the Federal Radio Commission which, in 1933, following the

Communications Act of that year, became the Federal Communications Commission (FCC). The Commission was in law an independent regulatory commission of the federal government required to function in such a way as to serve 'public convenience, interest or necessity'. There was therefore implicit in its terms of operation the idea of trusteeship on behalf of the public. In more recent times a member of the Commission, critical of its record, felt it necessary to restate the principles it should follow. 'The radio spectrum', he said, 'was meant to be a resource owned and retained by the people. Private interests were to pay [for access to the spectrum] by performance in the public interest.'

The impetus for political control

The situation was complicated, however, by the fact that the argument for public control of access to 'the ether' was not totally altruistic. There were other interpretations of public interest than those flowing from the concept of the electromagnetic spectrum as a scarce public resource and of broadcasting as a natural monopoly. They had to do with political control. The period when the arguments for the public control of broadcasting were first propounded was also one when there was considerable fear that the use of broadcasting might lead to the dissemination of subversive ideas. In Britain, 'owing to its proximity to a highly unstable Europe, the military and naval authorities considered it essential to prohibit for some while wireless experimental work by private persons'(Burrows 1924). The fear presumably was that amateur hams might pick up – and perhaps pass on – undesirable messages like the radio signal addressed To All by the Bolsheviks and similar signals broadcast by the Soldiers' Council which took over the high-power Berlin transmitter during the Spartacist rising. But there were also fears over what the wireless fans might transmit. It was a fear voiced at the Second Conference of Wireless Societies of Great Britain in 1921. Here a representative of the Cardiff and South Wales Wireless Society reported that he had been speaking to his MP who had declared that if transmission was made accessible to everyone 'he feared the Bolshevist element would very soon make full use of the opportunities given to the detriment of the country'. The Wireless Societies were highly respectable organizations and as such declared themselves ready to vet applications for radio licences, which had to be accompanied by testimonials of good character. In 1922 the Postmaster-General was still anxious, however, declaring that 'wireless communication admittedly cannot be kept secret but this seems no reason for making it easy for the general public to listen to everything that is passing in the ether' (Briggs 1961: 105). It was the same fear that made W. Inskip, a Conservative MP shortly to become a law officer of the Crown, to interject anxiously 'Who will be the censor?' when, in that same year, the PMG announced in the Commons on 4 August his intention to license a limited number of radio stations. The question was again raised shortly afterwards in the Sykes Commission on broadcasting. A Post Office official was able to give the Commission assurances that when drawing up the licence of the British Broadcasting Company they had tried 'to word [it] in such a way as to give us some right of objection'. He also spelled out the sanctions that lay to hand. The BBC, he explained, could be as partisan as it pleased about political or economic or other questions but if this were the case he was quite sure the licence would not be renewed (Briggs 1961: 169). The BBC recognized these fears and bent to them in accordance with that policy of self-censorship which is also central to the concept of public service.

In the United States the Radio Act, as we have seen, firmly stated that broadcasting was covered by the First Amendment. This, it was pointed out, should have meant that the government, in the shape of the FCC, was positively forbidden to interfere with the broadcasters' freedom of speech with certain exceptions to prevent the broadcasting of obscenity and material presenting 'a clear and present danger to the state'. In practice, however, government regulation has been more far-reaching in that the FCC has had the right to review programme services, to make rulings as to the balance between programmes and to apply to them the standards of 'public interest, convenience and necessity'. It cannot be said that the Commission has been overrigorous in its review function; it has, however, been argued that had government regulation as applied to broadcasting been applied to the press it could never have been defended successfully in the courts.

There was thus in both Britain and the United States, whatever the local differences in the rigour of the controls, a coincidence of concepts – that of public trusteeship and public control – which found the approval of the politicians of the consensus. There is no need to rehearse the criticisms which have been directed over the years at the BBC and the IBA in Britain or the FCC in the United States for the way in which they have discharged their public duties: criticisms of the degree of real public accountability they display; of their lack of openness to the societies on whose behalf they discharge their trusteeship; and of their bland denial of their role as managers of news and political mediators, although the active part played by public corporations and public agencies in Britain and elsewhere in defining the political, social and moral consensus is well documented. The argument produced by the institutions that their neutrality is guaranteed by the composition of their governing bodies does not bear examination. In this respect nothing has changed since the 1930s when one Fabian critic of the BBC wrote that its Board of Governors displayed 'an excessive homogeneity of age and type' (Robson 1937: 87) and described them as 'highly unreflective of the general outlook of the community' (*ibid.*). (The situation has not changed in the interval; the men and women chosen from the list of 'the great and good' compiled in Downing Street come from a narrow social sample in which bankers, retired Foreign Office officials, businessmen, academics and high Civil Service executives in retirement have figured largely.) It was in the 1930s, too, that the *Harvard Business News*, commenting on the performance of the FCC, opined that while talking in terms of public interest, convenience and necessity, the Commission actually chose to further the ends of the commercial broadcasters. It is a view which has been reiterated in more recent times.

The drive for deregulation

The concept of public service with its dubious yoking of trustee-ship and control is now under attack from two opposite directions – from the radical Left and the radical Right. The criticisms from the Left are directed in Britain towards libertarian solution. The call is for a wider range of opinions to be allowed access to the media, for the recognition of views at present repressed, mediated, or merely ignored, and for more democratic control over the broadcasting in-stitutions. To some, the development of the new information tech-nology and the possibility of a proliferation of channels appears to present an unproblematic opportunity to end the paternalism of the public service institutions. There are, however, radicals at the other end of the political spectrum who also look to the new tech-nology as a weapon to be used against the regulatory bodies: but for very different reasons. They speak for business interests which wish to exploit the new technology for reasons which have little to do with the social role of broadcasting and much to do with the uninhibited play of market forces in a monetarist economy. Now while it is clear that the argument from 'natural monopoly' is increasingly difficult to sustain it is still worth asking whether the concept of 'public service' must inevitably be jettisoned as a result of the campaign for deregulation, which would inevitably lead to the reduction of social control over the media.

It is only an apparent paradox – given the curiously close relations between the FCC and the American networks – that the case for deregulation was set out in the United States in 1982 by the chairman of the FCC, an agency which is still officially charged with trusteeship over broadcasting. His view is that the public interest would best be served if market forces were given freeplay and argues that communications policy 'should be directed towards maximising the services the public desires' for, as he puts it in a remarkable populist formulation, 'the public's interest . . . defines the public interest'. Addressing himself to the problem of the contradiction between the concept of public trusteeship and the First Amendment, he proposes that the Commission should 'refrain from insinuating itself in program decisions by the licensees' on the grounds that there is no reason to believe that the FCC is any more qualified to judge programmes than the advertisers or the subscribers who support them. This is entirely consonant with his view that the Commission should rely on the broadcasters' ability to determine the wants of their audiences through the normal mechanisms of the market-place. It is an argument that disregards the complicated question of how 'the public' knows what it wants and what opportunities it is given to make effective choices. It follows from this extremely consequent application of monetarist principles that he advocates the granting of squatter's rights on frequencies to existing licensees and moots the idea of a spectrum fee to be paid for access to the wavelengths which would thus put a price-tag on distribution. This is a very long way from Herbert Hoover's talk in the 1920s of 'the ether roads', which he defined as 'a great national asset'. It is not surprising that this line of thought leads to a proposal that the Public Broadcasting Service, which is seen as distorting the market, should be ghettoized and confined to transmitting programmes that might not find their way on to the air through the market mechanism.

In Britain there has been no such authoritative statement of the doctrine of deregulation, although *The Times* has devoted no less than five leading articles to attacks on the BBC which have a clear monetarist inspiration. The closest approach to an outline of how it might apply in Britain is contained in a report on communications policy produced by the Adam Smith Institute, a radical conservative organization which has set up the Omega Project 'to fill a significant gap in the field of public policy research' (Adam Smith Institute 1984: ii). The Project was designed 'to create and develop new policy initiatives, to research and analyze new ideas and to bring them forward for public discussion in ways which overcame the conventional shortcomings' (*ibid.*). The Institute hoped 'that the alternative possible solutions which emerge ... will enhance the nation's ability to deal with many of the serious problems which face it' (*ibid.*). The Omega Report on Communications is a document that combines extraordinary naivety with appalling frankness (which is welcome) and a strong admixture of right-wing populism. Thus the authors confidently state that the only criterion for judging programme quality is how many people liked it and not how much a few do. High ratings, they insist, should be the yardstick of what people want. But they are honest enough to admit that, were their policies to be adopted, there is no doubt that the average quality of programmes might decline. This, they optimistically believe, would be 'easily offset by the expansion of all sectors of the market that would inevitably follow the relaxation of controls' (*ibid.*: 39). The report disregards in saying so the abundant evidence that competition in broadcasting has so far produced not greater variety but greater homogeneity. A recent analysis by ORF, the Austrian public service broadcasting organization, of the output of material on offer from private satellites suggests that the proliferation of channels is more likely to lead to an illusion of plurality since, for economic reasons, private enterprise takes into programming material that has been rejected by public service organizations because it does not correspond to the standards it has adopted.

It may be true that the views of the Adam Smith Institute are more interesting as indications of the thinking of hard-core monetarist circles in Britain – from which rumours have emanated about the application of market forces to public service broadcasting – than as a blueprint of what a Conservative government might plan for the BBC. But prominent in the debate over the BBC's proposal to ask for a licence fee of £65 was a strong lobby for the introduction of commercials on the BBC, orchestrated by *The Times*, which accused the Corporation of failing 'to confront the issue of whether the BBC's current strategy (however successful in the past) is the best way to preserve public service broadcasting in a financial, technological, and political climate of which Lord Reith would scarcely have dreamed; and adding that 'cable, satellite, videos and computers make it harder to justify a universal licence to benefit the BBC alone' (*The Times*: 27 February 1984).

The argument for deregulation is closely connected, both in Britain and the United States, with the development of satellite broadcasting and cable and the desire to encourage what the Adam Smith Institute

report calls 'the legion of entrepreneurs' to invest in the new technology – something they have so far been reluctant to do – thus
allowing 'the British people ... to ride the wave of opportunity' (Adam
Smith Institute 1984: 1), although it is unlikely that the financial bodies
able to invest in such large-scale, high-risk enterprises would have a
wide popular base. What the report champions is the idea of 'a free
cable system' in which a number of traditional controls would be
relaxed or abolished – for instance, those forbidding ownership by
political parties or religious bodies. It does, however, propose that
certain restrictions on scheduling X-rated material before 10 p.m. and
locking systems to keep children from watching 'adult' channels may
be convenient. But the general thrust is towards what Stuart Hall has
defined as 'the libertarianism of the new Right'. Thus the report argues
that deregulated radio would encourage truly local stations and allow
'specialist stations, perhaps covering whole cities or parts of the
country, servicing ethnic and musical minorities. ... With a liberalisa-
tion of the existing licensing arrangements, a true freedom of choice
will come to exist and the power to choose ... will pass from the
bureaucrat and programme planner to the listener or viewer' (*ibid.*:
44). By discussing programmes at all the report is less narrow in its
approach than the report on cable systems produced by the Technological Advisory Panel for the Conservative government in 1982 which
discussed the introduction of cable almost exclusively in terms of large-
scale capital development and investment with a corresponding neglect
of questions relating to programme policies, to public interest and to
social responsibility. This narrowly financial approach was somewhat
diluted by the subsequent Hunt Committee Report and the legalization
in cable flowing from it – in particular the setting up of a licensing and
controlling body to oversee cable operations, albeit one that has less
powers than the older regulatory bodies in the field of broadcasting.

Free market/strong state

From whichever end of the political spectrum the pressures for some
form of deregulation come, they encounter certain obvious difficulties
expressed as political contradictions. Thus the right-wing radicals represent a tendency which wishes to apply the rules of the market-place
to broadcasting but they are also part of that new conservatism which is
strong on law and order and anxious to control what the public see –
witness the British legislation on the compulsory licensing of video
recordings – or read – as is demonstrated by police actions against

bookshops selling gay literature. There is some ground for thinking that the Right considers the present regulatory bodies too lax and that it wishes to use the courts more often as a control mechanism over broadcasting rather than working through oversight bodies like the BBC Board of Governors or the IBA. An example is the case against the IBA where the court found that the Director General of the Authority had committed a grave error of judgement and that the Authority itself was in breach of duty in that it did not satisfy itself that *Scum*, a film set in a boys' penal institution, did not offend – in the words of The Broadcasting Act – against 'good taste and decency'. The later timidity shown by the Authority in refusing to allow the broadcast on Channel 4 of a documentary containing revelations about the activities of the security services in Britain until the Attorney-General declared that he did not intend to proceed against the programme-makers or those taking part in the programme may also have been founded in fear of the courts. At government level, the contradiction in the right-wing attack on regulation is illustrated by the disagreement over the introduction of cable between the Department of Trade, which urged speed and the minimum of regulation, and the Home Office, which – as the department responsible for broadcasting – counselled caution and the need for controls.

Enzensberger argues in his highly relevant essay on the consciousness industry (Enzensberger 1976: 24) that technological developments will lead to a multiplication of outlets to the point where government of the media will become impossible.

The telephone is sometimes held up as an illustration of his thesis; but in Britain and elsewhere the tapping of telephone conversations has become widespread with official permission or tacit official agreement. It is difficult to believe that a government dedicated to the idea of a strong state would allow unbridled licence and unrestrained communication in the media. It comes back to the fear that haunted a British Postmaster in the 1920s that too many people were talking to each other. Nor is it probable, given the strong centripetal forces in our societies, that government will readily dispense altogether with something akin to the present centralized broadcasting organizations, if only for reasons of control, for ease of communication in times of crisis and no doubt (in the case of nuclear war) for the promulgation of orders from some underground command bunker in the planning of which there is every reason to believe that the BBC, for example, has long been involved, ready to assert its role as 'the national instrument of broadcasting' to the end. Not that the relationship between a strong

government and the broadcasting institutions will necessarily be altogether untroubled for, however accurate the descriptions of the part
these organizations play in the manufacture of the consensus, there
will always be the possibility of a degree of tension from time to time
between the requirements of the authorities and the professional aims
of the broadcasters. The moment of detached analysis displayed by the
BBC's *Panorama* programme during the Falklands/Malvinas War and
the suggestion that there was an Argentinian case as well as a British
one brought down Mrs Thatcher's wrath. From their side the institutions will be anxious to prolong their existence, although the current
Director General of the BBC is on record as thinking that the BBC is not
necessarily eternal. The danger of such a situation is that the requirements of government and the self-interest of the institutions will lead to
closer collaboration in a period marked by economic and political crisis
such as the present.

Technology and opportunity: the Left's dilemma

It is the perception of the symbiotic nature of the relationship between
licensed broadcasting institutions and government that has led critics of
the radical Left to believe that the dismemberment of the broadcasting
systems promised by the new technology is to be welcomed. But within
their position too there is a contradiction. It is that while being in many
respects libertarian they are not necessarily reconciled to the thought
that ideas might be promulgated amid the proliferation of channels
which, for one reason or another, they would find offensive on social,
moral, or political grounds. Thus they might well object to the dissemination of programmes which were imbued with racism, sexism, or
fascism. It is true that like the Right they would be able to have recourse
to the courts, but the judiciary has an unhappy record in censorship
cases where sexism and racism are considered and is unlikely, as at
present constituted, to show any great understanding of the problems.
This is a line of argument that leads one back to the question of the
regulatory bodies and the attitude that critics on the Left should adopt
towards them. The problem is that in Britain there is little sign that the
Left – a term which, straining it somewhat, can be extended to include
the Labour Party and the Trades Union Congress – is thinking practically about the future of the media and the alternative to a process of
deregulation which would amount to an erosion, or even the abolition,
of a system which, for all its faults, still contains elements worth
defending. There has been nothing, for instance, to match the formal

interventions by the West German trade unions in the debate over cable television and legislation covering it in the various Länder – interventions in which they have laid down their conditions for the introduction of cable, for its control and for the safeguarding of community and other interests. It would be sad if the fact that the radical Right has come up with certain solutions – like those proposed for local radio in the Omega Report – which are consonant with the libertarian demands of the Left were to inhibit debate or lead to an unwillingness to consider far-reaching change and reform to the organization and control of broadcasting. As Stuart Hall has rightly argued, the idea of liberty, on which the whole anti-state was predicated, does not belong exclusively to the Right. They appropriated a certain version of it and linked it with other reactionary ideas to make a 'whole' philosophy and connected it into the programme and the forces of the Right. The counter debate on the Left must come soon if it is not to be too late. It will have to be conducted in the knowledge that the new technology is less likely, in the present conjuncture, to offer opportunities to small, well-intentioned, high-minded groups than to highly organized business interests. It should start from the question: If deregulation offers freedom, to whom does it offer it and on what terms?

4

Journalists' Orientations to Political Institutions: the Case of Parliamentary Broadcasting*

Jay G. Blumler and Michael Gurevitch

*T*he idea that the mass media play a pivotal part in the nexus of power relations in society is by now largely accepted by most communication researchers, irrespective of theoretical differences. Nevertheless, analysis of the linkages between media organizations and other power-wielding institutions in society is still segmented and incomplete. Some scholars have operated within the economic power domain, examining, for example, how ownership structures, dependence on capitalist markets and competition for advertising and audiences may constrain the production of media content (Bagdikian 1983; Miliband 1969; Murdock and Golding 1977; Westergaard 1977). Others have operated within the political power domain, tracing variations of media roles to their differential relations to the state apparatus, government institutions and political parties (Blumler and Gurevitch 1975; Seymour-Ure 1974; Siebert *et al.* 1956; Smith 1979; Tracey 1978). Various individual case studies have also focused on media relations to a number of specific pressure groups, such as trade unions (Glasgow University Media Group 1976 and 1980), the women's movement (Tuchman *et al.* 1978) and the environmental lobby (Greenberg 1985), as well as organizations with either broadly consensual (Paletz and Entman 1981: ch. 8), reformist (Goldenberg 1975), or more radical political objectives (Gitlin 1980; Schlesinger *et al.* 1983; Schmid and de Graaf 1982). Lacking, however, has been a more enveloping

* This essay draws extensively on the research and insights of a number of colleagues, who worked on the several branches of the project, and for whose contributions the authors are greatly indebted: Dr James Cross, Mr Julian Ives, Mrs Sue Middleton, Mr Michael Pilsworth and Mrs Kathryn Rowan.

scheme, stretching across several power domains, and designed to explain differences in the orientations of the mass media to a range of diverse social groups and organizations.

This essay proposes an approach to the development of such a scheme. The empirical data on which it is based emerged from yet another case study – that of the launching of the sound braodcasting of Parliament in Britain in 1978. In the course of that inquiry, much evidence was gathered from different sorts of news and current affairs broadcasters about their attitudes towards coverage of Parliament, once the possibility of directly broadcasting its proceedings had been created. Generalizing from that study, and from the different viewpoints disclosed by it, we have sought to develop a conceptual framework, within which media portrayals of a variety of social and political institutions might be theorized.

Mass media relationships to news sources

In their daily routines, journalists engage with social and political institutions predominantly as potential sources of news. As Roshco (1975) has pointed out, 'The sociology of news must . . . be concerned with the basis for establishing reporter–source relationships as well as with the nature and consequences of subsequent interactions'. Yet our ability to analyse the structure of media–source relationships has been hampered by the absence of a fully considered analytical scheme. Several signs of such neglect are noticeable.

First, as deployed in the literature, the very notion of a 'source' is ambiguous. The term has been applied both to the organizations and groups, which often feature as *subjects* of news reports, and to the individuals, whose location within such institutions enable them to serve as *informants* about decisions and events which they have made or witnessed. Such a distinction alrady alerts us to a possible duality of journalistic response to sources: as subjects they will be judged for their newsworthiness, but as informants they will be assessed for their authority and credibility.

Secondly, although differential access to the news may be a key mechanism in public opinion formation (for example, through agenda-setting and status conferral), little attempt has been made systematically to specify the range of factors that could account for the varying treatment that diverse sources enjoy or suffer at the hands of news workers. In trying to explain the differences of news visibility between groups or individuals, different analysts tend to latch on to different single mechanisms, ignoring other potential influences. Media professionals, for example, usually refer to *news values* to explain why, say, presidents and prime ministers get more attention than miners and garbage collectors (except, of course, when the latter go on strike!). In offering such explanations, media professionals appear to be oblivious to the origins of news value judgements, tending to see them as inherent in the events or individuals they cover, rather than tracing them to their own collective professional assumptions and rules of thumb. Some scholars have suggested that the *personal predilections* of reporters towards 'the issues involved in the group's activities' may influence their contacts with and stories about their sources (Goldenberg 1975). Critical researchers tend to argue that a permeation of *ideological influences* ensures a reproduction in the news of differential power relations in society at large (Hall 1982). Yet another line of explanation attributes the greater ability of certain sources to attract favourable coverage to the more powerful *controls and sanctions* which they can exert – for example, the denial of information, advertising and other 'goods' valued by the news organization (Tunstall 1971). Little attention has been paid, however, to how these different explanatory mechanisms might be related to each other – whether as competing alternatives, as mutually complementary, or as diverse influences cutting across each other in a more complex field of forces.

Thirdly, the presumed uniformity of journalists' orientations to a given institutional source has rarely been questioned and probed. Do all media professionals, who are able to take or influence decisions about the reporting of a source's affairs, approach them in a more or less uniform manner? If so, how is such presumed uniformity achieved? To answer such questions, it is necessary to identify those roles in news organizations whose incumbents might react differentially to the source concerned and are in a position to affect its coverage. In the literature, this problem has mainly been addressed through a dichotomous distinction between specialist and generalist reporters or between news-gatherers and news-processors, depicting the former as more open to co-optation by source perspectives and interests than the latter.

Finally, in certain studies of news-making a too narrow view is taken of the journalistic role in relation to those of sources. Journalists are sometimes depicted as individuals, whose relations with their contacts are shaped by calculations of utility or preference, reflecting their professional goals (Grossman and Rourke 1976) or their political and ideological inclinations (Noelle-Neumann 1980). Omitted from such explanations are interpretations that take more broadly into account both the institutional structures, in which media professionals are employed, and the socio-political cultures, which may impinge on and shape their representations of social institutions, issues and actors.

In short, media-source relations may be even more complex than most analysts have so far imagined. Such was certainly an implication of our own attempt to understand the attitudes of British broadcasters to a central political institution in British society – Parliament – at a time when their access to its proceedings had significantly changed.

An inquiry into the broadcasting of Parliament

Parliament has long been a major site of information about political processes in Britain and hence a prominent topic of mass media coverage. Most decisions of government are announced there. Daily opportunities to elicit government reactions to breaking news stories and unfolding events are ever present in Questions to the Prime Minister and to other departmental ministers. Parliament is also the prime forum in which party differences over issues of the day are ventilated. The prestigious lobby of Westminster correspondents is based there. The main conventions and routines of reporting from Westminster are consequently long established and firmly rooted (Tunstall 1970).

For many years, however, British broadcasters had felt hamstrung in their ability to present Parliament to the viewing and listening public. As long as the tools of their trade – microphones and cameras – were excluded from Westminster, the coverage and colour they could provide was diminished and thwarted. Perhaps this situation also symbolized the restrictions of access and secrecy, under which the media laboured more generally, when trying to record the activities and decisions of the British government and bureaucracy. The introduction of the sound broadcasting of Parliament in 1978 was therefore perceived as something of a victory (albeit minor, perhaps) in the continuing struggle over media rights to collect and publish political information. Even such a minor victory was bound to be regarded as inaugurating a new departure in the communication of parliamentary affairs to the public and was initially greeted with some enthusiasm. The key change here was the possibility of *direct* coverage. For the first time members of the broadcast audience could listen to MPs' contributions to debates, either live and *in extenso* or in an edited form afterwards. Hopes ran high.

This innovation in political communication was sufficiently important and problematic to merit an investigation of the consequences and problems it would bring in its wake. Supported by a grant from the then Social Science Research Council, such an inquiry was designed and conducted by the Centre for Television Research at the University of Leeds and the Hansard Society for Parliamentary Government. A 'systematic' perspective was adopted, involving (a) observation of the production process at Westminster and in national and local radio newsrooms, (b) interviews with many broadcasters, including policy-makers and executives, those directly involved in reporting from Parliament (such as Westminster Correspondents) and those who, as controllers of radio channels, managers of local stations and editors of news and current affairs programmes, were mainly schedulers or trans-mitters of parliamentary items, (c) a content analysis of parliamentary reporting in a wide range of radio and television news and current affairs programmes during a single parliamentary session, and (d) a study of audience responses to extracts of parliamentary proceedings presented in a variety of ways.

Many findings from this research have already been reported else-where. An account of the influences and tensions that shaped the organization of parliamentary broadcasting appears in Blumler (1984), which also describes how parliamentary events were presented in tele-vision and radio news bulletins and the part played in the coverage by recorded excerpts of speeches. The range of audience reactions to parliamentary actuality in broadcast reports, including impressions formed of MPs' roles and behaviour in the House of Commons, has been charted by Cross (1982). In this essay, however, we consider the views and perceptions of Parliament that the broadcasters themselves expressed on the job and in interviews with members of the research team.

Broadcasters' orientations to Parliament: layers and levels

When examining the interview material, we were immediately im-pressed with the exceptionally varied sets of attitudes that broadcasters had displayed towards Parliament – or rather towards parliamentary proceedings as a source of programme material. Broadcasters' reactions to parliamentary events, and the recorded actuality of such events, appeared complex and multi-layered. In our attempt to structure their responses, three underlying dimensions of broadcaster orientation were identified.

First, broadcasters could regard Parliament simply as an important and rich source of information about politics in Britain: what the issues of the day are and how they are debated by the main parties, factions and their leaders; the policies that governments announce for coping with current problems and how these are received by the same forces; and as the arena in which fluctuating power relationships are mirrored and played out and the demands and viewpoints of key sub-groups of society confront each other and are resolved. At this level, broadcasters may be said to relate to Parliament as media professionals, regarding it primarily as a source of materials for selection and processing as news values dictate.

Holders of such an attitude tended to minimize the innovatory potential of recorded parliamentary material and often expressed modest expectations about its impact on public awareness. They were far more interested in the availability of short extracts for incorporation into news reports than in the transmission of entire debates. They appeared to regard Commons sound, then, as just another 'tool' in their professional kit, to be used mainly to illustrate and enliven their usual ways of presenting news from Parliament. In their eyes, parliamentary tape was rather like another wire service that could supplement, without radically altering, their customary approaches to political coverage. As one local radio station news editor told us at an early stage:

> We will cover exactly the same stories as before, but we will have a new tool at our disposal. It's just a new source of material for us. The use of actuality will make the news 'better radio' because it will be first-hand; it's far better to have Jill Knight actually speaking in the House rather than a repeat of what she said. However, the main point remains: What's the best way to do a story? This is nothing new; we have to do this all the time. We should apply the same news values to this material as we apply to all other material. Our judgement might be clouded to begin with, but we will reassert ourselves over this new material, and we will go back to our old values.

From such an outlook an emphasis on limited objectives naturally followed (as expressed a BBC Radio 4 executive):

> What we are doing is opening a window on the world through which people can peer if they wish. It will mainly be about what's happening today, and most people will just want to know what's happening *then*. Out of all that they may get some feel of what Parliament is all about and how MPs operate. But one has constantly to keep in view limited rather than more grand objectives.

Secondly, and overlaying this professional approach, there was the fact that, constitutionally, broadcasting organizations are ultimately accountable to Parliament. This is the central feature of the relationship of broadcasting to the state in Britain, distinguishing it on the one hand from those broadcasting systems which are directly subordinate to state organs or have party political appointees inside their own governing bodies, and on the other hand from those in which a diluted line of political accountability is channelled through a relatively weak regulatory agency. Of course broadcasting organizations everywhere are exposed to pressures and influences from a whole range of powerful bodies in society, such as political parties, industrial and trade union interests and many other civic groups. But the further element of constitutional subordination in their relationship to Parliament obliges British broadcasters to bear in mind the acceptability of how they work and what they produce to those who are ultimately in a position to determine their organizational futures. The need to ensure and demonstrate that their uses of recorded extracts from parliamentary debates will be 'responsible' reflects this unique relationship – the influence of which was probably reinforced by the establishment of a House of Commons Select Committee on Sound Broadcasting to monitor and report on the service.

Thirdly, we identified yet another extra-professional layer to the relationship, which stemmed from the symbolic position that Parliament occupies in society, standing as the presumed institutional embodiment of the central values of British democracy. At this level, partly out of civic commitment to the national political system, and partly because in their eyes the values that British broadcasting stands for flow integrally from the values of 'parliamentary democracy', some broadcasters tended to treat the institutional symbol of that system with a certain deference and respect – as if imbued with a degree of sacredness.

Holders of such an attitude were inclined to assess the sound broadcasting innovation for its prospects of acquainting the audience more fully with what Parliament represented in the British system. Sometimes such assessments were relatively hopeful. Notes of reserve chiefly stemmed from fears that actuality clips in news reports might limit the ability of parliamentary correspondents to provide explanation and analysis in their own words, as well as from concerns about audience reaction to the sound of background noise and boisterousness in Commons debates. But the broadcasters attuned to this dimension also discerned enlarged opportunities for civic education in the service. As one correspondent put it: 'The broadcasting of Parliament provides a great opportunity for us. Most people have never been to Parliament and have not seen how intimate a place it is. They should get a feel of the peculiar quality of the House of Commons and of MPs themselves and realise that they are Members of something a bit different and special.'

The fact that broadcasters could relate to Parliament along these different dimensions implies that they were caught up in a web of tensions emanating from the different, and sometimes incompatible, claims on their loyalties of professional norms, embedded in the first layer of the relationship, and the extra-professional values and considerations represented by the other layers. Professionally, Parliament was viewed primarily as a source of raw material for the journalistic mill. But the extra-professional attitudes implied that Parliament was entitled to treatment in a manner that would uphold its symbolic value in the political system and not undermine its dignity. At this stage, it is worth noting a similar distinction that emerged from a previous study of broadcasters' attitudes towards coverage of an election campaign. Like Parliament, election campaigns symbolize the values of a democratic political system and can therefore provoke equivalent contrasts of perspective among broadcasters involved in their coverage. In that study, Blumler (1969) distinguished between 'sacerdotal' and 'pragmatic' responses to the claims of campaign reports for inclusion in the nightly current affairs programme, 24 Hours. So-called 'sacerdotalists' largely comprised those political specialists and commentators who considered that campaign developments deserved a regular and prominent airing almost as an inherent right and regardless of news-value calculations. 'Pragmatists', on the other hand, were those editors and producers who regarded themselves as having a wider programme brief to tend, were keen to cover non-election stories when news values justified their inclusion and aimed to serve an audience, many members of which, they argued, were less than fully interested in election news as such.

Broadcasters' organizational roles and attitudes to Parliament

The preceding discussion has depicted broadcasters as swayed by different sentiments towards Parliament. It is reasonable to assume, however, that they do not perform their duties under a continual buffeting of cross-pressures. Rather will each broadcaster resolve these attitudinal conflicts for himself or herself in a relatively consistent manner. As the case of 24 Hours suggested, the mode of resolution could reflect the demands placed on the broadcaster concerned by his or her position and role inside the broadcasting organization.

Elsewhere, we have proposed the notion of 'role relationships' as a tool for analysing complex interactions between mass media professionals and politicians in the production of political messages (Blumler and Gurevitch 1981). This implies that the behaviour of people in roles is prescribed by the requirements of such roles and is guided by the socially defined expectations which govern them. Two advantages of analysing the behaviour of broadcasters (as well as politicians) in such terms were identified by us. First, 'Such an approach draws attention to influences on political communicators that derive from their respective organisational settings, in which their roles are largely defined and performed'. In other words, broadcasters are anchored in a framework of tasks assigned to them by their organizations, and their reactions to other political institutions and communicators will stem in large part from their occupancy of defined positions in the organizational hierarchy. Secondly, 'A focus on roles as regulators of behaviour also links . . . media professionals . . . back to the surrounding political culture of the society concerned'. This helps to explain the continuity of professional behaviour over time, as well as the diversity of patterns of professional behaviour when viewed across different societies. Thus, the relationship of British broadcasters to Parliament is largely specific to the British political system, which has shaped both the place of Parliament in British society and the purposes and structure of British broadcasting itself.

For our present purpose, adoption of a 'role perspective' has the further advantage of sensitizing us to the *multiplicity* of broadcasters' roles that may have a bearing on how Westminster materials will be used. Up to this point, we have referred to the broadcasters as if they comprised an undifferentiated group, all enmeshed in the tensions arising from conflicting orientations to Parliament. But this appeared not to be the case. Interviews with many broadcasters, involved in different capacities in the processing of parliamentary material, suggested that their outlook on the institution and on the value, in broadcasting terms, of its proceedings as captured by the microphones in the Chambers, varied according to the roles they occupied in their organizations.

At least three groups of broadcaster roles appeared distinguishable by this evidence: first, there were the editors, correspondents and commentators who worked at Westminster, including those based in the new Units that were established there by the BBC and Independent

Radio News to receive, listen to and prepare news items and packages from the taped recordings of parliamentary proceedings. These individuals were closest to the institution of Parliament both geographically – working as they did in 'the belly of the beast' – and socially – through frequent and often intensive interactions with MPs. Of course, their professional identities and reputations were also bound up with the number and prominence of the parliamentary stories that were eventually broadcast.

Secondly, there were the newsmen, editors, managers and channel controllers who were positioned on what might be described (from this standpoint) as the periphery of the broadcasting organizations, working with the various local radio stations and networked news and current affairs programmes (on both radio and television), into the output of which parliamentary items were often inserted. Such broadcasters were more remote from Parliament than their Westminster colleagues, not only geographically and culturally but also occupationally. They were less exposed to the 'culture of Parliament', and parliamentary proceedings comprised but one among a quite wide range of news sources and broadcastable material with which they had to concern themselves.

Thirdly, there were the higher executives and policy-makers in the broadcasting organizations. Although such individuals were not directly involved in processing parliamentary material, they had an overall responsibility to ensure that the broadcasting of Parliament was seen by the main clients that their institutions had to satisfy – principally MPs and audience members – as in some sense a 'success'.

So far as we could tell, the differing attitudes to Parliament that had been identified were not distributed at random across broadcasting staffs. There was a tendency for broadcasters in certain roles to adopt one set of attitudes, while incumbents of others exhibited different orientations. This is not to claim that we can precisely measure the strength of this association, for the distinctions proposed here have emerged from an analysis of originally unstructured interview material. Nevertheless, important differences across broadcasters did seem to emerge from the evidence, drawing attention to three main lines of linkage between their organizational roles and their attitudes to Parliament.

First, the outlook characterized as 'professional', that is to say, relating to Parliament primarily as a source of political information and stories, seemed far more prevalent among those broadcasters who worked on the 'periphery' of the system – that is, for the local radio stations and the networked news and current affairs programmes which present parliamentary items as part of a wider service to listeners and viewers. More distanced from Parliament, these individuals worked closely on the interface between the broadcasting organization and the mass audience. Not surprisingly, a central preoccupation was winning and keeping the loyalties of their listeners and viewers, in whose hierarchy of interests parliamentary material was assumed to occupy a relatively low place. As one newsman in a local station described his audience: 'They're not interested unless it is something that affects them. The example I would give here is the Budget, because taxes affect them – taxes on cigarettes, sweets and drink. But the general run of parliamentary business is of no relevance to them.' Consequently, Westminster material should normally be projected only in a news perspective: 'I'm a bit cynical really about the role of Parliament. I think Parliament on radio has been very overrated and has far too much importance attached to it. It has its uses along with other components of news, but that is how it should be seen.' And the concern of higher authorities to encourage a substantial use of parliamentary material could provoke a certain amount of irritation and resentment:

> The IBA pressurise us a lot more than we would like from the programming point of view. They do try and take an editorial role. And they certainly pressure us about parliamentary material. What they don't understand and what I try to make clear to them is the idea of prolonged live audio from the House of Commons – it's really not for a station like this. This station has a variety of interests, so unless the material is of exceptional relevance we wouldn't want to take it. . . . We find ourselves being subject to pressures which are demonstrably remote from public reality. . . . The station's overall policy has to relate to all the various pressures on us, and of course the prominent one here is the audience and the fact that the public likes a certain kind of music, and the type of talk they like is of a companionable kind.

The second orientation, according to which Parliament was perceived as the sovereign authority to which broadcasting was ultimately accountable, appeared to be more salient to broadcasting executives and policy-makers. A prime task of this echelon is to represent the organization to their 'political masters' and to cultivate as positive and conflict-free a relationship with them as possible. It followed that among the reference groups to whom they would turn when assessing the success or failure of the sound broadcasting of Parliament, MPs would be central. This is not to imply that interviewed executives often expressed such views to us in unqualified form. Nevertheless, other broadcasters sometimes perceived them as if naturally motivated by such impulses:

> The service we provide for BBC central management in using parliamentary material and maintaining contact with the MPs, they see as a purely political function. They are only too pleased that there are these nice chaps down in —— who are talking to MPs and actually know them. After all, we must not forget the licence fee and the importance of keeping Parliament sweet. We act as lobbyists on behalf of the BBC, and that is how we are seen.

Thirdly, the more 'sacerdotal' orientation to emerge from the interview material was expressed most often by parliamentary correspondents stationed at Westminster. A number of factors – including the fact that they worked and had their offices in the Palace of Westminster, their dependence on daily access to MPs to do their job and their total immersion in the affairs of Parliament – all probably conspired to encourage a view of Parliament, not only as an information source, but also as a keystone of the British political system and the repository of its core values. These broadcasters were often depicted by their colleagues as well as carriers of Westminster values, less likely, for example, to provide a stringent commentary on certain parliamentary developments than would their less inhibited colleagues in the written press.

Varying attitudes to Parliament, however, were not purely differentiated by organizational role. Broadcasters who perform different roles are naturally dependent on each other and on the organizational structure as a whole in carrying out their tasks. For example, the parliamentary correspondent at Westminster is in daily contact with editors and producers on the periphery and is thus thoroughly accustomed to fashioning his or her output in approaches, lengths and styles that will suit the needs of the programmes in which the items are to be slotted. In addition, they realize that they stand in the front line of their organization's relationships with ministers, Opposition spokesmen and MPs generally, having to defend or justify reports that may from time to time be criticized. Similarly, many producers and editors on the periphery will have become accustomed to the regular receipt of parliamentary stories, impregnated with a Westminster viewpoint, as a sheer fact of programming life. Like other members of the organization, they too must appreciate the desirability of keeping on tolerably good terms with Parliament. And for their part, the higher executives are aware of the need to support the professional troops in the field, on whose commitment and dedication the regular production of attractive programming depends. Thus, the three sets of broadcasters, though differently preoccupied and oriented, were also aware that they belonged to the same organization, sharing certain corporate interests in common, which the policies and practices of parliamentary broadcasting should, so far as possible, promote.

Professional versus extra-professional orientations

Nevertheless, conflicts naturally arose from time to time over policy issues and practical news judgements from a situation in which broadcasters' differing attitudes to Parliament were to some extent aligned with their organizational roles. When such clashes surfaced, which orientations would prevail? We now aim to specify those factors which may have strengthened or weakened the influence of the several orientations on the organization and output of parliamentary broadcasting.

Factors supporting an extra-professional approach

Permission to record and broadcast the proceedings of Parliament was conceded only after many years of lobbying and exhortation (spiced by several cliff-hanging votes in the House of Commons), and the circumstances in which it was granted put broadcasters on their mettle to vindicate their trustworthiness. Special assurances, not applicable to any other form of content, were given about the preparation and use of parliamentary actuality. Before Parliament was won over, a four-week on-air experiment was organized in 1976, during which broadcasters of all sorts set aside their differences and pulled out all the stops in order to show how fully, interestingly and responsibly they could present parliamentary debates to the listening nation. Afterwards, speaking in a Radio 3 discussion of the experiment, a senior executive of the BBC proudly drew attention to the Corporation's record of having represented in the output the voices of 350 of the 599 MPs who had contributed to Commons debates in the period. The broadcasters also had to look to the future. Some may have reckoned that the chances of realizing their still unfulfilled ambition of televising proceedings at Westminster could turn on how sound broadcasting was perceived to have been handled. In addition, it was evident that MPs differed over how best to oversee the service. Although a Unit under the control of Parliament itself was rejected by a Commons vote, the arguments of its more articulate proponents may have sharpened the need to demonstrate that broadcasters were not inveterate trivializers, attracted only to the spillage of political blood. In any case, a Select Committee was established by the Commons to keep a watching brief on the service, and although its interventions thereafter were sporadic, uneven and circumspect, showing much respect for journalists' editorial freedom, it was assumed that it might one day deliver its verdict in the form of a report on how the broadcasters had fulfilled their responsibilities.

In this context, the assertion of 'extra-professional' influences took several forms. First, policy-makers on both sides of the British broadcasting system strove to ensure that, through use of the new facility, Parliament would not be treated solely as an object of daily news attention. In the BBC, this concern focused on attempts to devise ways of showing Parliament at work through the live coverage of some of its debates. That concern went through many twists and turns during the period of the research. In advance of the introduction of parliamentary broadcasting, the BBC decided to schedule *Prime Minister's Question Time* twice weekly live, but after some – not many – weeks, the Corporation began to receive a number of calls and letters from listeners who found it uninteresting and objected to the resulting displacement of popular plays in Radio 4 schedules. Initially, the Director General of the BBC stoutly rebutted these complaints by proclaiming a higher duty of public service broadcasting to show parliamentary democracy at work. Not long after, however, certain MPs also expressed alarm over the unfavourable impressions of their conduct that the noisy background to *Prime Minister's Question Time* might be conveying, noting as well that this set-piece occasion was hardly 'representative' of the mainstream of their business. Although live coverage of *Prime Minister's Question Time* was kept on the air through to the summer recess of 1979, it was dropped at the outset of the following parliamentary session. In terms of the conceptual framework outlined earlier in this chapter the initial decision to present *Prime Minister's Question Time* reflected a 'sacerdotal' attitude to the broadcasting of Parliament, while the later decision to abandon it reflected both a professional response to perceived audience reception and a prudential response to the authority of Parliament. Even so, the BBC continued to seek other ways of meeting 'sacerdotal' needs – at one point, for example, devising a so-called 'Match of the Day' format, whereby a mixture of edited and live portions of parliamentary debates could occasionally be transmitted before and during the 10.00 p.m. news on Radio 4 without unduly disrupting its schedules.

Independent Broadcasting faced similar problems in the context of a quite different system. It wanted to institute a regular service of parliamentary broadcasting and to make sure that it would actually be drawn on by Independent Local Radio stations. Yet the operation could not be prohibitively costly, and the form of the provision had to blend in with ILR broadcasting styles. The adopted solution entailed transmission from Westminster, at periodic intervals throughout every parliamentary day without exception, of short packages of Commons and Lords materials (called 'wraps'), whether or not, according to journalistic judgements, the newsworthiness of the events taking place on that day warranted that amount of attention. The Independent Radio News Unit at Westminster was accordingly set up to prepare at least three such 'wraps' daily, including actuality and commentary, and lasting about three minutes, in order to fit smoothly into the stream of ILR bulletins and news flashes. This clearly reflected a commitment to reporting from Parliament that was above and beyond what news values would dictate and implied that the local stations themselves should similarly report parliamentary events regardless of news-value considerations. Moreover, although it was not supposed that all stations would broadcast every 'wrap', the Independent Broadcasting Authority conveyed its expectation that they would make a 'regular' use of Westminster material, and it required the stations to keep a log of their uses of such material, returning it periodically to IBA headquarters for deposit and review. So far as we are aware, no other form of content has been accorded such privileged status in the Independent system.

Secondly, unique understandings were given by BBC and Independent broadcasters alike about procedures to ensure 'responsible' uses of parliamentary tapes. Excerpts would not be broadcast in 'unsuitable' outlets, like entertainment and satire programmes. Editing of the tapes, the fashioning of reports and the provision of commentary would all be undertaken by Westminster staffs – without subsequent re-editing by other broadcasters elsewhere. Creatively, then, the output would be under the control of those broadcasters who were closest to Parliament in location and most socialized to its values. In the words of a BBC executive, this ensured that their judgements would be made 'in the light of the pressures of their own superiors and others, Members of Parliament, who come up to them all of the time and say, "Why did you use that rather than this?" They are not working in a vacuum.'

A third manifestation of 'extra-professional' influence is perhaps more difficult to identify precisely. But in the months before April 1978 (when parliamentary broadcasting was due to start), excitement noticeably quickened in certain quarters about the onset of the new venture and the availability of a new source of programme material. It was as if the freshness and challenge of the impending development had

encouraged some broadcasters to lift their sights above mere professional routine and to contemplate an enlarged vision of their political
task. In something like a spirit of 'public service' for civic enlightenment
(as defined by Burns 1977), they mused on the possibilities of using
their new access to Parliament to inform audience members about
political affairs more fully and to enable them to play their part in
democracy more effectively. As an IRN informant told us at an early
stage: 'I sincerely believe that parliamentary broadcasting will be a very
good thing for the broadcasters, for the public and also for the MPs,
provided it is done intelligibly and fairly.'

It should be noted, however, that such initial awareness of the new
potential was countered by the lack of much advance planning to guide
optimal exploitation of the innovation. Of course, certain broad policy
decisions were amply deliberated, and the new Westminster Units
were carefully designed, staffed and accommodated. But at programme
and station levels, many editors and producers were more inclined
to 'suck and see' what would happen on 3 April 1978 (the date of
the launch) than they were to imagine alternative programming
approaches beforehand. Thus, in the months before that date, conceptions of the parliamentary broadcasting service were infused with a
spirit of innovation without a corresponding practice of *planning* for
innovation.

Factors supporting a professional approach

Despite the 'sacred' face of Parliament's authority, professional attitudes heavily permeated the daily work of the service. Few programme
innovations and relatively little sustained live coverage followed from
the installation of microphones at Westminster. Sound tapes of parliamentary proceedings came to be regarded chiefly as a resource for radio
and television news reports to be drawn on in line with customary
routine and practice. What influences promoted such an outcome?

First, a more strictly professional approach was favoured by the fact
that the broadcasting of Parliament was not brought forth in a vacuum.
The new facility, which enabled broadcasters to transmit the voices of
MPs instead of merely reporting their words, was introduced into an
already well-formed broadcasting system, in which the main ground
rules of parliamentary reporting, methods of taking extracts from the
proceedings of major political occasions (such as party conference
debates) and ways of structuring political discussion were firmly established. Although it was a richly varied system, it was not necessarily a
highly malleable one, wide open to innovatory effort. 'Professional'

perspectives permeated it and were likely to dominate the uses made of a new source of material, especially if the latter was perceived as neither outstandingly appealing nor radically different from other forms of political information. The framework, in other words, was already given. This is not to suggest that more professionally minded broadcasters tended to denigrate the contribution to programming of their new ability to relay the actual sound of parliamentary speeches and debates to the audience. From a professional viewpoint, such actuality might even be highly valued – for its ability to convey immediacy, colour and the excitement of specially big parliamentary occasions, for example. Nevertheless, it would mainly be prized for its contribution to already fixed patterns of news provision, and that is why it came to be regarded almost as another wire service, snippets from which could be stitched into reports that in form and substance were little changed otherwise.

This is also not to ignore the fact that the policy-makers considered ways of using the facility beyond what might be involved in merely 'raiding' the tapes for news points. But the clearing of space to transmit significant debates live continually bumped up against the constraints of traditional scheduling routines, into which they were difficult to fit, and for which quite powerful channel Controllers were responsible. The twice-weekly afternoon broadcasting of *Prime Minister's Question Time* became the professionally favoured solution to this problem in 1978, partly because, being relatively short, fixed and predictable in timing and duration, it was less disruptive of the schedules than any other form of live broadcasting would be.

Secondly, the presentation of parliamentary news to the public depended on an entrenched principle of the British broadcasting system, namely, that responsibility for programme content is lodged with programme editors and station managers. Thus, each editor of a news bulletin, current affairs sequence, or local radio strand is supposed to decide on merit the day-to-day make-up of his programme, although in certain cases his decisions may be scrutinized by executives after the fact. Of course both the BBC and the IBA had given assurances that items incorporationg parliamentary actuality would be prepared only by Westminster staffs, whose responsibility would include not only editing and cutting Commons material, but also 'packaging' it. But the convergence of these two principles ensured that parliamentary reporting (particularly in the BBC) would stem in daily practice from a whole host of consultations and negotiations between the 'suppliers', based at the Westminster Unit end, and the programme and station 'consumers' at the other end of the system. Such discussions would consider both the 'what' (which Commons events merited attention) and the 'how' (item lengths, favoured excerpts, lines to take in surrounding commentary, and so on) of parliamentary coverage. But because the 'consumers' (the programmed editors) had the last word, their more professionally defined needs would normally be paramount. In line with these influences were the organizational arrangements that were made for the Westminster Units. The BBC Unit was structured around four desks, one each for Radio News, Radio Current Affairs, Television News and Local Radio. With the exception of the one for Local Radio, these desks were staffed by members of programme teams, who were assigned to this duty for specified periods of time in rotation. Thus, the creation of the Unit entailed an extension of the territory of the different programme departments into Westminster, from which they had previously been excluded. To put it in another way, the new facility from Parliament opened doors into Westminster for those broadcasters who were less wedded to the parliamentary ethos than were the specialist correspondents who had always 'lived' there.

Thirdly, the subjection of parliamentary material to more 'professional' routines and approaches may have been encouraged by the political climate prevalent in the late 1970s, when parliamentary broadcasting was launched. In the eyes of many political commentators, this was not exactly a buoyant, hopeful, or politically exciting period. On the contrary, some broadcasters considered that the political vitality of Britain was at a low ebb at that time. This may have caused them to be more sceptical than they might have been at other times about the likely audience appeal of the sound of MPs clashing in debate – and therefore also more content to do little more with parliamentary actuality than fit it into tried and tested reporting formats.

Fourthly, in the conflict between intangible ideals and aims (like 'educating the audience' and 'promoting political awareness'), on the one side, and organizational, scheduling and programme format constraints, on the other, the latter may tend to prevail, if only because they have behind them the cumulated weight of institutional experience and inertia. Professional self-confidence then becomes a powerful ally of such inertia, for if the established approaches of news and current affairs broadcasting have stood the test of time, why should more adventurous forms of programming be contemplated?

Fifthly, when balanced against professional motives, extra-professional ones, reflecting the broadcasters' more personal value orientations, may seem suspect and dubious, as if involving a desire to 'make propaganda for Parliament', or to oblige audience members to follow politics more heavily than they would if they were guided by their own inclinations alone.

Sixthly, some ebbing of the traditional 'public service' spirit of British broadcasting may have also played a part. The argument here is intangible (and contestable), but if, as Burns (1977) maintains, that ethos has indeed lost some of its previous vigour, the motivation of broadcasters to provide a service of parliamentary coverage that would not bow to (real or imagined) audience constraints could also have been undermined. Ironically, the original 'knock on Parliament's door' by broadcasters demanding entry to Westminster occurred at a time when, according to Burns's analysis, many broadcasters were more animated by public service concerns. Then, with the passage of years, they may have pressed their demand for access more routinely as something to which they simply felt entitled, so that by the time it was finally conceded, they were in a mood to celebrate the new opportunity more as a technical than as a moral victory.

In sum, although certain broadcasters undoubtedly wished to use parliamentary actuality more imaginatively and innovatively, their aspirations had to be accommodated to a set of intra-organizational and 'ideological' constraints, operative in turn within a somewhat depressed political environment. The marginality inside the organization of the roles of some of those broadcasters who might have been more keen to use the service as an instrument of civic education may also have been a factor. The parliamentary correspondents were, in a sense, marginal not only geographically (for example, at the BBC physically distanced from both Broadcasting House and the Television Centre), but also because they dealt with materials which, by professional wisdom, were regarded as 'marginal' for large sections of the audience. Their proximity to the centre of parliamentary affairs, then, did not in all ways enhance their position and power within their own organizations.

Parliamentary broadcasting 'compromised'

In both the organization and the output of parliamentary broadcasting, the result of all these tensions was something of a compromise. Though professionalism was infiltrated and supplemented, it was never overridden. This impression of broadcasting organizations striving to reconcile respect for Parliament with professional attitudes and routines is conveyed by several features of the service as it developed and emerged in practice:

(1) When initially they were considering what form of live coverage should be regularly given to parliamentary proceedings, *Prime Minister's Question Time* was chosen by the BBC and LBC (the ILR all-news station in London) not only because it was supposed to illustrate the account-ability function of the House of Commons. More to the point, it also had several qualities which satisfied essentially professional standards. It was dramatic and theatrical; it generated conflict and excitement; and it brought together in regular confrontation the top party leaders of the country. In addition, it had the eminent merit for schedule-conscious broadcasters of being relatively short (20 minutes) and utterly depen-dable, almost always starting and finishing at an exact time.

(2) The alternative 'Match of the Day' approach to the same goal that was envisioned for a time after *Prime Minister's Questions* was cancelled, offered a relatively tidy way of packaging a potentially chaotic set of events, facilitating audience comprehension by focusing on a pin-pointed start followed by coherent movement towards a conclusion.

(3) IRN's three-minute parliamentary 'wrap' was also a device to reconcile conflicting needs. On the one hand, it was a way, extra-professionally, of ensuring the regular reporting of Parliament, above and beyond what news values alone would prescribe. On the other hand, it was tailored as a format to harmonize with the professional presentation styles of much of Independent Local Radio's verbal out-put. It was compatible in length with other items that audience mem-bers would be hearing regularly and would not tax their supposedly limited tolerance of sustained exposition.

(4) Other more demanding uses of parliamentary material were sometimes scheduled in slots which ensured that, while the 'afficion-ados' of parliamentary affairs were catered for, the professionals' hold over the mass audience would not be jeopardized. Such was the case with *Inside Parliament*, a weekly 45-minute programme that the BBC introduced in 1979, aiming thereby to counter the charge that it was not covering the full range of parliamentary activity, in particular the work of Select Committees. Often composed of relatively long items, this programme was initially transmitted on VHF Radio 4 on Saturday mornings and subsequently moved to a late Sunday night hour. Such timings avoided the risk of challenging the average listener's presumed indifference to the complexities of the political process while allowing political credit to be banked by serving a specialist audience of above-average political interest and weight.

(5) The notion of a compromise even applies to the substance of daily news reports from Westminster. On the one hand, parliamentary

stories conformed closely to the lengths and styles of a typical news item. The following passage from a project report of a spell of observation at the BBC Westminster Unit describes the ease of parliamentary correspondents' working relations with news producers and their sensitivity to news bulletins' format requirements:

> A central feature of the work was the producers' daily interaction with parliamentary correspondents. During the observation period we were impressed with the relative smoothness and amicability of this relationship. . . . Essentially, it was due to the fact that when working together on tape-recorded political content, they shared a common set of objectives and occupational values, which stemmed in turn from a shared understanding of what they were looking for and how to get it. A decisive factor here was awareness and acceptance of programmes' requirements: actuality passages that provide arresting 'quotable quotes', are audible, intelligible, pithily expressed and clearly edited; plus a succinct overall package (including correspondent commentary), adding up in total to no more than a certain number of minutes and seconds. It is true that in producing such a package, the correspondent's analytical judgement, though expressed only in a few sentences perhaps, counted for much. He was the parliamentary expert, and, within bounds set by conventions of impartiality and non-editorialising, he was free to provide his own interpretation of a parliamentary event – and indeed to express that interpretation in terms different from those that might have been used by one or more of his fellow-correspondents in packages on the same event prepared for other programmes. But when listening to taped Commons sound for striking parliamentary turns of phrase, it was as if the news programmes' requirements for such qualities as force, crispness and vivid metaphor were paramount.

On the other hand, a content analysis of the correspondents' own remarks within such stories has shown that, more often than not, they emphasized the importance and seriousness of the reported debates, in this way at least according Parliament its symbolic deserts (Blumler 1984).

Journalists' orientations to political institutions

We now turn to the larger issue to which this essay is addressed, namely, media professionals' orientations to the broad range of social institutions and organizations, whose activities they follow and report. What might we learn from this case study of parliamentary broadcasting about the structuring and application of such attitudes? Are the sensitivities to cross-cutting, sometimes contradictory, loyalties specific to the reporting of the British Parliament? Or do similarly conflicting orientations shape their reactions to other organizations and groups as well? Can the framework outlined in this study extend our understanding of the place of the mass media in the web of power relationships in society?

Two opposed explanatory frameworks are often pitted against each other in interpretations of newsmen's relations to prominent power groupings in society: the more conventional journalistic paradigm (Hackett 1984) and the critical approach. The former stipulates that media professionalism requires an 'above the battle', objective and impartial stance towards the objects of media coverage. Media professionals are expected to ignore or subordinate all loyalties implicit in their other roles, such as support for a given partisan position or preference for the interests and causes of other groups in society. The main exception is support for the core values of society, as in the familiar BBC dictum that as between democracy and totalitarianism impartiality is inconceivable. The critical alternative rejects this position as an expression of a professional ideology, which obscures and provides a 'cover up' for the true loyalties of media professionals to the prevailing status quo. Allegiance to the core values of society translates, in this view, into propagation of a 'dominant ideology'.

We perceive difficulties in both perspectives. However convincing in suggesting reasons why journalism reproduces and reinforces the contours of social power, the critical approach is too dismissive of the attempt by media professionals to apply universalistic criteria to the social and political actors, whose affairs they report. Consequently, they cannot explain the many instances when even highly prestigious institutions and personalities attract negative news coverage.

For their part, many journalists in Western media systems would probably regard the evidence in the parliamentary broadcasting case study as highlighting little more than a minor exception to their usual rules. And one sees what they could mean. There does seem to be a tendency for reporters to apply similar yardsticks to all groups and institutions, whenever they are embroiled in episodes of conflict, drama, failure, hypocrisy and scandal that can be related in news-story form. Yet that is not all that is involved in news-making. Media organizations develop and express distinctive policies, which are reflected not only in their editorial positions, but also in their reporting perspectives. Much news has a normative function as well as an informative one, relating reported events, explicitly or by implication, back to issues in which societal values are at stake (Lazarsfeld and Merton 1957; Alexander 1981). Moreover, certain groups *persistently* attract certain forms of coverage in the media, whether positive or pejorative. The structured and internally consistent treatment of, say, the recipients of welfare (Golding and Middleton 1982), soccer hooligans and other perpetrators of deviant behaviour cannot be plausibly explained as an outcome of the application of news values alone.

We therefore contend that journalists react to all special groups and institutions, not only via news-value criteria, but also according to the degree of respect (or lack of it) to which they are regarded as entitled by the dominant value system. The utility of this perspective for theorizing and analysing media relationships with other social institutions is reflected in the following five major implications which flow from it.

First, it might be possible to arrange all social institutions and groups on a continuum, according to the degree to which their representation in the media betrays a more sacerdotal or more pragmatic orientation by those assigned to report their activities. The monarchy, for example, probably receives more sacerdotal treatment in the British media than do most other social institutions. This is not to deny that the Royal Family may occasionally be subjected to more 'professional' coverage, as exemplified in attempts by the press to intrude into the privacy of its members. But such behaviour is episodic, normally confined to the more 'popular' end of the British press and (more to the point) is sometimes frowned upon, even censured, by other sectors of the media. A similarly sacerdotal treatment may be accorded the Church, though again more pragmatic perspectives may be applied when its spokesmen express unorthodox views, engage in political controversy, or indulge in 'unseemly' conduct. Slightly lower down the sacerdotal ladder, we may find the central institutions of the state and government, including Parliament. It should be emphasized that their status does not preclude a critical, even hostile, media stance towards the policies and personalities of such institutions. But the treatment meted out to policies and personalities should be distinguished from a more sacerdotal orientation towards institutions *qua* institutions, which in this case will often attract the respect to which they are entitled by virtue of their symbolic embodiment of the value system of society. Then perhaps there are a number of 'half-way' institutions, recognized as part of the legitimate fabric of society, often entitled to voice their views on current issues, yet mainly reported in pragmatic terms. In Britain, perhaps the trade unions are an outstanding example of this mid-point category. Finally, some groups seem to occupy the other end of the reporting spectrum. Every society has its pet villains – those groups and organizations which are most remote from, indeed stand in opposition to, the central values of society. In Britain, this role has been assumed in recent years by certain deviant groups, such as 'welfare spongers' (Golding and Middleton 1982), 'muggers' (Hall *et al.* 1978), teenage hooligans (Cohen and Young 1973) and IRA 'terrorists'.

Secondly, as the above examples suggest, journalism is inherently, not just incidentally, a several-sided enterprise. Media coverage of a given institution will reflect the interaction between two sets of influences – its more or less abiding sacerdotal standing in the scale of social values and its momentary weight on news-value scales.

The validity of such a dualistic perspective is strengthened by its compatibility with other tensions in which journalism is enmeshed. One arises from the intermediary position of the news media in society, dependent on sources yet professionally committed to cater for presumed audience needs and interests. Exposed to pressures from both sides, then, journalists will naturally respond, more or less sacerdotally, to differences of prestige and power among source institutions *and*, via news-value calculations, according to what they think audiences will find most exciting and significant.

The field of forces within which journalists operate contains another source of potential tension – that between their professional loyalties and their need to sustain a continuing relationship with their sources. On the one hand, they look to their own colleagues for daily stimulus on the job, confirmation of their news-value decisions and an affirmation of their professional standing. On the other hand, they enter into 'role relationships' with their prime news sources, building up a shared 'emergent culture' with them, including various mutually accepted groundrules and criteria of publicity appropriateness and fairness (Blumler and Gurevitch 1981). It stands to reason that in such relationships, the more esteemed sources will be able to exert greater 'clout'.

This dualistic view of journalism may help to clarify its much-disputed relationship to the socio-political status quo. Does it tend to uphold or to undermine, legitimize or discredit the dominant institutions and ideology of society? In our view, the least simplistic answer is that it performs both functions in different ways and at different times. Both potentially and in practice mass media workways have both legitimizing and disruptive implications for the social order. They are involved in processes of both social control and social change.

Thirdly, the sacerdotal orientation could be said to prescribe that some institutions should be reported by the media according to what those institutions regard as their *inherent deserts* and not merely according to what they *do* and how that chimes with conventional news values. It follows that the more sacerdotal the media's orientation towards a given institution, the more likely it is that that institution will be represented through its own perspective, that is, in ways which reflect its own view of its purposes, values, activities and relations to society. Perhaps this proposition sheds fresh light on those intensifying conflicts that have recently erupted in many Western societies between the mass media and a host of aggrieved parties, such as trade unions, spokespersons of ethnic minorities, women's liberation and many others. The root of such conflicts may be traced to a desire on the part of the groups concerned for a more sacerdotal treatment of their affairs by reporters, who, faced with criticism, may resist such demands by refusing to acknowledge that they are involved in the sacerdotal game at all, claiming instead to be impartially guided by news values. Such conflicts are peculiarly intractable, because the grounds to which the contesting parties appeal are radically different without always being openly professed.

Fourthly, the outlook advanced here may clarify the sources of cross-national similarities and differences in how journalists present the news. In Western societies, news values as such tend to be transculturally uniform. Although such an assertion is largely speculative at present, some evidence in its support has emerged from a study of the contributions made by television journalists in nine Common Market countries to the broadcast coverage of the European Parliamentary elections of 1979 (Blumler 1983). But it is primarily due to the specificity of cultural factors, entailing different rankings of social institutions in different countries (for example, Congress is probably lower in the American pecking order than Parliament in the British hierarchy of institutional prestige), that news output can seem quite divergent and varied when compared across a number of different societies.

Finally, this framework alerts us to the fact, little explored so far in the literature, that media institutions themselves may be on the receiving end as well as on the originating end of the orientations discussed in this essay. If, as we believe, all social institutions evoke in the members of society a varying mixture of sacerdotal and pragmatic attitudes, then the news media are no exception. They too are regarded by their audiences, and more importantly by their sources, in a mixture of lights, combining sacerdotal respect for the principle of freedom of expression with a pragmatic recognition that the media can distort and trivialize and may be harnessed to the service of particular interests. Important consequences for the political functioning of the media in society could flow from how this balance is struck. The readiness of the leaders of powerful institutions uninhibitedly to indulge in news management practices may turn on it. The course of the previously mentioned conflicts between media professionals and groups wanting to be represented in the press and broadcasting 'through their own eyes' may be affected by it. And ultimately, it may determine society's response to the claims of the news media to the respect, independence and other privileges to which they feel they are entitled by virtue of their own embodiment of certain sacerdotal values.

5

The Problems of Making Political Television: A Practitioner's Perspective

Roger Bolton

*P*olitical television is getting better, as are media studies of broadcasting. That point must be made first as any study of the problems of political programme-making will make the whole enterprise seem impossible. The problems range from the internal and external constraints a journalist faces to the problems of his own limited experience and understanding, the technical demands of his medium, the limited attention span of his audience and their different levels of knowledge and intelligence.

Then there are the manifold temptations along the way: money, ambition, self-publicity. Occasionally there is a test of courage and, without glamorizing the business or mistaking careless rashness for bravery, there are moments when the individual is tested in a way that rarely happens in other parts of television. However, despite all the problems it's getting better all the time and there is tonight's programme to get on the air. Broadcasters are eternal optimists, always believing that yesterday's disaster will be wiped out by today's success.

The internal constraints

Most practitioners are aware of the limitations of the medium and the internal constraints faced by broadcasters and in particular by makers of political television programmes. Television is a 'mass' medium, its audience has a wide range of intelligence and knowledge. Despite the widespread belief that most of the viewers for serious current affairs programmes must be of more than average income and education, audience research studies show that the majority of the audience for

93

the BBC's flagship current affairs programme *Panorama* comes from the lower reaches of the class structure. Broadcasters cannot assume too much but if they assume ignorance it severely limits what they can get across in what is a very limited period, the ordinary attention span. The eternal compromise begins, and it is compounded by the need to keep a frequently tired audience attentive. Nobody *has* to watch, and most people wish to be entertained as well as informed. I plead guilty to forgetting that on many occasions.

As one cannot re-read a television paragraph the programme-maker must signpost with particular care, summarizing at frequent intervals. It is hard to avoid simplifying and there are sirens to be heard calling the producer away from the difficult and the complex.

'Television can't cope with ideas, it's for story-telling, for facts not issues.' I have heard this siren song from the mouths of most distinguished broadcasting figures. It has to be admitted that the argument has some force. For every *Civilisation* and *Ascent of Man* there are many failures, but those two series stand as beacons and surely demand of all practitioners of political journalism an answer to the question, Why hasn't there been a series about political ideas of equal distinction? *The Sea of Faith* provides a further example, presented by Don Cupitt, Dean of Emmanuel College, Cambridge, a leading theologian who some believe can no longer be considered a Christian. It had its difficult moments, but it demonstrated that television and complex ideas need not be incompatible, and can be watched with enjoyment by significant numbers. Another siren voice sings, 'You've got to have a villain, it's got to be us against them.' Investigative and consumer journalists are particularly prone to the overwhelming compulsion to nail a villain in the last frame. Narrow chauvinism is often present; if in doubt blame the *Frogs*. Other voices: 'Forget the issues, it's the personalities that matter.' 'Make the facts fit the story the public want to hear.' 'Oh God that's boring.'

'Yield not to temptation'

In some ways television can encourage a superficial approach to political television. A 'scandal' is more attractive than a complex and difficult argument. For example, it is much easier to make a moving short film about the closure of a hospital (usually attributed to 'grey unfeeling bureaucrats') with understandably angry and emotional parents and moving pictures of child patients, than to explain the conflict of priorities in a declining economy. This is not to argue that such films are bad, simply that they are not sufficient. The situations they portray must be placed in context.

A programme which is on the side of the suffering and which focuses the public's anger on a target is often thought successful. It has brought an 'evil' out into the open and the 'guilty' persons have been identified. This 'accusatory' form of television gives the viewer and the makers a glow of satisfaction but I fear it is often close to the satisfaction given by unscrupulous politicians to a bewildered public. The need to blame rather than to understand is shared among politicians and broadcasters. It leads to a quieter mind, and a more straightforward film, if only the prosecution's case is heard – and the defence doesn't get a word in edgeways.

I do not mean to suggest that investigative programmes that champion consumer rights, like BBC 1's *Watchdog* or Radio 4's *Checkpoint*, do a disservice: far from it. They do a genuinely good job on behalf of the public, for they deal with areas where the truth and the facts can often be established. This product *is* dangerous, that man *did* defraud his company, this unemployed person *was* cheated by a loan shark. Nor do I argue that broadcasters should be afraid to put conclusions at the end of their programmes. All I wish to do is to point out the tendency of the medium to push one into black-and-white programme-making. One should not go with the tide unless the necessary thought, research and open-minded consideration of alternative arguments has been carried out. In addition, this 'black and white' approach usually draws one away from the major issues to the more dramatic and visible ones. This does democracy a disservice, makes sensible political decision-making more difficult and plays into the hands of those who wish to see us frolic on the surface while they carry on unobserved in the depths.

Consider. You are a young programme-maker. You are faced with the choice between making a film about Dr Armand Hammer, friend of Lenin, Brezhnev, American presidents, the Chinese, Prince Charles, patron of the arts, oil tycoon, etc., etc., with a PR Company pushing glamorous material, free jet flights around the world and an 'exclusive' interview, or trying to explain the coming crisis in the funding of pensions. One way lies pleasure, the applause of audience and editors, and good ratings. And the other? I sometimes think Mephistopheles sits in the cutting rooms. It is to the credit of many programme-makers that they do resist the temptation.

An expensive business

The economics of the medium are a further, obvious constraint, as is what I often regard as an obsession with overmanning and productivity. People are expensive, cameras don't charge overtime or eat, so there is an understandable tendency to hold down numbers of those elements of production upon which one cannot charge capital depreciation.

The BBC is particularly bothered about this, especially at licence fee time. Some newspapers seem to positively enjoy taunting the Corporation over the numbers of people it employs, as if a number, say 30,000, were a good or bad thing in itself. At Party Conference time there are always articles about BBC overmanning. However, they often fail to relate the numbers to the range of broadcasting the BBC does on the External Services, four national radio networks, two national television networks, regional television and local radio. The same person cannot service *Breakfast Time* and *Newsnight* and sleep as well. Nor do they take into account the complex technical facilities required. A television producer has to take more than a typewriter to get his programme on the air; in effect he has to take his whole printing press.

So there is considerable pressure to restrict the number of production staff, and the expansion of daily programming makes it even more difficult for departmental heads to husband their human resources and give broadcast journalists the time to do original research. One can end up simply reprocessing someone else's 'facts'. Increasingly too the complex technical requirements of television mean that more and more time has to be spent on mastering the 'television typewriter', using the complex graphics, and so on, rather than on the subject material itself. In such circumstances it is not necessarily the best journalists who rise to the top. Sadly this problem is often compounded by Luddite political journalists who sometimes refuse to learn initial production techniques, though, to be fair, there is little training to help them do so. It is usually sink or swim in television, even today. The late entry from Fleet Street, or elsewhere, is rarely able to catch up on the techniques required. His political knowledge, insights and enthusiasms may then go to waste.

The mote in the eye

There is a further potential internal constraint on broadcasters and indeed all journalists, the difficulty of reporting the affairs of our own workplace and of acknowledging the pressures upon us. One has to acknowledge that the journalistic integrity of an organization does sometimes come into conflict with what is perceived as its institutional interest. Or put another way, do media organizations report themselves as freely as they report other groups? I have my doubts. Or put a third way, does the BBC in the licence fee application period act with greater caution than at other times? The answer is yes. Such damage can be limited by a more honest approach to the audience, acknowledging the conflict. And, to be fair, many 'difficult' programmes are transmitted and some only temporarily postponed. One ought not to be surprised: we would be angels or possibly masochists if we gladly scored what in the business is known as 'own goals', and no one is objective about themselves or their own organization.

I have to admit that I felt betrayed by my BBC News colleagues when they published a factual statement about my involvement in a particular controversy. The statement was accurate but necessarily brief and therefore the context was not supplied. 'But you don't understand, you're giving a misleading impression.' I found myself mouthing the words my 'victims' must have used about investigative programmes I've made. It's a salutary experience. When we know something about a subject we become aware of how superficial the reporting of this is. Hence our anger. None the less, the news report had been accurate.

In the case of the broadcasting institutions such sensitivity is often heightened by a mistrust of the fairness of the reporting of certain newspapers who are thought to be opposed to the Broadcasting duopoly and the licence fee and to have a financial interest in its dismemberment. Can it be coincidence that the Rupert Murdoch-owned *Times* published so many leaders critical of the BBC during the 1985 licence fee campaign? This tends to make management defensive and wary of public debate. Still the BBC management has a decent record of going on to the air to be 'clobbered' over an issue, although the producers of review programmes like BBC 2's *Did you see . . . ?* and BBC Radio 4's *Feedback* must be aware of the limits of their critical independence. I admire the way they explore the cliff edges. There is another problem hindering open discussion. Far too many of us making programmes are both too proud and too scared to admit mistakes. Our apparent arrogance irritates the public but we fear an admission will be exploited by our enemies, and the press.

Corporate ethos and self-censorship

The BBC itself has no opinions on matters of public debate but it does demand of its employees professional adherence to certain principles. It supports parliamentary democracy, for example, it opposes racial discrimination, it defines objectivity and balance and requires both of its journalists.

Those who do not believe in these things will believe that the pursuit of them involves censorship of other ideas and beliefs, will believe that the organization recruits in its own image, and perpetuates its 'bias'. However, even as I acknowledge this, I still believe that very few facts and opinions do not get through. I have participated in the selection of some very iconoclastic *and* independently minded people, who are frequently a pain in the neck but who make stimulating and irreverent programmes.

There remains self-censorship, which I believe is the most significant form of censorship that exists. It comes in many forms. When *I* cut something it's an editorial decision, when *you* do it's censorship.

We were sitting in a conference room in BBC Manchester Network Production Centre, discussing our journalistic output. We do spend rather a lot of our time gazing at navels rather than any other part of the anatomy, but I had thought that our output, in programmes like *File on 4*, the leading BBC radio weekly reporting programme, and *Brass Tacks*, the bi-weekly, television journalism programme which goes out on BBC 2, was quite decent. However, I was feeling uncomfortable. I had walked into the room feeling one of 'us', the scars of long-ago battles on my face, fresh blood on my hands from the latest skirmish in defence of the spirit of BBC journalism. I was now being labelled quite clearly as one of 'them' – the censors, the conspirators, trying to trample upon the public's right to know, ally of Government, the Establishment, the Bosses. 'Them.'

A 24-year-old researcher was clearly accusing me of censoring a programme on Northern Ireland, by cutting a folk singer saying that some members of the IRA were regarded as 'good boys' by Catholics in Northern Ireland. I had tried to explain the programme was much overlength; the point had been made elsewhere (although less directly) by more representative figures. Hadn't I . . . but why should I expect him to remember? He did look and sound very much as I did 15 years ago. Had I changed or had nothing changed?

I have mentioned earlier that as licence fee time comes around a greater sense of caution is felt within the BBC. But actual censorship? What subjects dare we not touch, what subjects are forbidden to touch? I asked for examples. The Royal Family? Touchy certainly, but the BBC had made features about the Royal Finances, and Willie Hamilton, the Labour MP and a vocal critic of public spending on the monarchy, wasn't banned. Incest? Rather a lot of programmes on that I thought, indeed recently sexual issues had seemed to be disproportionately covered. Anyway, I couldn't get very worked up about whether trans-vestites had received their fair share of air time.

Later I began to wonder about what were the difficult sensitive issues. There clearly were some, the Security Services and Ireland, for example, but these issues were covered in some form. I found, and still find, great difficulty in thinking of *issues* which are censored. What one *is* aware of is the fact that many producers don't have the heart, or the stamina, to take on some of the difficult areas of broadcasting where politicians, and increasingly lawyers, lie in wait.

When Editor of *Panorama*, I got a bit fed up with a particular producer who was always complaining of what we didn't cover in Northern Ireland but who never volunteered to go there himself. I doubt if he was a coward, I suspect he thought it would be easier to make a successful and glamorous film about crime in many interesting foreign countries, preferably the United States.

More worrying, some producers may be afraid of the effects on their career of the controversy which is inevitable in some areas. Instead of probing the more sensitive areas of domestic life, where there is little common ground, it is easier to go abroad and confirm our prejudices about a foreign country.

For those of us who proclaim the independence of the BBC's journalism the summer of 1985 was a terrible time. First came the 'Real Lives' row and then allegations in the *Observer* about the vetting of BBC staff by MI5. To many it felt as though we had shot ourselves in the foot. A colleague remarked that he now knew what it was like to be a member of the crew of the Titanic.

The 'Real Lives' row

It was the 'silly season' in Fleet Street. *Sunday Times* journalist Barry Penrose needed a front-page story for that week's paper. He says that 'contacts' rang him up about a programme to be shown in the BBC 1 'Real Lives' series of documentaries, two weeks hence. As a result he picked up a copy of the *Radio Times*, the weekly magazine of BBC programme schedules, and read there an extensive feature about the two contrasted figures in the programme, Martin McGuinness and Gregory Campbell: both elected representatives, the former a past and probably present member of the IRA committed to the use of the 'Armalite' rifle as well as the ballot box, the latter a hard-line Unionist who advocates the killing of IRA members.

Where was the 'story'? McGuinness himself, and his party, had frequently appeared on network television programmes and even more frequently in programmes in Ulster.

The government had not chosen to ban the party, nor to ban broadcasts which included Sinn Fein representatives (although this was the policy of the Dublin government).

Penrose had not seen the programme but those television previewers who had would have told him that it was a low-key, sad and depressing film which revealed the irreconcilability of the two extremes in the north. It contained no 'secret' interviews with hooded men, no secret filming with terrorists. The security forces in Ulster were well informed and had co-operated in the filming.

The one thing going for the story was a general concern, voiced by President Reagan in the wake of the hijack of airline hostages in Lebanon earlier in 1985, that the American media had been manipulated by the hijackers. The US networks, extraordinarily competitive in their news programmes, had been involved in unedifying scrambles at press conferences and had carried extensive interviews with hostages, their families and hijackers. The great media-manipulator, Ronald Reagan, found himself being out-manipulated. In a speech to the American Bar Association Mrs Thatcher had been quick to join in the complaints that extensive television coverage gave terrorists 'the oxygen of publicity'.

We were still a long way from a *Sunday Times* scoop. So Penrose began to act as the catalyst, if not the creator of the story. He got Mark Hosenball, a *Sunday Times* journalist based in the United States, to ask Mrs Thatcher a hypothetical question about what her reaction would be to a film which featured the alleged Chief of Staff of the IRA. The Prime Minister, caught off-guard, gave a typically robust reply. She still did not know about the BBC film, but that did not prevent the *Sunday Times* printing a story with the headline: 'THATCHER SLAMS IRA FILM'. Then a catastrophic number of balls started rolling quickly downhill.

The then Home Secretary, Mr Leon Brittan, wrote to the Chairman of the BBC Governors asking him to stop the programme going out and included the following incredible statement in his letter: 'Even if the programme and any surrounding material were to present terrorist organisations in a wholly unfavourable light, I would still ask you not to permit it to be broadcast.' If any coverage was wrong, why hadn't the government passed the appropriate legislation, banning either Sinn Fein or the broadcasting of interviews with its members?

Still Mr Brittan was only playing the politicians' game. The BBC's Board of Governors should and could have politely replied that if the Home Secretary wished he could exercise his legal right and ban the programme, but since the BBC management, having seen the film, regarded it as suitable for transmission, with a couple of changes, the programme would go ahead.

The governors would then review the programme after transmission and decide whether the management's decision was right. If not they would consider policy changes and/or replacing any executives concerned.

Alas, the governors did not do this. They insisted on seeing the programme themselves before transmission, thus effectively passing a vote of no confidence in the Board of Management and taking direct editorial control themselves. Worse still they then voted 10:1 not to show it. Radio Moscow and Libyan Radio had a field day saying that the BBC's much vaunted independence had been shown to be a sham. Most of the newspapers, including the *Sunday Times*, criticized the decision. The Board of Management, and the Director General in particular, were left high and dry.

The opponents of public service broadcasting made the most of their opportunity, many staff went on strike and desperate efforts were made to get the programme transmitted. In the writer's view, not transmitting the programme clearly amounted to censorship.

As it is, three issues were raised which will not go away: first, who runs the BBC? second, are the principles of its journalism to be altered? and third, are the governors representative of society and are they capable of defending Public Service Broadcasting against party politics, and a frequently hysterical press?

Two reassuring things did happen, however. First, a great many staff were prepared to lose a day's pay by striking, not over wages or conditions, but over the issue of the principle of the independence of the BBC's journalism; secondly, the Director General immediately authorized a *Panorama* programme about Sinn Fein and the Anglo-Irish Summit for October 1985, a programme which would include interviews with Sinn Fein leaders.

After several weeks' uncertainty the BBC announced in September 1985 that the film would be screened after all (in October). Two changes in the programme were made (to show the violent effects of IRA action and the limited extent of Sinn Fein's share of the vote) and in a rather lame statement it was claimed that 'the Board of Governors now believes that the general climate is such that an early showing of the programme is acceptable'. Though hailed as a victory by many journalists the outcome left many unanswered questions about the relationship between the government and the BBC, and about the role of the BBC governors.

The 'vetting row'

The MI5 episode which followed shortly afterwards was a cruel kick in the face when the victim was already on the floor. Its origins lay in the curious dichotomy which lies at the heart of the BBC. On the one side are those involved in production and journalism. On the other is the administrative and institutional support system. The former prides itself on its independence, and is concerned with day to day programming, the latter is inevitably concerned with the survival of the institution and so with matters like the renewal of the licence fee which provides the Corporation's income. Part of the personnel and administrative system is also involved in the preparations for the event of war when a system of communications must be safeguarded.

Since about 1937 the BBC has had a relationship with the intelligence Service department MI5, mainly to safeguard the system of communications in the event of war. The involvement had clearly grown and most staff knew that there was some sort of vetting somewhere. Programme-makers rarely came across it, and found it rather absurd, irrelevant and ineffective. I came across it twice in 18 years in the Corporation. On both occasions the questions raised against candidates for jobs were dismissed by those in charge. It was largely an unnecessary hangover from the war, which had not seen reform because of 'administrative inertia'. None the less, when two *Observer* journalists investigated the story they found some disturbing cases where individual careers had been blocked on security grounds without their knowing anything about it and on the basis of inaccurate information. The BBC promised a review and reform.

To the writer it seemed three things were required: first, the reduction of those jobs requiring vetting to a handful, primarily concerned with engineering responsibilities in the event of war; secondly, the public identification of those jobs which require vetting so that candidates would know they were to be vetted; thirdly, a system of appeal which would allow candidates to discover what was alleged against them and give them the opportunity to challenge what could well be erroneous material.

The public outcry was particularly irritating as the effect of vetting had been minimal and had not affected significantly the independence of the journalism – but try telling that to press journalists and the public in the summer of 1985!

Despite the two disasters, an objective viewer would notice that the

BBC continued to interview Sinn Fein, continued to incur the government's displeasure and continued to do thorough and effective journalism in its programmes. Conservative MPs were further convinced of the ineptitude of MI5 since it was well known 'that BBC producers were a bunch of "Trots"'.

There is another insidious form of self-censorship, which comes with the desire to preserve 'contacts'. It is akin to the self-censorship of the cricket correspondent who keeps quiet about the drunkenness, womanizing and occasional hooliganism of a touring side because he must ensure the continuation of 'exclusives'. Perhaps like the parliamentary 'lobby' correspondent or the specialist correspondent he feels he can sip with a long spoon. I believe it is always shorter than he thinks.

What such a lobby correspondent must always do is let the public know the limitations of his reporting and the bargain he has struck. It may be a necessary one but he should be open about it. Why not name Bernard Ingham, the Prime Minister's personal press secretary, instead of 'informed sources'? Or, in the case of cricket, David Gower, the Test team captain rather, than 'a leading member of England's cricket team'.

But there may be some self-censorship which comes from experience, or despair, or mistrust. Those of us who inspire this reaction stand condemned. All editors and broadcasting authorities can do is try to earn the trust and then say to the doubters 'try me'. Or more crudely, put up or shut up.

So let us summon up our confidence, if we have any left, aware of our subjectivity and the limitations of the medium, and self-censorship, and try to make political television. What are the problems facing us in the outside world?

The outside world

Reporting is often not the problem, it is analysis that poses the difficulty. The facts can often be established, the causes may be matters of opinion. But simply to state the facts, 'two people were shot in Northern Ireland today', isn't enough. Why were *they* shot, why is anyone shot in Northern Ireland? The question 'why?' is arguably the most important one.

So have the opinions, the various analyses, been given air time? It is here that we must acknowledge that the range of voices, of opinions, is too narrow. The desire, sometimes encouraged by the main political parties, to ensure that discussions are representative of percentages and power groups means that the radical, minority, or new opinion is less well represented. The debate is therefore often too narrow, deprived of the richness of the unorthodox. Conservative maverick Enoch Powell on the nuclear deterrent or on the Russians is seldom heard. The distinguished historian and anti-nuclear polemicist E. P. Thompson struggles in relative silence until the Campaign for Nuclear Disarmament flourishes. Too often ideas wait upon political backing before reaching the airways.

The BBC does keep a list of appearances by MPs in its journalistic programmes and it does try to keep a balance between them. It is perhaps inevitable that news and current affairs programmes tend to feature representatives of groups that decide whether ideas will be put into effect, rather than those with simply fresh or interesting ideas. The difficulty of access can be explained by a lack of intellectual curiosity by producers as well as by external pressures, but the BBC Community Programme Unit and Channel 4 are ensuring that many more voices are heard.

Facts? – what facts?

Let us turn to the 'missing' facts then. The laws of libel, 'D–Notices' and the Official Secrets Act keep some matters from the public, and an expensively lost libel case is a powerful incentive to adopt a much more cautious approach in giving legal advice. In April 1985 the BBC settled a libel case brought against one of its programmes, *That's Life*, by a Dr Gee. The BBC's costs were reported to be over £1 million. It gave many pause for thought, and it would not be surprising if some journalists decided to take a break from 'investigations' in the consumer area leaving many stories untouched.

A further problem is our sources of information. They are limited, and government and most institutional bodies, from the trade unions to Whitehall, want to keep it that way. Information is to be released on *their* terms. J. Downing writes elsewhere in this volume about government secrecy and the media, and the legislation in operation. However, ministers break some of these Acts continually with 'leaks' and with impunity. The price of the 'leak' for journalists is often the inability to check it against the facts. The reward for politicians is either setting the agenda and dictating the terms of the argument, or testing an idea before publicly backing it; or, of course, the cowardly dissociation of a Cabinet member from his Cabinet without the inconvenience of leaving it, a technique pushed to its limits and beyond in the Thatcher Cabinet in early 1986. So journalists are well advised to treat *all* sources of information with suspicion. I hope we are as energetic in discovering information as we are in receiving it.

Those who give us information are increasingly aware of the mechanics of broadcasting and are therefore in a much improved position to manipulate it. And of course Whitehall is full of people who are paid to release information only in the interests of governments. Even prime ministers' press secretaries ('sources close to the Prime Minister') have been known to tell terminological inexactitudes. Harold Wilson 'let it be known' how he had 'read the Riot Act' to the Parliamentary Labour Party on many occasions. On one famous day he was reported as threatening to take their 'dog licences' away, that is, withdraw the whip. These accounts were often read with amazement by MPs who were present and remembered things very differently.

Harold Wilson was also extremely well informed about newspaper deadlines and frequently captured headlines with a last-minute story. Nowadays most politicians play that game. Get your retaliation in first, said the late Bill Shankley, Manager of Liverpool Football Club. Most inhabitants of governments don't need to be told that.

There are various other tricks which can be used in the PR offensive. Ring up a television programme and offer an 'exclusive' interview. The producers rarely say no if they think they will beat a rival. Go on current affairs programmes like *Weekend World* or *The World This Weekend* on Sunday as Monday morning's newspaper headlines are the easiest ones to capture. Issue a very long and complicated white paper to journalists only on the day of publication, and hold a press conference close to the news deadline. The journalists will not have time to absorb it all, they will have to accept the summary given by the politicians and a day or so later when the difficult questions are beginning to be formed in the broadcaster's mind, who cares? The headlines have been won, the terms of the argument established in favour of the politician concerned.

If a difficult television discussion is proposed – refuse to take part, say you were misled about the nature of the programme, and if it goes ahead say it is obviously biased. If you are a Cabinet minister refuse to participate in a discussion with anyone less senior than yourself. It limits the field. The other trick in this area is to demand a separate interview. Programme makers can be so desperate to get the minister that they agree. I have buckled to such pressures, I'm afraid.

Another technique is to do only a 'live' interview on the news. That way you can't be edited and in the two or three minutes available it is unlikely that the questioner will be able to put you on the spot. During the Falklands War, television was sometimes taking the Ministry of Defence pressman Ian MacDonald's statements 'live', thus frustrating any attempt to put the remarks into context. The dangers of such 'live' interviews are well understood by the broadcasting authorities who have tried to ensure that they do not recur.

A significant blow to informed political discussion and debate was struck by the emergence of Mr (later Sir Gordon) Reece and the Saatchi Brothers at Conservative Central Office. While they were amateurs compared with Ronald Reagan's entourage, they signalled a concentration on image rather than content. They were concerned with winning elections not arguments.

Attention was switched from the quality press in Fleet Street to the mass circulation newspapers. Knighthoods and ennoblements followed. In broadcasting, Jimmy Young on Radio 2 was favoured rather more than *Panorama,* chat shows rather than Robin Day. Mr Young frequently asked difficult questions and occasionally Sir Robin or Sir Alastair *was* allowed in but, this aside, the overall result was a gentler ride in more relaxed surroundings for a larger audience. Eminently sensible if you are Mrs Thatcher, extremely frustrating if you are a political journalist. And 'tough' interviews are getting tougher – for the interviewer. For example, Mrs Thatcher has invented her own way of dealing with questions. Don't take a breath, or halt, at the end of sentences. This means that the interviewer either can't get his question in or seems to be rudely interrupting if he is. If the programme is live the time soon runs out, and accountability is evaded.

What politics does television cover?

So the problems of making political television are considerable. What sort of political television do we make? How successful has news management, image-making and pressure groups' lobbying been? Of course, those who are employed in making political television have a vested interest in proclaiming its success. Perhaps it is successful only in the short term, and in the margins. The pendulum swings and governments are ejected from office as the signs of their failure become apparent, or through simple boredom on the voters' part. Eventually the truth may come out but a lot of damage can be done in the short term, a lot of decisions taken and a lot of time and energy spent on isolating the PR and pressures, time and energy which ought to have been spent addressing the issues and informing the public.

Yesterday is, well, yesterday, say the PR men. Today's headlines are what matters.

It all acts as a sort of camouflage to hide the real political debate which should be taking place. Harold Wilson is reported as saying that the Labour Party was rather like a stage-coach. The important thing was to keep it going. If you did that then the passengers inside would talk to each other and leave the driver to get on with it. However, if the stage-coach stopped at the crossroads then the passengers would get out, argue about which direction to go and never get back in again. I would suggest that while it is the politicians' job to drive the coach, it is the journalists' responsibility to ensure that the passengers have seen the signpost.

All of this leads to two tiers of political debate, the public and the private. The public debate usually starts when the decision has been taken; sometimes it may never happen at all. On the surface statements are made, images created, poses struck, insults exchanged. Underneath the reality is often the opposite. One of my main frustrations as a political journalist and editor has been my frequent failure to help the public get into the real debate while it is going on, while it is undecided in Cabinet, party and Parliament.

At the time of writing there is a real debate to be had about the forthcoming defence crises where once more our commitments exceed our capacities. It is also clear that unemployment is unlikely to go down significantly in the long term, let alone the short term, but where is the debate about how society should adjust to that fact? The Conservative and Labour Parties, for differing reasons, find it difficult to accept this publicly, although they must know it to be true. The real problems of managing economic decline cannot be addressed without acknowledging this decline, but this is hardly the best prescription for re-election. Anyway it has to be admitted that much of the public is just not interested. Does this suggest that the media provide a platform for the sound and the fury, while elsewhere 'real politics' goes on?

That would be unfair to many parts of the media. It would be wrong to lump the *Financial Times* in with the *Sun*, or *Newsnight* with *TV–am*. Somewhere in the media most of the important issues are dealt with at one time or another. The problem is one of priority, not presence. Getting the important issues to the forefront of the debate, ahead of the peripheral and transient, is the problem.

Political television should be about the way countries are governed, or could be governed, their political systems and the important decisions which are being taken, or which need to be taken. Many argue that political coverage is too much about personalities rather than politics. Others argue that television's political coverage is too Westminster- or Whitehall-dominated, not enough of the 'real' world and people's ordinary experience. I believe political television should be, and is, about all these things. It is the proportions we should argue about and which are wrong.

Our domestic political coverage is obviously hampered by the fact that none of us is objective about our own country. We must try to become more so but we must first acknowledge the subjective impulses. As I have mentioned earlier, the BBC acknowledges a bias – towards parliamentary democracy, a bias which I welcome. But we must acknowledge, if we are to begin from that standpoint, that voices outside that form of democracy must be heard.

However, some people believe that broadcast journalism has taken a knock to its collective confidence because it is now being said that there is no such thing as objectivity. The trained observer is now being told that all his judgements are subjective, and he is still recovering from the shock. The Glasgow University Media Group has perhaps had the greatest influence here although *its* own subjectivity and lack of broadcasting experience has limited its effects upon many practitioners.

Still younger broadcast journalists have been affected and have tried to cope in various ways. One of my assistant producers, Haydn Shaughnessy, put it this way: 'Journalists have tried going out to the masses in order to let them have their say, without the interjections of a journalist. They have tried using groups of the general public as a check on journalists' judgements – this was the method of Channel 4's *Friday Alternative* in its early days. They have tried to lay all their emphasis on "alternatives" as a means of forcing change on to the agenda. They have abdicated responsibility and become biased. They have attempted to redefine the agenda by referring to provincial rather than London pre-occupations. I believe these approaches are diversions, albeit valuable ones, from the main responsibility of political journalists.'

For although it may be simply my opinion that the miners' leader Arthur Scargill deliberately did not hold a national ballot of his members before the 1984 coal strike began because he feared he might be defeated, the facts are there to be discovered. It is just as poor journalism to present an 'on the one hand, on the other hand' type of report because you don't attempt to establish the facts as it is to present opinion *as* fact. Media research has made thoughtful practitioners pause for thought, before I hope resuming the search for objectivity and accuracy.

Let me make a few points about our coverage of *foreign* politics. First, and most importantly, it is increasingly expensive to do, as the pound slips in value. It is undoubtedly easier to make political films abroad, to get it wrong and go unremarked. Few people who know the real situation see the films, and foreign complaints are less effective than domestic ones.

More programmes are made about the United States than is justified, because Americans speak English, are a television society and most producers like going there. Most people will agree to be interviewed and information is more accessible. Far too few programmes are made about Europe, mainly because those countries don't have English as the national language, and because our dominant culture influence is the United States, not Europe.

Our coverage of Eastern Bloc countries (particularly the Soviet Union) is too one-dimensional. This is partly our fault. Sometimes one feels we only do stories about the Soviet military machines or dissidents. However, I believe the main fault lies with the Soviet authorities. Their censorship, general restrictions and disregard for the truth puts off all but the heroic or the ideologically sympathetic. Either way the coverage is inadequate. There is too little coverage of South America or Africa, or Asia, because such coverage is very expensive, and unless there is a British connection or a particularly nasty war going on, our basic insularity triumphs.

Real attempts are made to redress the balance, mainly on radio, but many examples can be found on television in the attempt to disprove the point: David Harrison's *Afrikaners* and his new series *The Africans*, recent Chinese documentaries, Jonathan Dimbleby's South American series or film from Central Africa, the distinguished foreign reporting of Jon Snow for ITN and Tim Sebastian for the BBC. However, I believe the generalization that our foreign coverage is insufficient is accurate, and the financial cost of such programme-making is increasingly reducing our ability to make our own reports, and making us more dependent on 'buying in material', which is difficult to verify. The result of this is that the programme-makers back home on daily and weekly programmes sometimes commission foreign stories that fit the popular conceptions of a country, rather than the reality.

There is a further problem. If one's coverage of a foreign country is very occasional it lays open the individual programme-maker to the charge of being 'unfair' and 'selective'. A 1985 BBC programme on Turkey illustrates this point. The programme was concerned with the issue of whether or not Turkey should be readmitted to the European

Council in view of her record on civil rights. The programme therefore looked at torture in Turkey. It found a great deal and didn't pull its punches. The programme, for which I was responsible, polarized the audience. To some it was a brave and good piece of journalism, a view I naturally agree with. To some, British holidaymakers who had experienced the delightful Turkish hospitality, it was incomprehensible. To supporters of Turkey, however, it was a most unfair programme, and, true to form, the words 'bias', 'unfair', 'travesty' came forth.

I understand their views while standing by the film. The problem was that this programme was not 'balanced' by others to give a rounded picture of the country. Necessarily the political background of the generals' take-over in 1980 was only sketched in. A very narrow view of Turkey was put forward, but I believe that the programme was fair and accurate within its given area. However, if we do not increase our general coverage of such countries, such partly justifiable complaints will continue to be heard.

How would we feel if the only programme about these islands transmitted on television in the last few years was about the torture in Castlereagh Barracks in Northern Ireland? If some Eastern European countries still believe life in Britain is Dickensian or at least like that shown in the Forsyte Saga, is it not possible that our coverage of them is similarly distorting in its effect?

Our foreign coverage *is* usually better than theirs, more accurate and objective, but not by as much as we think. Some would argue from this that we should not therefore make programmes like the *Brass Tacks* on Turkey. This would be an even more dangerous approach I believe. After all the torture victims in Turkey are part of our common humanity. Television may often be an island, but no man is. The answer is not to cut back but somehow to increase our coverage. This will be very difficult to do in the present circumstances.

What can the broadcaster do?

Faced with these problems of internal and external restraint and with the inadequacy of much that we do, broadcast journalists should be asking themselves some very hard questions. How much better can we do, even given these problems?

We broadcasters should blame ourselves as well as the politicians for the state of political broadcasting. Their responsibility is to manage change not ensure a good debate and one should accept that there are many issues where it would be politically irresponsible to be frank in public, although governments frequently do use the cover of 'the national interest' simply to conceal mistakes and cover embarrassment. Arms limitations talks and discussions over Zimbabwe or Ireland are examples where political discretion is vital in order to achieve the end result. However, if we recognize the need for such discretion by politicans, yet also recognize the need for the public to be properly informed about these issues, while they are current, then I believe it must fall to journalists to place these items on the public agenda.

A former Director-General of the BBC disagreed. In his view it was the duty of Parliament, as an elected body, to decide the agenda. It was not an issue, in his view, if there was no real debate about it in the Commons. Thus the unification of Ireland was not an issue because the front benches of both major parties had agreed that it was not, despite the views of a very large minority recorded in public opinion polls, not to mention many people in Ireland, north and south.

I disagree with him. Broadcasters have no right to place the issues they regard as important before everything else but they do have a duty to put them on the list. This duty derives from the knowledge they have of the real political debate that goes on outside the Chamber or the studio, and the facts they unearth in their reports. The broadcasters' responsibility to the audience is to speak the truth as they see it, to be more open about their procedures and limitations, to be more aware of their own subjectivity. The broadcaster is privileged with information and he must share it.

In the light of all these formidable problems and duties, how qualified are television's producers to produce political journalism? Well, they are mostly white, middle class and relatively young, and they are almost as likely to be female as male. A large number will have gone to Oxbridge, they will be instinctively suspicious of authority, liberal on social issues, uncertain on economic ones. They will be independent, ambitious and intelligent. They will probably have arts or politics degrees. They are not representative, but they are often highly skilled, and the vast majority try not to wield private prejudices and do strive for the truth. And of course they are not alone. They have editors above them (who will probably be 35–45, almost exclusively male) who are well advanced on the road to cynicism! And they work with presenters and reporters who are often highly qualified and rather older.

What they do require is far more time to think and far more training. In my view young producers should be shipped to Party Conferences and made to listen to every debate, and go to evening meetings. Such attendance is an essential part of political education regardless of what the *Sun* or the *Mail* or the *Daily Telegraph* will say. Producers should frequently attend the House of Commons and also get out of London. Above all, television management should arrange that the best authorities in different fields should be brought to them, a wide variety of political thought and analysis placed before them. In short, we must ensure that a continuing political education is built into a producer's career, to supplement his practical experience. Those political specialists in broadcasting must also share their knowledge, not just with their audience, but also with their colleagues.

It is a tragedy that Philip Elliott is no longer here to make his always pertinent contribution. I found his writing full of sympathy, understanding and good sense, even when it hurt. He eschewed the easy gibe and the easy answer and he was never deflected from the central questions. He underlined our limitations without self-righteousness. He knew that broadcasters and media academics have a responsibility to educate each other, as well as to educate themselves. And it is here that media academics can play a part. They must reach the parts of the BBC they haven't reached so far, the daily and weekly practitioners, as well as managers like myself. They will meet some prejudice and antagonism within the Corporation and they will have to make sacrifices! They must write in simple, direct English. They must acknowledge their lack of practical knowledge and attempt to remedy it. They must look for the cock-up rather than the conspiracy. Perhaps the result of this dialogue will be a temporary loss of confidence by both parties in old certainties, but it is an essential prelude to our being able to discharge our joint duty, to pursue the truth more rigorously and to inform our democracy more fully.

Part Two

---

*Citizens
as
Audiences*

6
The Symbolic Form of Ritual in Mass Communication

David Chaney

*A*n element in conventional understanding of what makes a society modern is the idea that collective beliefs, primarily religious beliefs, become less important and that associated collective celebrations of those beliefs are less widely practised or valued. In this perspective rituals are archaic, almost superstitious survivals of a pre-modern consciousness, fundamentally inappropriate to the rationalist, secular and individualist social formations of urban-industrial societies. Recently, however, a number of authors have used the concept of ritual to illuminate the maintenance of social order or the ways in which social conflict is stabilized and contained in modern society. It has even been found relevant to understanding that quint-essentially modern institution of mass communication. Philip Elliott's paper on the genre of press ritual is an important contribution to the development of this perspective and in what follows I will use his definition of ritual: 'rule-governed activity of a symbolic character in-volving mystical notions which draws the attention of participants to objects of thought or feeling which the leadership of the society or group hold to be of special significance' (Elliott 1980: 147). I shall discuss the relevance of a concept of ritual to studies of the significance of mass communiction and in particular the implications for public drama of the spectacular character of ceremonialization in mass society.

Ritual in mass communication

An initial distinction must be made between reports of rituals which exist independently and can be described or represented in the media, and features of media performances which, regardless of content, are ritual-like in character. Thus, for example, the difference between a television broadcast of a religious rite and the representation of violence other than by authorized agents of the state through ritualized categories of 'terrorism' (Elliott *et al.* 1983).

Another possible distinction is whether there is a functional equivalence between sacred and secular ritual. In the mainstream of anthropological research 'the association between those formalities we call "ritual" and their religious or magical purposes has been so strong that analysis of the two has almost invariably proceeded together' (Moore and Myerhoff 1977: 3), but such an association would be inappropriate in a structurally complex urban-industrial society. Sacred rituals do persist in mass society but they are one type in a much broader class of collective ceremonies. Increasingly, in the course of the twentieth century these ceremonies have either been deliberately staged as performances for mass media of communication, or audiences for their performance have been greatly enlarged by access available through mass media. It is arguable that if this is so, sacred rituals are effectively secularized through the dominant mode of participation being transformed by media access.

It seems, therefore, inappropriate to begin a definition of contemporary ritual by reference to function. The message of a ritual might assert the existence of worlds beyond the here-and-now, but the essence of ritual performance is to affirm the experience of a collectivity which would otherwise have only an ambiguous cultural location. The form of the performance constitutes the category. Moore and Myerhoff list six characteristic formal properties: repetition; acting; 'special' behaviour or stylization; order; evocative presentational style – staging; and the 'collective' dimension (*ibid.*: 7–8): 'All of these formal properties make it an ideal vehicle for the conveying of messages in an authentic and arresting manner' (*loc. cit.*). The mode of authentication is through an implied continuity which transcends particular contingencies to generate a sense of tradition as legitimacy; an interaction between performance and symbolized historicity which is particularly appropriate for communal politics in which interests are imaginatively rather than personally represented. Not only is it empirically mistaken to believe that ritual will become less significant in secular society, it is precisely because identity has now to be invented (in Anderson's pithy definition the nation 'is an imagined political community' (1983: 15) and has to be so because the citizenry cannot be personally acquainted) that ritual becomes *more salient* as a mode of dramatizing the community. As

Anderson goes on to argue, it is not that there were once 'real' communities (or that they should be aspired to), rather that 'communities are to be distinguished, not only by their falsity/genuineness, but by *the style in which they are imagined*' (*loc. cit.*, my emphasis).

Anderson argues that in order to be thinkable the modern nation required, amongst other developments, a shift in consciousness concerning time, 'in which simultaneity is, as it were, transverse, cross-time, marked not by prefiguring and fulfilment, but by temporal coincidence, and measured by clock and calendar' (*ibid.*: 30). The collectivity is the parallel activities of a mass of individuals who while not knowing each other can still be confident of their common membership of the imagined community. The interdependence of time, imagination and community is displayed through the cultural form of the newspaper where heterogeneous events jostle for space grouped only by the dateline: 'Reading a newspaper is like reading a novel whose author has abandoned thought of a coherent plot' (*ibid.*: 37, n. 53). The readers of a newspaper are thereby symbolically integrated into a public whose common concerns are shown by the narrative of the world represented. Aptly the symbolic integration is marked by ritualistic repetition and renewal: 'The obsolescence of the newspaper on the morrow of its printing . . . creates this extraordinary mass ceremony: the almost precisely simultaneous consumption ('imagining') of the newspaper-as-fiction. . . . Furthermore, this ceremony is incessantly repeated at daily or half-daily intervals throughout the calendar. What more vivid figure for the secular, historically-clocked, imagined community can be envisioned?' (*ibid.*: 39).

This, then, is a third sense to ritual in mass communication. First, there are rituals which are to be reported; secondly, there are ways of reporting which are themselves rituals; and thirdly, the medium may itself be a ritual or collective ceremony.

In the anthropological tradition, in addition to the presupposition of an interdependence between ritual and religious or magical concerns there has been a stress upon ritual as a mode of functional integration. This has partly been because of the small scale of societies usually studied by anthropologists and partly because of a dominant theoretical tradition which presumed functional consensus as a norm. In more institutionally complex urban-industrial societies a stress upon ceremonies as integrative mechanisms leads to an unjustified consensualist, and implicitly conservative, view in which symbolic integration is assumed to be of equal value to all members of the community (cf. Birnbaum's (1955) criticisms of the complacency of Shils and Young's interpretation of the Coronation of the present monarch (1953)). Elliott argues that even if we recognize a distinction between authority rites and oppositional rites there is a common element of active subordination in favour of the privileges of dominant elites: 'Both require participants to become parts of the whole and in both cases the whole is greater than the sum of its parts. Recognition of this element of subordination is necessary to escape the Durkheiminan paradigm [leading to a] . . . recognition that ritual itself is a structured performance in which all participants are not equal' (Elliott 1980: 145).

This point is brought out in Lane's study of ritual in contemporary Soviet society. The affirmative force of collective ceremonies is used not only to suppress latent conflict but also to achieve 'a consensus in values (expressed in ritual action and symbols) which, at best, were only weakly affirmed prior to the ritual and, at worst, were viewed indifferently. . . . Ritual will be adopted as a tool of cultural management' (Lane 1981: 13). Different judgements of value consensus help to account for the inconsistency which Lane notes within Soviet sociological accounts of ritual which in capitalist societies is dismissed as mystifying and reactionary while equivalent rituals in Soviet society are enlightening and progressive. In a climate of deliberate consensus it is only likely that there will be strong consistency between ritual forms and other appeals to conformity: 'Cultural management through ritual supports, and is supported by, the inculcation of fundamental value orientations by other means (e.g. education, literature and art, mass communication, propaganda) and thus endows ritual with added authority' (*ibid.*: 259).

The reason that political elites in Soviet society have embarked upon such a radical programme of cultural management is that (1) they are committed to far-reaching social change which, in an unfavourable context, requires (2) a strong centralized state with homogeneous political institutions and (3) political values which emphasize the relative insignificance of the individual vis-à-vis collectivity. Undoubtedly ritual performances of the various types described by Lane are an attempt to create normative integration, but it is not a pre-existing equilibrium, temporarily disturbed, which is being regained but a denial of structural tensions in favour of an idealized cohesion (a transformation of a functionalist perspective). And in this sense of providing a selective reconstruction of social experience, ritual performances come close to our conventional sense of an ideology. Lane suggests that ritual performances will highlight certain features of a dominant ideology and may well change the relative emphasis of different components. In a social order in which there is a high degree of institutional integration, shifts of emphasis in performance may well provide indicators of ideological development, but in a less normatively coherent social order there is no need to assume a 'natural' consistency between ritualized values and ideology.

Elliott draws a stronger distinction between ritual and ideology. It is inappropriate to read the symbolism of ritual as a representation of rational interests. He argues that, following current anthropological conceptualization, we have to allow that 'ritual cannot simply be reduced to the rational. It draws on what is customary, familiar and traditional in the culture. It tries to add spiritual and emotional communion to any sense of political unity, though from any single point of view it may not work' (Elliott 1980: 146). This is an essential element in accounting for its dramatic force. Elliott is dissatisfied with those who see ritual as merely a distinctive type of vehicle for more general ideological concerns because they use ideology too glibly to explain the relationship between modes of expression and material social interests: 'Conceptual elaboration and investigation are necessary to provide the discriminatory links between ideology and power which ideology itself cannot provide because of its generality and because it is itself one of the terms of the equation' (*ibid.*: 169). In studying how the ideological trick of production and effect is turned we must attend to the interaction between form and symbolism in the lived world of audiences as well as to the constraints and presuppositions of structural commitments. He suggests a concept of symbolic form which 'is based on the cultural and social experiences of the people who participate, whether they are producers, performers or audience. It breaks down those distinctions' (*ibid.*: 147), to overcome the static presuppositions of content analysis in which content is treated as exclusively the work of producers and is therefore easily read as a rational redefinition of social reality in favour of sectional interests.

Ritual is in essence a collective ceremony and its performances are particularly relevant to public life. I have noted above that the repetitious character of ritual will tend to give a gloss of age and authenticity to performances and thus may act as instances of what Hobsbawm has recently characterized as invention of tradition: '"Invented tradition" is taken to mean a set of practices, normally governed by overtly or tacitly accepted rules and of a ritual or symbolic nature, which seeks to inculcate certain values and norms of behaviour by repetition, which automatically implies continuity with the past' (Hobsbawm 1983: 1). Hobsbawm argues that traditions are particularly likely to be invented in situations where innovation has undermined the stability of existing structures of authority or where new collectivities seek to establish their legitimacy. In this sense he sees these 'traditions' as a way of imagining the national community in Anderson's terms. Invented traditions are a mode of integration which can to some extent fill the vacuum of normative consensus left by processes of secularization. In assessing the significance of new traditions, Hobsbawm argues, we need a distinction between private lives and 'the public life of the citizen (including to some extent public forms of socialization, such as the schools, as distinct from private ones such as the mass media)' (*ibid.*: 11–12); thus in relation to public life neo-traditional practices have retained their force, while traditions and their associated rituals should be less significant in more private forms of socialization.

The best reason for describing mass media as privatizing agencies is that the audience is usually atomized, either attending individually or in small groups such as the family or peer group (and even in forms which have retained collective performance, such as the cinema, video-cassettes are privatizing audience reception). This is true and is likely to become truer, and yet it seems equally legitimate for McQuail to argue that 'the media operate almost exclusively in the public sphere – they comprise an open institution in which all can participate as receivers and, under certain conditions, even as senders. The media institution also has a public character in that mass media deal with matters on which public opinion exists or can properly be formed (i.e. not with personal or private matters or those which are essentially for expert or scientific judgement)' (McQuail 1983: 33–4). The most fundamental implication of the development of mass forms of communication for political institutions has been the creation of political publics and a public sphere (cf. Gouldner 1976). There is, however, no contradiction between Hobsbawm and McQuail because in important respects the politics of mass society have been privatized except as they are publicly dramatized through the media, and it is in the possibility of mediating private response to public forms that the symbolic form of ritual will be particularly crucial.

David Cannadine's study of changes in the context, performance and meaning of ritual performances involving the British monarchy 1820–1977 is directly relevant to this thesis (Cannadine 1983). He argues that in the course of the nineteenth century there was a slow development of a coherent ceremonial language in which the monarch's position was transformed from the head of society to the head of the nation. In part this was because effective political power was relinquished so that the ritualistic idiom of the monarchy could enshrine personal integrity in ceremonial splendour in a display of national uniqueness and institutional legitimacy. The context within which this change took place was the emergence of a modern nation-state: 'It was at the end, rather than the beginning, of the nineteenth century that Britain became a predominantly urban, industrial, mass society, with class loyalties and class conflicts set in a genuinely national framework for the first time' (*ibid.*: 122). Marking this development, and heralding the gradual acceptance of government by elites based on mass electorates, was the growth of a national, populist press which despite its vulgarity was consistently obsequious towards and a faithful publicist of the Royal Family and their ceremonials. The pomp and circumstance of institutional ritual provided a framework for the incorporation of new political publics.

Cannadine's methodology is based upon a conceptualization of ceremonial as a cultural form (and it seems to me that his use makes it virtually equivalent to Elliott's concept of ritual as symbolic form): 'for if, indeed, cultural forms are to be treated as texts, as imaginative works built out of social materials, then it is to an investigation of those social materials and of the people who – consciously or unawares – do the building, that our attention needs to be directed, rather than to an intricate and decontextualized analysis of the texts themselves' (*ibid.*: 162). He points towards the extent and attitude of the media in providing a framework for distinguishing changes in ritual meaning. I would wish to go further and suggest that the involvement of the media in public ceremonials is more than a diffusion of attitude and access. To the extent that there is an interdependence between these ceremonials and the constitution of political publics in mass society, then the media play a crucial role in providing a cultural form for the rhetoric of democratization. As an example I can cite a previously published study of my own in which I look at the efforts of the public broadcasting service to represent three postwar festivals in Britain, one of which is the Coronation of the present monarch in 1953 (Chaney 1983). I suggest that the innovation of television in becoming the main mode of public access to this ritual gave an anonymous mass public a better view than the elite and through the immediacy of live coverage transformed the meaning of public drama. What I call the quasi-democracy of intimate access provided for a personalization of symbolic ritual in which public figures are simultaneously humanized through vicarious observation but also distanced through the dramatic conventions of media presentation.

This brings us back to Anderson's argument that communities differ in the styles in which they are imagined. Rituals are a representation of the collectivity, a collective performance in which certain significant aspects of social relationships are given symbolic form and force. Public ceremonies are events in the world and thereby news as happenings but the rhetoric of news is itself part of that happening: 'To recognise news as a form of literature is to be forced to come to terms with what Geertz has called "the autonomous process of symbolic formation"' (Elliott 1980: 171). In order to follow the constitution of social experience in different modes of representation we have to follow Elliott's distinction between a sociology of knowledge and a sociology of meaning. The former implies a completeness, an effect for which we can locate causal determinations, the latter a more active sense of the terms upon which public life is presupposed: 'to consider the newspaper as a vehicle for symbolic forms in which large parts are occasionally preempted for ritual performances or as itself a symbolic form which occasionally takes itself seriously as the "Voice of the People" or "The Voice of Britain"' (*ibid.*). In part what this means in practice, I think, is that we need studies of the language of ritual – its performance, its staging and interpretation by commentators and publicists, and expectations and responses amongst audiences: what Elliott calls public as opposed to private meanings.

The promise of Elliott's paper is that the interdependence of ritual and media of mass communication concerns more than the detection of a particular type of media event: it points towards a symbolic form, a means of expression, for a version of popular and/or national community which collects what could otherwise not be expressed. We can initially locate that form in the distinctive language through which collective ceremonies are constructed and reported, the language of imagination in media accounts, but unless we are content to just note and rewrite the selectivity of such accounts, we have to go further and address the constitution of festivities as shared occasions mediated between public performance and personal experience. As an example of an unusual attempt in this direction I shall describe and discuss a book published by Mass Observation purporting to describe the day George VI was crowned King of the British Empire (Jennings and Madge 1937).

Another way of seeing: Mass Observation

The book is centrally concerned with activities and experiences of anonymous members of society and the ways in which the Coronation impinged on their lives on that day, 12 May. There are very few details, and these incidentally, of the Coronation ceremony. In order to provide a representation of the day the editors drew upon notes and diaries which individuals had agreed to keep for that purpose. It is because the editors were concerned with a public occasion, to document ceremonial performance in a particular society as cumulative experience not as news of what happened, that they were forced to experiment editorially to construct a communal response out of individual observations: 'the results of this survey, *May 12*, did give a picture of Coronation Day as ordinary people experienced it, which no other method then devised could have done' (Willcock 1943: 446). In documenting the occasion through the experiences of anonymous individuals they attempted to treat the social as a mode of discourse as well as an object of discourse. The editors offer us an opportunity to reflect upon the manner of our participation in the rhetoric of collective activities, and thereby ask fundamental questions about the participation of the public as spectators.

The immediate stimulus for Mass Observation's project was provided by the Abdication crisis which dragged on throughout most of 1936. The pronouncements of the principal actors and commentators were punctuated by references to the British people, the nature of public opinion and the norms of collective morality, and so on. Madge, one of the founders of Mass Observation, was at the time working as a reporter on the *Daily Mirror,* and has since confirmed that it was the discrepancy between experience of public opinion being formed on the streets and in the bars, and the articulation of that opinion in national newspapers, that led him to explore the idea of an organization that would help this public to accurately express itself.

On 12 December 1936 Geoffrey Pyke published a letter in the *New Statesman* commenting on the public response to the Abdication crisis, a response which he felt provided 'in a relatively limited form . . . some of the material for that anthropological study of our own civilisation of which we stand in such desperate need' (Pyke 1936: 974). Three weeks later Charles Madge replied that a group had already been formed for this purpose – in practice it was a group of friends loosely based on Madge's home in Blackheath. In his letter Madge argued that if English anthropology is to deal with 'mass wish-suggestions' then a new method must be evolved, a method which would utilize the ephemera of coincidence on a mass scale to escape the repression of conventional knowledge: 'Only mass observations can create mass science' (Madge 1937: 12). Tom Harrisson replied enthusiasticaly to Madge's letter and travelled down from Bolton to meet the Blackheath group, with the consequence that another letter was published in the *New Statesman*, this time over the names of Harrisson, Humphrey Jennings and Madge. This letter announces the formation of Mass Observation as a group of observers from a wide background to study physical behaviour, mental phenomena and symbolism: 'The Observers will also provide the points from which can be plotted weather-maps of public feeling in a crisis' (Madge and Harrisson 1937: 155). The method to be used would combine the distinctive virtues of both artists and scientists working with the 'maximum of objectivity'.

This correspondence and other references in the media were followed by the publication of a pamphlet over the names of Madge and Harrisson with a cover designed by Jennings and with a foreword by Julian Huxley. In this they clarified the method to be adopted: 'Mass Observation intends to ... make use not only of the trained scientific observer, but of the untrained observer, the man in the street. Ideally, it is the observation by everyone of everyone, including themselves' (*ibid.*: 10). The approach they propose will attempt to explore the interdependence between instance and consciousness; the detail, however squalid, of everyday experience will be recorded so that collective experience can be accumulated. They use the metaphor of detection to describe the method although there will be no privileged object such as a class of criminals; rather, every member of society is of equal interest, therefore 'we do not intend to intrude on the private life of any individual, as individual. Collective habits and social behaviour are our field of inquiry, and individuals are only of interest in so far as they are typical of groups.' (*ibid.*: 30). They believed that the common grounds of individual experience is provided by media of mass communication so that the focusing of attention upon certain crucial events, such as the Abdication, provides for a more unified social consciousness. Mass Observation is in this sense intended to serve a neutral role between the individual and the collectivity of which he is a part. The observers will be monitoring social processes in ways that will help to elucidate the constitution of those processes: 'To make the scheme work, not only must facts be collected over the widest possible field, but they must be made known to the widest possible public' (*ibid.*: 40; see also Chaney and Pickering 1986).

In a contemporary article that is generally critical of Mass Observation, T. H. Marshall remarks of the *May 12* study that it proceeds as though selection and interpretation can be exploited, instead of taking the more appropriate course of attempting to control them by use of a scientific plan: 'the great need today is not for observation by the masses, but for observation by teams of fully-trained scientists who can unite the methods of different scientific disciplines' (Marshall 1937: 50). The alternative Marshall is offering (a) inserts the social scientist as a technician between the collectivity and social experience, and (b) endorses an editorial role for the publications of social scientists in which meaning is transformed into technical knowledge. Both attitudes to public experience were enshrined in later sociological practice, with the consequence that the nature of public imagery as lived experience practically disappeared from the sociological agenda. The symbolic form of media ritual is not just a picture of artful performances, it is in differing ways and to differing degrees the language through which individuals can participate as members of political publics.

The symbolic form of ritual: the May 12 study

In order to clarify the editors' remark that their account of George VI's Coronation treated the social as a mode as well as an object of discourse, we can compare the day survey with a conventional newspaper report. One can say that the day survey was composed of individual observations which were then edited into coherence, and yet this is also the essence of newspaper reports. The individuality of observations in newspapers is usually not stressed (unless it is an 'exclusive') in order not to detract from the authority of the account. The newspaper implicitly claims – this, to the best of our ability to know, is what happened; the observer merely reports that this is what I saw. The authority of the newspaper account is therefore bound up with the editorial process. In deciding which stories are to be used and which aspects are to be emphasized newspapers see themselves as responding to the imperatives of the situation, they recognize the activities of fellow journalists in creating news and stereotyping reportable features, but this is still a professional response to an independently existing world of news. Mass observers in contrast treat the news media as constituting in part at least the occasion; they are an essential element in the experience of the relevance. This is so just because mass media are the arteries of the community the observers are attempting to report, but also because their existence implies the anonymity, potential equality and the artificiality of a rhetoric of community which makes an anthropology of ourselves imperative. The need for a project like Mass Observation could not be perceived before the democratization of the nation made possible through media of mass communication; and yet that very democratization called into question ritual performances celebrating the stability of a social order symbolized by feudal inheritance and monarchical rule.

The four chapters of the Coronation study are divided in the following way. In the first, reports are used to 'set the scene', that is, the preparations for the Coronation and the range of expectations for the forthcoming occasion are described, mainly by intercutting clippings from a range of newspapers. In the second chapter the experience of the Coronation in London is described. The third chapter offers a survey of national actions and reactions to the events taking place in London. The spread obviously suffers from the geographical concentration of the observers but clever interweaving disguises this. In the final chapter individual reactions to the national occasions are described.

The chapter reporting preparations is very 'filmic' in style in that the organization of clippings can be seen as a rhythmically structured form of film editing. (Throughout the Coronation study the material is organized within each chapter into a series of numbered paragraphs of uneven length, and we can therefore use this numbering system as an organization frame for description.) In general we can say that the first hundred paragraphs of this chapter report clippings from newspapers. Within this total there is the following pattern: items 2–13 emphasizing the 'national-ness' of the occasions; 14–28 planning by public authorities; 29–38 international arrivals; 39–49 intercutting pageantry with arrivals; 50–71 intercutting commercial exploitation with plans for local celebrations; 73–99 local irritants such as reports of individuals or groups querying preparations. It does not require a lot of imagination to see these as visual themes in which diversity and detail are cleverly contrasted in order to illustrate the scale of the occasion. Following this long opening section there is a switch in style to a group of observers' reports which alternate a flurry of short reports of pessimistic rumours, followed by a long report of a local council deliberating its festivities, followed by more homely reports of local interest, with again three more long reports on preparations in Scotland and Africa. The last two sections return to newspaper clippings, one group 133–58 concerned with the minutiae of preparation, and the next, 159–75, being an overview of the relevant days leading up to the Coronation in which within each paragraph there is an intercutting of items from different sources, a practice not usually followed. The effect of this last section is one of gathering pace, an effect heightened by two concluding paragraphs in which a fairly long quotation from *The Times* editorial on the day of the Coronation is followed by Harry Pollitt's message in the *Daily Worker* on the same day. I have described this organization of material as filmic because the interweaving of clippings provides a very rudimentary montage of theme, style and detail, the cumulative effect of which is to set up in the reader's (viewer's) mind an expectation of an occasion of unusual significance.

If this chapter is seen as an overture, a stage-setting, it is legitimate to ask about the themes that are introduced at this stage – what is being promised. I think there are four clear themes, although I do not think one could rank them in order of importance. In the first theme, we are continually being reminded that the occasion dwarfs predecessors and involves a degree of preparation and involvement on a previously unrealized scale. It is not just that the Empire and the world beyond were mobilized to send representatives but that within Britain the events were virtually inescapable. The second theme is that of pomp: the occasion is seen to involve a manner and style of participation so that people from a wide range of social backgrounds are forced to act in terms of roles they are often uncomfortable with. (I think it is part of this theme to be sensitive to the jarring notes introduced by those who refused to recognize ceremonial implications, such as the bus strikers.) Part of the force of this concern with pomp is a belief that the Corona-tion symbolizes feelings of national identity, feelings which were an important element in Jennings's later films. Thirdly, there is a theme of individual fascination – reports of individuals being drawn into the occasion almost against their will. The idea that individuals were gradually caught up is, of course, an extension of the themes of scale and pomp. Finally, there is the fourth theme of a concern with the mechanism of staging the event. This is the typically documentary idea that festivities require back-stage work. A related concern is the com-mercial exploitation that accompanies the events, the way the occasion is adapted to individual entrepreneurial advantage. Besides these themes which emerge from the content of newspaper items, a second dimension of significance is provided by the source of the material. The use of newspaper cuttings is an implicit display of the degree of national interest and also the impossibility of escaping that interest. Much of the style of the occasion as it is to be observed is anticipated by the resources that are drawn upon in describing the occasion being assembled.

In the introduction to the second chapter the sources of observers' reports are briefly described. As well as 43 observers who had already volunteered to take part in the day survey, 77 further reports were recruited by distributing a questionnaire at random which invited those who read it to reply to certain very general questions. (Many of those who returned questionnaires went on to become regular observers for the organization.) Finally a group 12 individuals already known to each other and based on Madge's house in Blackheath went up to central London and mingled with the crowds, submitting reports on the day so that they effectively covered midnight to midnight. In the paragraphs based on reports by the Blackheath groups there is a characteristic 'camera-eye' style. In relation to the reports on London this approach is exemplified through externals: dress; indices of status; colours, snatches of conversation; details of deportment. The sense of observational distance comes across most clearly in their frequent reports of fragments of sexual interaction – flirting, gestures of affection, ogling, etc. Part of the same idea that everyday life continues through major occasions comes in reports of the crowds' often ironic response to the pageantry, such as cheering horse droppings.

The character of this 'camera style' is brought out more clearly by the contrast with reports from observers and questionnaire respondents. This contrast is not between cynicism and endorsement. The predominant response within all three groups is a feeling that the Coronation is beng enjoyed as an aesthetic occasion, a magnificent show, but that it is quite possible to remain at least agnostic about the institution of the monarch. The contrast between friends and observers is that only amongst the latter group do we find confessions of individuals being caught up in the occasion so that, often to their own surprise, they find themselves cheering the monarch's coach, or feel emotionally moved at one of the frequent renditions of the national anthem. I do not know to what extent there is cause and effect in this as part of the chapter that makes heaviest use of observers' reports is that section concerned with the progress of the procession and the service of crowning. Obviously these provide more opportunities for emotional identification than the rest of the day.

In the third chapter on national activities on 12 May reports from friends of the editors are absent and the bulk of the material is taken from the observers' reports. Confirming the differences in style noted above the observations in this chapter are generally more personal in reference, with a greater consciousness of personal response to circumstances. The perspective is consistently local and very individual: the reader cannot escape the awareness that he is being introduced by an individual to a situation the latter is familiar with. It is this perspective that often gives the reports the feeling of diary entries. Diarists always have to choose between writing for themselves and thus recording events which are only personally significant, or writing for an eventual audience, in which case recorded events may be described for their significance in their social context. This choice is one that observers here often seem to be struggling with; they necessarily record personal experience but continually feel the need to make clear that this is experience of 'the public at large'. In some cases there is clear recognition that this is an individual searching out of 'public' experience. Thus although many of the same details as were noted in the London reports – public singing and activities in public bars, and so on – recur, the tone has changed: the pattern that is being accumulated is more biographical and of a life being lived rather than observed. It is relevant that several observers, particularly women, gave as one of their reasons for co-operating with Mass Observation the fact that they hoped that the need to write observational reports would provide a suitable opportunity for the pleasure of writing and personal expression. The editors exploit the way reports become more intimate by interweaving material in another rudimentary montage. The chapter opens with a number of overlapping 'waking-ups', what individuals first saw and felt, and so on. This section is followed by one consisting of shorter reports of the questionnaire replies given by the respondents who were presumably, at least at this stage, less committed to the enterprise. This is followed by a long section of longer reports from volunteer observers. Here the cutting between observers is much slower and it is at this stage that the material is most biographical. In a concluding section the pace is picked up once more with overlapping segments as the day draws to a close.

The chapter on individual reactions is concerned with how the prescriptive force of national celebrations impinged on individual circumstances, whether they were resented or enjoyed and how the day took on a significance in personal fantasy. The unifying feature of observers' reports here is the significance of radio in making the occasion truly national: 'The most potent means of unifying behaviour was the broadcasting of the ceremony and processions, and of the King's speech. It meant that a very high proportion of the population spent the day listening in and thus partaking in the central events' (Jennings and Madge 1937: 267). There is little concern with the accuracy of the broadcast or the attitudes of commentators, more with when and how it intruded on and sometimes dominated everyday experience and at what points listeners found themselves stirred by the ritual, often despite an initial scepticism. The effectiveness of the radio as a means of mobilizing individual interest was frequently through its presence in public settings such as pubs, cafés, shops, cinemas, or overheard in the street. Sometimes this public attention was deliberate, as when people went to special broadcasts in cinemas, but it was also sometimes reluctantly engaged: 'At 12.30 came the words "The King is acclaimed". A rather noisy hail-fellow-well-met man in plus-fours shouted "The King God bless him". People stood for a minute, then resumed their seats, continued drinking, and apparently forgot there was a Coronation' (*ibid.*: 278).

Different modes of mass communication are seen to have served different functions in 1937. Newspapers set the agenda for a day of national celebration while the radio acted to draw the nation in during the course of the day. The editors stress the novelty of this extension of the public for ritual (and note uncertainties over appropriate response: 'Certain problems of behaviour, which are inherent in all occasions when people sit in a room listening in (especially now that loud speakers have replaced earphones), were more than usually apparent. For example: Is it permissible to eat during a "sacred broadcast"?' (*ibid.*: 269–70), and thereby highlight the specificity of each dramatic occasion. For this Coronation a unique feature was the extent to which members of the public thought that it should have been Edward VIII rather than his brother George being crowned, and whether the necessity for the Abdication was an index of the power of the Church and the Conservative establishment. Not only was this Coronation important in developing a tradition for a new form of public drama, it was also a deliberate attempt to stabilize the monarchy as a political institution. Finally, the editors pull together a number of incidents recorded, 'which have a peculiar quality, or a quality which is in some sense an amalgam of funny, peculiar and stirring; perhaps what they have in common is that they illustrate a somehow disturbing attitude towards the day' (*ibid.*: 325). The common element in these incidents and dreams is the Coronation as symbolic drama; they represent 'that residuum of the day which ... is important as giving its dominant tone or character, a character which is made up of the totality of the fantasy and image-making of all the individuals' (*ibid.*: 328).

The representation of the Coronation is organized on a number of dimensions simultaneously. The first is a progression from anticipation to response. The first chapter sets up the occasion followed by two chapters on the day itself, both using an internal order of the day from midnight to midnight, one day report concentrating on London as the setting, the other on the day in the provinces thereby distanced from the occasion; the last chapter completes the movement by exclusively reporting reactions and responses. There is a second progression in the use of material for these chapters in that the unfolding of the occasion is paralled by a move from impersonality to individuality. The latter progression works in a number of ways through the tone, voice and style of selections as well as the source of observations. The first chapter is largely made up of clippings from newspapers while the last contains a number of reported dreams. Even within the middle chapters there is, as I have noted, a consistent shift from a neutral to a more personalized focus of observation. The nature of these progressions is completed by a further level of development in which the medium of representation gradually shifts from form to content. By this I mean a change in focus from the organization of ceremonial to degree of involvement. At the beginning it is how we as readers are to be given an occasion, by the end our collaboration in the meaning of what we have experienced is taken for granted. The narrative order of representation is therefore structurally consistent whilst encompassing a number of perspectives.

I have not described the Mass Observation study of the Coronation in 1937 because I believe it to be an exemplary approach either to studies of public opinion or to the implications of mass communication for public drama. It is, however, extremely unusual as an attempt to get to grips with the experience of changing forms of public ritualization. The 'failure' of the Coronation study – and everybody concerned seems to have agreed that it was at least unsuccessful – effectively directed attention away from the public as the *subject* of everyday experience and substituted the public as *audience*, that is, as a group of readers to whom 'results', as descriptive profiles, would be reported.

Public forms and private experience

The thesis of this paper is that the use of a concept of ritual in relation to studies of mass communication enhances our understanding of the significant implications of mass communication for political order. As one of these we can suggest that national media provide a means of participation which is both personal and yet presupposes a national political community. The sociology of urban life has arguably concentrated on private negotiations of meaning and reward to the detriment of public forms and occasions (Lofland 1983). To the extent that the mass media have been seen as privatizing agencies, the study of their effects has quite naturally been individualized. It is, however, true that the development of mass entertainment has added further layers of imagination to urban experience. Collective ceremonies have patently

not disappeared from the calendar of institutional identity and reproduction, indeed they have been made more accessible and less arcane
through their dramatization as media performances. It is not that the
functions of public drama have become unnecessary in contemporary
bureaucracies, but that a rhetoric of democratic egalitarianism paradoxi-
cally displays the form of institutionalized power as private participation in rituals of consensus: 'the bureaucratic process, fostered at first
by absolutist state ceremonies and subsequently by nationalistic par-
ades of soldiers and now by television performances of high state
dignitaries, is ritual at its core, a repeated exercise of political power
effective because affective, a force said to be impersonal because it
is rooted on the consensually accepted authority of a fascinating
righteous executive' (Trexler 1980: xxii). The political publics of mass
society are less *audiences* for political debates than vicariously engaged
spectators. The city as the stage for ritual performance has dematerialized
to be replaced by an infinite suburban fragmentation of opportunities
for employment, consumption and entertainment. The spectacular
forms of mass communication are the public life of a privatized mass
culture.

Two brief points in conclusion are, first, that rationally we may be
uncomfortable with the politics of ritual, an attitude expressed well in
one of the Mass Observation reports: 'Reviewing it all calmly afterwards, one sees how very dangerous all this is . . . although people will
probably always like pageantry, colour, little princesses, etc., and it
seems a pity to rob them of this colourful make-believe element –
nevertheless because it makes it in the end harder for us to think and
behave as rational beings when we are exposed to this strain and
tension – I would definitely vote agin [sic] it' (Jennings and Madge 1937:
304–5). Nevertheless, we may need to use irrational forms of mobilization to work towards a more rational political order. And secondly,
there is no need to assume *a priori* an ideological homogeneity to these
performances. 'Television does not provide society with an homogeneous integrative *gestalt* so much as with a variety of ways of managing and assimilating knowledge and opinion.' (Elliott 1972: 145). This
variety does not provide a diversity which facilitates democratic pluralism; it is rather that the discourse of mass communication has become
an autonomous form of imagination: 'the dominant means of communication in society is tending more and more to be conrolled by
people who have nothing to say, or if they have, cannot use the media
to say it' (*ibid.*: 166).

7

Diversity in Political Communication: Its Sources, Forms and Future

Denis McQuail

*A*t *various* points in his work, Philip Elliott deployed a notion of mass communication as society addressing itself. This appeared, for instance, in his framework for analysing the relative autonomy of television producers, vis-à-vis society, in relation to the flow of messages from 'society as source' to 'society as receiver', the audience (Elliott 1972). He indicated several degrees of competence or freedom for mass communicators to determine what message would reach a public, ranging from direct access for society, as in the case of party political broadcasts, through news and documentaries, in which the message from society is shaped or interpreted, to the case of artistic creation in which the message is entirely determined within the media and society has no claim to shape content. In that context, Elliott was concerned to emphasize the limited possibilities for society as source to speak directly to society as audience and the restrictive part which media tend to play in diminishing this contact yet further. He also expressed a view of the audience as mainly a passive receiver of mass communication, at best a contented spectator, at worst a victim of manipulation. He wrote: 'The mass communicators draw on society for material suitable for their purposes, the audience is largely left on its own to respond to the material put before it' (Elliott 1972: 164).

Subsequently, Philip Elliott looked more closely at possible sources of variation in 'media culture', drawing upon an analysis of media organizations and occupations (Elliott 1977). These sources were held to include: a degree of institutional autonomy; competition; overproduction; economic slack in times of prosperity; ownership prerogatives;

professionalism; patronage and subsidy; the values of novelty and individualism. He completed the list by naming the audience as a source of variation, noting that 'it would be incorrect to argue that media culture is simply imposed on the public without reference to its wishes'. In general, he saw these various sources of variation, including the last mentioned, as somewhat marginal to the general condition: 'they are relatively rare, unstable and grounded in the margins of the cultural production process in democratic, capitalist, society'.

The overall impression left by Elliott's treatment of the media is that they have relatively little freedom of manoeuvre and operate within narrow constraints imposed by the pressures to produce for markets, or by the other institutional arrangements within which they operate. This impression is reinforced by his research on media content, whose patterned regularities are seen as reflecting either the constraints mentioned or are the result of external social and political pressures (Golding and Elliott 1979). The nature of these pressures is not explicated in detail, but it looks as if they follow lines of force established by dominant holders of political and economic power in a class society. If mass communication is 'society addressing itself' then the 'society as source' which has most access is not very diversified in practice, but restricted largely to those who claim access by right of ownership, elite position, or some other legitimating principle. A relatively narrow range of voices dominates what 'goes into' established mass media and the mass media themselves have only limited freedom to filter out, change or add to this flow. This may be an overstatement, but it helps in dealing with the question of the third element in the society – media relationship – 'society as receiver'.

On the whole, a correspondingly bleak view of the audience presents itself. The audience emerges either as a body of non-participant spectators largely manipulated by media performers, or as so dependent on what the media offer as to be incapable of independent choice. The 'spectator' image is derived from an assessment of the mass communication process as so devoted to the primary task of claiming and keeping attention as to lose sight of the aim of actually communicating, in the sense of effecting an 'ordered transfer of meaning'. In his critique of 'uses and gratifications' research Elliott attacked the assumption of audience activity and emphasized its dependence on what is made available to it (Elliott 1974). Although this critique was mainly directed at the theoretical assumptions and methodological failings of that research tradition, it includes an expression of the view that the tastes and interests of the audience are so much shaped by what the media, out of their own dynamic, choose to offer that it makes little sense to try to examine them independently of that offer or to try to base any proposal for alternative provision on such evidence. A thorough analysis of the audience is largely missing from Elliott's work, but such reference as there is represents it, despite the caveat noted above, as largely passive, malleable and at most reactive, in the face of content provided according to the imperatives of market systems and the requirements of media for large audiences and cost-effective production. Such a view does not allow much scope for the existence and expression of audience diversity. In so far as there is variety in the audience it is to be found in social class and in the situations directly confronted by audience members. Thus, the differential choices of, and response to, media content predominantly reflect differences in social structure and in the social distribution of opportunity.

The condition of political communication

These materials offer a perspective on political communication, in its broadest sense, which calls for some examination. It is a pessimistic view, which suggests that political content as distributed in its various forms by mass media to large audiences is dominated at source by a limited range of interests and outlooks and is little changed in the mediating process except in the direction of accentuating features for maximizing audience attention for the sake of the media themselves, rather than in the interests of citizens or of the democratic process. There is limited scope for mass communicators to add political substance or spice, because of the constraints mentioned or because of the increased influence of professional norms of objectivity. The undue influence of attention-gaining features in the direct coverage of politics has been documented, for instance, in the form of imbalance of time/ space devoted to procedures and personalities compared to issues of political substance (Graber 1971). The increasing use of techniques derived from advertising, which are also primarily attention-gaining, have shifted the balance also from communicating to impression-forming. One might be justified in linking to these observations an impression of the audience for political communication as attached to sources more by habit, ritual and duty than by strong and varied motivation. Much evidence seems to indicate a rather low level of audience interest in overtly political content and presenters tend to struggle to make politics minimally attractive. Politics appears to be a minority interest which goes with more favoured educational

135

background and higher income instead of being of universal concern, as should be the case in democracies. It could well be argued that the main variation in the audience for political communication is simply a taste for news and politics and the main cause is to be found in a combination of socialization through media and social structure, as Philip Elliott more or less suggested.

It is important to consider this view carefully, not only to check its validity but also to avoid missing what may be significant, although less salient, types of variation and their sources. This is essentially a normative matter, since what is at issue is not only what has happened until now, as mass media have taken over many tasks of established political institutions, but also what chances there are for satisfactory political communication under conditions of change in media. It is desirable to clarify the normative frame of reference by setting out some criteria of satisfactoriness. Implicit in this discussion is a view that 'better' political communication would at least involve more active interest, involvement and participation by the public in choosing and responding to political messages of a diverse and often opposed kind about issues of substance. The content of political communication should stem from the real political divisions of society and give voice to them, should expose and carry forward debate. For its part, a more 'healthy' audience situation would be one in which the members of different publics would be firmly attached to each other by ties of political belief and action on the basis of information and ideas readily available. Political communication by mass media would be a living and integral part of the political institution rather than an adjunct of show business and media commerce, an empty ritual, a tool of manipulation, or a means of controlling politics itself.

This idealized version at least offers some guidelines for exploring the degrees of freedom which audiences have or might have. If nothing else, it is a reminder that this matter is closely intertwined with questions of the freedom enjoyed by mass media and the producers, since some of the conditions for audience freedom are certainly established by the media. Essentially what has to be examined is any possible basis for more choice for an audience to seek, find and respond to relevant political messages. This reconnaissance has to be carried out with an eye to media innovation and to social change. It involves looking at media structures and the work of communicators as well as at audiences, thus trying to identify positive and negative features of the whole situation affecting the audience. It means taking account of different kinds of message: news and information; expressions of value, belief and opinion; interpretation and criticism by journalists or others; and also politically relevant messages contained in fiction and creative forms.

Sources of variation from the side of the 'sender'

The naming of several main sources of audience variation should help to make the theme more concrete and illustrate the diversity of factors which has to be taken into account. First of all, there is the question of quantity of channels and media sources, plus the range of these sources and the volume of political messages. Other things being equal, the more political communication that is genuinely available, thus really accessible to people, the more chances there are for audience members to make relevant choices or to recognize, and connect with, some strand of political belief. An essential matter here is the criteria by which quantity is assessed and the level of provision at which one makes an assessment. Are there many channels, more different points of view, more kinds and items of information, and so on? By certain measures, the decades of the post-war era in liberal democracies, especially Europe, have seen a clear increase in some of the respects mentioned. Newspapers are larger; there are more kinds of publication, including many minority, alternative and critical ones at local as well as national levels; more book titles are being published; there are many new radio and television channels and much more broadcasting time. In short, there is probably more political content, however defined, readily available than at any point when it would be sensible to make a comparison. Of course, 'other things' are usually not equal and one cannot assume that *more* means more diversity. However, there has probably been a dual process of homogenization and of differentiation which needs more precise attention to elucidate.

A second matter concerns forms and formats for presenting political content, and a widening in this respect can also be a source of audience diversity. Examples of this kind of diversity include, additional to straightforward news and commentary about political events and direct address by politicians, such things as televised debates and discussion programmes on television, politically relevant press supplements, various forms of political advertising, political satire shows, phone-ins, chat shows, documentaries, films, plays and stories on political themes, public demonstrations reported via media, and so on. It is hard to doubt that the range of types of format for political communication has been extended as television has taken its place alongside other media, however much it has been subject to restriction, and other media have responded competitively. It is also not very plausible to suppose that a period which has seen such a qualitative development of a major new medium has not added something both to the quality of choice for audience members or extended the range of tasks carried out by media in linking citizens to political actors and conditions. There are more ways in which politics can be received and some of these new ways not only benefit the politically interested but have probably enabled political messages of substance to reach some sections in a population which might otherwise be unreachable by politics. In other words, new developments in the presentation and distribution of politics could have helped to compensate for some deficiencies in realizing 'communication potential' which have their origin in social inequality. More arguable is the extent to which the developments referred to belong to the category of superficial attention-gaining devices or to that which concerns enhanced participation, relevance and greater attachment to politics. There is surely an element of the former, but the second cannot be ruled out. In one of his comments on the uses and gratifications research, Philip Elliott referred to the possibility (specifically concerning the BBC discovery of satire) that the media may have a 'creative role in contributing to social change' (Elliott 1974: 265).

In this connection, one can also mention the strengthening of relatively new communicator roles, associated especially with the growth of public service television – for instance, that of 'gatekeeper', giving and withholding channel access to political advocates, and that of interpreter for, or representative of, citizens. This kind of development represents an increase in the mediating activity as between political elites and public and possibly a taking away of some competence from both political advocates and citizens. The trend, associated with professionalization and the greater power attained by the media institution, must be viewed ambivalently according to the norm outlined above. It may have the effect of attenuating direct links between would-be political leaders and followers and it may relieve the latter of some burden of selection and interpretation. The trend does not in itself enlarge freedom and may reduce diversity by resolving inconsistencies and presenting rather similar, sanitized and consensual versions of issues, by relativism and by secularizing ideological conflicts. The point is at least a caution against reading too much into evidence of apparently qualitative change without a similar close analysis as called for by evidence of quantitative change.

Audience-side factors

The factors so far discussed have been on the 'offer' side, concerning media themselves first of all, rather than audiences. If one turns to the latter, the most obvious source of variation has already been mentioned – that of social structure, whether in terms of class, life-cycle, gender, race, and so on. Social structure still distributes people according to political-economic experience and governs the pattern of relevance of political messages and, to some extent, their differential accessibility. Much attention has been paid to the matter of apparent decline of class politics and there is a good deal of evidence to suggest that class-based loyalties are weaker and less predictive of political behaviour, the content of politics itself less ideological and more pragmatic. Elliott wrote in 1974 of this phenomenon: 'In Europe generally this de-radicalization has coincided with a period in which the party press and other direct channels of communication between political parties and public have disappeared. In their place, mass media have developed, more closely integrated into the corporate economic structure of society, and standing between the mass audience and political activities and other sources of radical or class ideologies. In this intermediate position they have been able to comment on and interpret political developments and so contribute to the process of de-radicalization' (Elliott 1974: 263). This thesis would imply a weakening in the influence of social structure as a source of audience diversity and as a determinant of access to political messages. However, another version of what has happened is more a fragmentation of and differentiation of a large working class and a consolidation and growth of a middle class around more or less traditional bourgeois policies, together with the articulation of minority political movements. It does not follow that social structural influences no longer bear on the formation of political interest groups in relation to mass communication.

There could be more opportunities going with enhanced supply *and* with the looser grip of traditional political divisions on political communication for new kinds of audience groupings to emerge based on social circumstances and political interests. Thus, the trend towards fragmentation of mass audiences and specialization of provision does not necessarily work against the provision of political linkages through mass media or reduce the total public for messages of an overtly political kind. Audience groupings based on gender, youth, or certain kinds of 'taste culture' may also be available for politicized versions of content consistent with the given audience definition. One should also add the obvious point that one kind of audience grouping which attracts an enhanced offer consists of the minority of politically interested – of various persuasions and of varying intensity. These are certainly more catered for now in broadcasting than in its early days and specialized print media provision is also substantial.

A second relevant audience-located factor concerns issues, causes and movements around which citizens may cluster and organize. The growth of issue-related politics has often been remarked on, with prominent examples to be found in matters to do with nuclear weapons, the environment, the women's movement, and so on. Opinion-forming on such matters is less likely than in the past to be monopolized by political parties, even if they do have to take stands on such issues. Essentially, these issues are on the political agenda because of their base in publics which are also audiences, and mass media are often important for the consciousness and the political activity associated with such issues, even where they work 'negatively' rather than 'positively'. The relevant point here is that, in their capacity as audience members, those involved in such issues set up a demand which mass media have some necessity as well as freedom to meet, in various forms: through news, documentary and drama. The pull or pressure from below is more clearly felt in such matters than is the case with conventional, party-originated, political content, where the main factor is a 'push' from above. The media supply which results does increase the chance for audiences to differentiate, develop and recruit in politically relevant ways. This may well work as a process of reaction, where what is offered is unacceptable or inconsistent with experience.

Two further sources of audience diversity are less matters of public discussion and less clearly observable, but are indicated by theory and research. One has to do with the variety of uses and motivations which audiences can bring to the political communication 'offer'. Much research testifies to the existence of alternative definitions of the utility or satisfaction associated with political communication. One familiar scheme distinguishes between the following motives: information-seeking, keeping up with political events; assessing the quality of leaders and the merits of alternative policies or programmes; looking for advice in a political choice; reinforcement of values and confirmation of allegiance; entertainment and spectator satisfaction associated with political contests and conflicts (Blumler and McQuail 1968). These are categories which can classify the orientations of audience members and together they describe a familiar framework within which people are able to locate themselves in relation to communicated politics. They describe stable or changing audience roles which are adopted by preference and as occasion seems to call for. They indicate one or more preferred orientation to political communication and although in part they are a response to the alternative forms in which politics is offered by the media and politicians themselves, they also correspond to a range of different purposes. They can best be regarded as originating with the political institution, since this guides and connects both supply and demand for political messages. The point here is that these categories express a variety of options for audiences, ranging from more to less active involvement and from more cognitive to more normative concerns. A given audience member in a given case does not have to be viewed or have to view herself or himself exclusively and inevitably either as an object of propaganda or a detached spectator. There are clues in most messages as to the appropriate response, but there is no need to respond in this way. If one relates this to what has been said about the enlargement of the range of formats in which politics is presented, especially on television, then one might conclude that potential audience freedom has been extended rather than otherwise and that there is no one dominant mode in which mass communication seems to require an audience response or attachment. Socialization into the role of audience member does not necessarily mean manipulation to uniform spectatorship.

The second relevant matter on which theory rather than research has something to say concerns variations in response or 'decoding' by audiences. The relevant line of thought is that messages are encoded in a certain way so that they have an underlying organizing message which presents the receiver with a 'preferred reading', an ideological meaning which may not be apparent on the surface. Possibly 'proferred reading' would be a more appropriate term for this, emphasizing the element of sender determination. According to this view, communication is primarily the production and reproduction of meaning and implies a preference for one interpretation of facts, items, or separate 'signals'. At the 'encoding' end information cannot be neutral, but involves choices guided by values. This is the view advanced by critical theorists who see mass media as essentially ideological in the way they work in the interests of an established class or political order (Hartley 1982). The analysis of preferred, or proferred, meaning is usually applied to content which does not openly set out to propagate a world view or an ideology, such as 'objective' news and information. To that extent, it is relatively superfluous to many categories of political communication which do openly seek to communicate political views. Yet it may acquire relevance in circumstances where much such content is negotiated through self-designated neutral gatekeepers, as noted above.

Actual research on 'decoding' is at a very early stage, but it is relevant to the present discussion because it offers the possibility that audiences have alternatives in what they can choose to take as the meaning of political content. The notion of a 'dominant' or a 'preferred' reading logically entails the correlate that there are alternative or subordinate meanings and readings. Content can be accepted at its face value or reinterpreted according to the standpoint and wishes of the receiver. Viewed from a class perspective, readings can be arrived at according to either the dominant code, or a 'negotiated' code (that of neutral information), or an 'oppositional' code, within which information is understood according to opposed class interests (Hall 1980). The extent to which alternatives are taken up has not yet been empirically established and even the process itself awaits confirmation. Nevertheless, it opens a further possibility for audience freedom, albeit a last-ditch defence against ideologically biased information or covert propaganda. When all else fails, even under conditions of monolithic control,it is possible for receivers to discount what is offered and even reverse the intended meaning, so that a more relevant understanding is arrived at. In such an extreme case, propaganda would usually be held to be counter productive – reinforcing the opposition rather than gaining acceptance. More relevant to the present discussion is the intermediate case where information is ambiguous or incomplete and where oppositional readings depend on a high degree of consciousness and the availability or learning of an alternative framework for giving meaning to information. As seen by critics, the problem is often that much political communication is ambiguous or the meaning and reading confused by the adoption of 'professional', objective, modes and formats of presentation. The degree to which alternative decoding can take place depends to a certain extent on some organized political consciousness and thus on supra-individual circumstances.

A framework for diversity research

These potential sources of diversity, in the sense of possibilities for choice or differential response on the part of the audience for political communication are in reality interdependent, interactive and of varying strength. A mere listing is not a sufficient basis for approaching any conclusion, as if the more sources of diversity, the more degrees of freedom for the audience. Much depends on the structure of society and media. It is not easy to relate the different elements together within one framework. A Marxist-critical perspective would direct attention (on the sending side) towards broad tendencies towards concentration and homogenization of what is offered, to consensual tendencies in the public sector of media and to the sharpening of lines of class conflict. On the audience side, it would emphasize trends towards fragmentation of non-ruling class interests and consciousness and, whatever the surface freedoms on offer, the most significant bases of choice would have to be related in some way to class interest. This perspective does, however, limit the possibilities for assessing tendencies in political communication in capitalist, democratic societies, partly because it is not very media-sensitive and recognizes only one dominant dimension in the structure of media and in media–audience linkages.

An alternative approach is by applying considerations of degree and type of media diversity more consistent with pluralistic models. The relevant question is whether media offer opportunities for politically diverse audiences and/or audience interests to flourish. The more diversity, the more degrees of freedom for the audience, based on any of the sources listed above. The somewhat negative perspective on the audience sketched at the start is essentially one which posits low diversity of offer and of take-up. To go beyond assertion to assessment or diagnosis and prognosis one needs an analytic tool beyond that of the very general notion of diversity. One such tool is provided by the distinction between 'external' and 'internal' diversity, which lies at the heart of the problem for critical as well as pluralistic theory, since one represents a more conflictual, the other a more consensual version of how diversity should be institutionalized and express itself (McQuail and Van Cuilenburg 1983). The ideal type of external diversity is represented by a system in which sharply differentiated political or world views are carried more or less mutually exclusively by separate media channels to their own chosen publics composed of like-minded persons. Media and audiences are thus likely to be distributed along a spectrum with much debate and conflict between separate media voices and between publics associated with them. Generally, the media act as means of expression, debate and organization for their own publics. Such a system of the kind represented by an extensive party-linked press, would be associated with high political consciousness and strong normative ties between media and their audiences. The choice offered to audiences would be a sharp one *between* differentiated media sources, but within the audience for a given medium a high degree of uniformity would be expected.

This is a model favoured by many who regret the seeming decline of class politics and the trend to massive media which tend towards a homogenizing of taste and an incorporation of opposed interests into a dominant consensus. It certainly seems as if the model has been in retreat and has only locally and temporarily ever held sway in Europe. However, there are a number of possible partial versions of the idea of 'external' diversity and it would be worthwhile to try to recognize the different forms it might take, especially, perhaps, the alternative kinds of relationship between a medium and a political party or belief. If there has been a depoliticization and de-radicalization of media, one must recognize several possible causes: simple market economics; journalistic professionalism; the rise of television as a journalistic instrument; social changes, which bring new preferences, higher living standards, more 'secular' ways of thinking. In other words, the decline is not likely to be the result of change in the media or a turn in the tide of the class struggle. Amongst the costs attributed to a decline in 'external diversity' are the loss of relatively exclusive control by parties over their links with followers, and the loss of clear anchorage points for political beliefs. Political beliefs risk becoming diluted and relativized and simple faith is likely to be weakened.

The alternative model – of 'internal' diversity – is typified by a system in which all or most points of view and kinds of information are made available in a range of media which overlap with each other and reach audiences which do not differ very much in social composition and which are also internally heterogeneous. If such audiences are structured, it is not according to political belief but according to variables of life-style, social-economic position and so on. The internal diversity model also generally characterizes public broadcasting systems, which are supposed to represent and express all main strands of thought and interests on a more or less fair and proportional basis, within programmes or over a period of time. Audiences for political content, for instance, are not addressed as if they belonged exclusively to one persuasion, rather they are addressed as if they belonged to no persuasion. There are no politically alternative news programmes and direct access for political parties is presumed to mean access to the whole public. In the newspaper press, the model is represented increasingly by newspapers which seek either to provide an educated professional public with much 'objective' information and dispassionate analysis or by the larger-circulation, 'middle of the road' newspaper which is uncommitted politically and essentially commercial in its goals as well as consensual in tone and substance. Choice for audiences is supposed to be assured by competition to meet needs and interests and media tend to try to satisfy the largest number within their own complete 'package'. The trend towards internal diversity, coupled with, or fuelled by, commercialism has troubled some politically critical observers of the scene (for reasons already noted), although it has often been hailed as a mark of progress away from a more bigoted, narrow and ideological kind of politics and as a trend which goes with high journalistic standards of objectivity and independence. An argument sometimes advanced is that in reality people usually only read one newspaper and it is better for democracy that this should offer a range of alternative points of view within its pages.

In discussing forms of diversity as evidenced in media structure, content, or audience, there is another relevant distinction to be made. This involves a separation between the principles of 'open' and of 'reflective' diversity. Should media offer a more or less equal access to all serious or legitimate viewpoints or should access reflect proportionately the distribution of strength or allegiance of parties or the range of existing public opinion? The second is the more common goal of public broadcasting systems and is what commercial systems under free market conditions are supposed to arrive at, although they often do not. It seems the most 'natural' way and the most easy to justify as a goal of practical public policy. It should not set any severe limit to audience choice, yet below a certain threshold (which may well be high) it does tend to do so. The open access principle – an outlet for every voice – seems most consistent with libertarian principles, but is not likely to be promoted by either commercialism or totalitarianism. Its characteristics, which are most consistent with external diversity forms, are also least easy to promote institutionally under open conditions. It is a principle which may also not appeal to those who want to see ordered democratic change based on strong coalitions of interest, since a babel of voices may be divisive, confusing and ineffective. Yet it does have the great advantage of promoting change and undermining consensualism and ritualism in political communication. The choice between open and reflective forms is one that has to be faced if one wants to evaluate available degrees of freedom or to promote more freedom.

As noted already, there seems to have been a rather general shift from external diversity forms towards the internal variety, especially promoted by public broadcasting which has limited channel capacity, carries an obligation to be fair to different points of view, promotes a notion of a general public interest and is usually obliged to reflect the main divisions of politics and culture in society. The trends mentioned give some support for the somewhat more pessimistic interpretation of the audience situation in respect of diversity. Requirements of impartiality, balance and reflection of established interests are quite likely to lead to a bland presentation of issues, as if these were open to alternative pragmatic solutions rather than resulting from irreconcilable differences. The existing distribution of power or the rules of the game are not likely to be placed centrally on the agenda of political action. Political messages under conditions of internal diversity and reflection are often received in a context of entertainment and tend to be an optional and easily avoidable component of a package of media messages. The 'mainstreaming' effect on political beliefs which some researchers have detected as a result of dependence on television in the USA is in line with these observations (Gerbner, Gross *et al.* 1980).

Assessment

The question of future prospects for audience diversity must be considered with some attention to developments in new electronic media currently under way. These may offer politically relevant services and affect the working of existing media. The main changes in prospect are: more of the same or very similar, via new cable and satellite channels; more entertainment and advertising; new specialized information services via teletext and videotex; a multiplication of sources, challenging existing public or commercial monopolies; a fragmentation of television audiences; much greater cross-border flow of television. These and other conditions have been hailed by some as representing a significant widening of choice of audio-visual content for many individuals and also an improved chance of access for local or minority voices so far rarely heard, in Europe at least. There can also be a shift of balance from passive reception to active search, which can tell in favour of an improved political communication situation in the terms described above. The potential has been viewed with less favour on several grounds: as enlarging the role of the private sector and promoting commercialism; as weakening the public sector in broadcasting and the powers of control for public ends; as promoting further privatization and consumerism in place of a public political life; as shifting the advantage of acquiring valuable political and economic information towards elites and the more economically powerful, and strengthening lines of communication alternative to those available in democratic politics and in the public sphere.

Given the uncertainty about the direction, extent and timing of prospective change and the variety of criteria indicated it would be difficult to reach any definitive assessment of the issue under discussion without leaning heavily on pre-judgement, a favourite theory, or pure guesswork, especially in the absence of much systematic research directly focused on the question of audience diversity in the matter of political communication. There are several possible degrees of assessment, ranging from the most pessimistic to the most optimistic, which could be consistent with what has been presented in this essay. At the negative end of the spectrum, one sees only a growing attenuation of channels and an impoverishment of chances for most citizens to acquire relevant and useful information and to interact with chosen leaders on the basis of common political beliefs. What is especially missing is the normative 'glue' for political attachments. From this point of view, the main source of variety open to the citizen/audience member would be that of an oppositional reading of what is offered and a turning to non-mainstream sources for alternatives. An intermediate assessment would recognize that, whatever the validity of the criticism of the broadcast media, as they have grown they have also developed mechanisms for mediating between citizens and political power. It would recognize too that relevant journalist communication roles have helped to encourage a degree of exposure to, and participation in, political life, which have made the political world comprehensible, have represented the point of view of ordinary citizens and have preserved at least the possibility of a 'healthy' public sphere, in which issues can be discussed and opinion formed on the basis of common information. Yet more positively, one might accept the inevitability of changed conditions of political communication, especially in the move to 'internal' forms of diversity and the 'secularization' of social and political life, and look to possibilities within these given conditions for new and expanded opportunities for political communication based especially on new media.

It is not inevitable that media which are less overtly partisan or more general-interest oriented and consensual should exclude such possibilities. It is also not yet inevitable that new media should simply offer more of the same or take away from what has been achieved. On the first matter, there is a difference between bland, opinion-free, consensual media trying to appeal to everyone and offend no one (or no one with power) and relatively open channels which lack a single editorial line, but which offer opportunities to diverse groups, points of view and new forms of content. Experience with the fourth television channel in Britain has demonstrated both the potential of this institutional form and the obstacles to achievement. In the newspaper sector, there is also evidence that the tendency to open columns to alternative, sometimes conflicting, points of view can be viable within the framework of an internal diversity model. It may even, at the same time, be interesting for readers, not commercially harmful and stimulating for political debate. The formula seems to work both in North America, where local newspaper monopolies are the rule, and in Europe, where there is still some choice between alternative, politically active newspapers. In respect of new electronic media, the benefits of potential diversity of source material may yet have a more general effect of reducing the reliance on monopolistic sources and help alternative media to retain an independence. Early experience of satellite channel multiplication in the United States is not especially negative, since politically informative channels can operate on the basis of rather small and dispersed audiences. Minority politics by way of electronic media may be economically viable in a commercial system. One may need to face the possibility that the tried and tested European method for guaranteeing minimum political communication standards from electronic media needs to be reconsidered. One could at least reasonably hold the view that some potential growth points still exist and not all is gloom.

Conclusion

Possibly enough has been said to support a contention that tendencies towards concentration and homogenization and 'internal' forms of diversity in media supply have not necessarily reduced possibilities for the exercise of audience choice. This is due partly to three developments: the continual addition of new, initially minority, sources and of new media; the absolute increase in the volume of mass media on offer; the invention of new forms within established media and of new arrangements to compensate for structural rigidities and unwanted tendencies. The audience itself should not be left out of account in this assessment since it (in so far as it is an it) has also changed in the period under review, in respect of political communication as in other matters. The change has several aspects, including the normal turnover of generations with changed expectations and interests and, almost everywhere, a growth in sophistication resulting from wider educational opportunity and a speeded-up cultural experience. It would be foolish to ignore the extent of structural communicational disadvantage, the tendencies towards fragmentation, trivialization and manipulation which are intrinsic to the commercial competition for new audiences which has fuelled much of the media growth. It would be equally unjustified to assume that structured inequality was greater than before or that the public has become more passive, gullible and manipulable, certainly on the basis of considering the media alone. It is also most implausible to suppose that politics itself is in some way in decline.

The roots of political diversity within the great or the many small media publics are in the 'soil' of the society, the media having some climatic or other artificial influence of a fertilizing or suppressive kind. Without going as far with this image as Chance the gardener in the film *Being There*, to suggest that spring will follow winter, one can say at least that the condition of the political system itself, independently of the media, is more important as a key to the future of audience diversity. Theory in these matters does not seem to have advanced a great deal since C. W. Mills analysed the condition of 'mass society' thirty years ago, and concepts and methods for monitoring the condition of audience reception of political communication are not much further on. It is unlikely that the actual conditions of society or media are essentially the same as then, so we are left with a rather large and open question which believers in media pluralism at least ought to set about answering. Critical theorists might also have to accept that there is no return to the situation of 'external diversity', leading to the emergence of a single right way (or, more likely, single wrong way against which to react) and they also have an interest in mapping the encroaching jungle of media abundance, if it cannot be held back. This essay has attempted to open debate in an area marked out by Philip Elliott, but not explored by him. It is certainly a task for which his observations, conceptualizations and insight have helped to prepare the way.

Part Three

---

*Reporting the State
and the
State of Reporting*

8

Government Secrecy and the Media in the United States and Britain*

John Downing

*I*n 1984 Senator Barry Goldwater, conservative Republican chairman of the Senate Intelligence Committee, made public a letter he had just written to the Director of the Central Intelligence Agency. In it he asked the director: 'What the hell is going on?' He was referring to the CIA's secret decision to mine Nicaraguan ports. Senator Moynihan, vice-chairman, threatened resignation over the issue. In the same year, a junior British civil servant, Sarah Tisdall, was sacked and gaoled for six months for divulging to the *Guardian* the plans of the then Defence Minister Michael Heseltine to make a deliberately confusing statement to the House of Commons concerning the arrival of US cruise missiles at Greenham Common.

Secrecy was not total. Both cases were widely reported in the respective countries. After an international outcry, the CIA desisted from this form of subversion against Nicaragua. In Britain Ms Tisdall served her sentence, despite the national outcry. The US case was only the latest in a twenty-year series of clashes between Congress and executive agencies over the waging of undeclared war. The British case was a classic of the UK's omnibus definition of secrecy rights, even to the point of effective judicial endorsement of a government minister's right to deceive the House of Commons. Neither case should be taken to summarize the entire character of government secrecy in the country concerned.

* My gratitude to Philip Schlesinger for his continuing acute comments on my writing, and also to Jim Aronson, Ash Corea, Donna Demac, Philip Matters and Andrew Polsky.

British debate over the comparison of government secrecy and the media in the USA and the UK is usually framed around the prior positions of reformers and traditionalists. Reformers point triumphantly to aspects of the US system to underpin their claim that openness in government is not tantamount to social revolution. Traditionalists look sniffily at the appearances – for example, the US Freedom of Information Act (1974) and the Government in the Sunshine Act (1977) – and insist that everyday information realities are much the same in both nations. In the USA, whilst one wing of opinion would regard Britain as politically immature in this area, another would envy its quaintly charming stability, its heartwarming trust in government's 'knowing what is best', its small volume of infuriating leaks.

Only one sure conclusion can be drawn from these long-standing *prises de position*, namely, that the British traditionalists – rightly or wrongly – are quite alone in awarding equal force to government secrecy in both nations. The task I have set myself here is not so much to add another arrow to the quiver for this fray, but to raise certain questions concerning government secrecy and the media which are often passed over in the policy debates. I shall illustrate these issues from both countries.

There are, however, some brief conceptual observations which must preface the main discussion.

Fundamental to this analysis is my assumption that government secrecy is not a given, an absolute, but a battleground. Its extent fluctuates between societies and over time and by issue and with varying political conditions. The assumption is common but misguided that there exists an organic logic at work in the classification of documents and information, rather than an administrative machine which responds to shocks, crises, diktats and disaffection.

Equally fundamental is the relation of political mobilization to information and secrecy. By 'mobilization' I mean the involvement of large numbers of people, in many settings, at many levels, in pursuit of a political objective (or many). Such involvement may be autonomously organized, but much more often will be summoned into action through a political party, trade union, public interest group, alternative media, or a combination of two or more of these. Without the likelihood of political mobilization, then, information can be less carefully controlled, for its dissemination will not lead to organized movements of opinion. Here again we see the importance of conceptualizing government secrecy as a battleground.

With these clarifications in mind, let us proceed to a more detailed discussion.

Corporate and government secrecy

A paradox of the understanding of power in classical liberal theory is that it assumes a free flow of information in the political realm, a free flow of goods in the economic realm, but carefully restricted information flow in the economic realm. No doubt corporate secrecy derives from predictable concerns, such as corporate leaders' anxieties lest competitors steal a march on them, or lest unions and/or environmentalists should force them to narrow their profit-margins for safety's sake. None the less, the corporate power-structure does run the economy, in various forms of conjunction with the state, and thus exercises astonishing power over citizens' everyday lives. Secrecy is considered its birthright, with the result that the impact of major corporate decisions may be practically irreversible by the time they become public knowledge. In a contemporary political economy, where the leading sectors are generally in a close, though not always friendly, relation with the state, the practices of secrecy in the corporate and political spheres generally reinforce each other. In these 'forward sectors' military, scientific and technological developments often have a tight interconnection, and thus corporate secrecy can be justified in the name of national and state security. A classic case in point has always been the nuclear industry (see Hilgartner *et al.* 1983; Hertsgaard 1983; Gowing 1978; Williams 1980; Aubrey 1982).

So much may well be self-evident to readers. There are some important examples of how business and government elites operate to support each other's secrecy, drawn from the USA, which usefully illuminate the issue and indicate some of its complexities.

The first such is the October 1984 proposal of the National Security Agency to equip government and the corporate sector with half a million very expensive, specially designed 'spy-proof' telephones. Espionage by the Soviet Union and by unnamed capitalist powers was the reason cited, though the surveillance technology aimed at is also capable of purely domestic deployment by rival firms (Burnham 1984d).

The second instance is the legislative assistance given to corporate secrecy by the Reagan administration from its earliest days in office. In the name of cutting down bloated bureaucracies, of leaving the managers free to manage, and of opening up the economy to healthy competition, Reagan's team managed to cancel the publication of many series of statistics with a direct bearing on health and safety at work and in the environment. The combination of deregulation measures and the use made of the 1980 Paperwork Reduction Act has enabled corporations to retreat much more behind their veils, and has robbed unions

155

and environmentalists of much of their most useful documentation of national trends (Demac 1984).

A third aspect to be considered is the role of the Securities and Exchange Commission, an institution under consideration in late 1984 for introduction into Britain's financial world. In Britain there is sometimes a misplaced impression that the SEC is constantly enforcing corporate disclosures in the public interest. While Roosevelt may have originally viewed this as its purpose, in 50 years of existence its actual function has been to promote the kind of disclosure that would stimulate investors' confidence, thus lubricating the overall flow of investment capital. This is a communication service to investors, but not primarily to the public at large. Even so, its most significant service is to the leading investors, a reality thrown into further relief by the SEC's consistent failure to develop procedures to illuminate the financial performance of the biggest, most diversified firms. Corporate secrecy is not under attack at its most sensitive points, or in its most powerful representatives, as a result of the SEC's operations (see Seligman 1982).

Lastly, an ironic twist in the battle for free communication is provided by the intensive use of the 1974 Freedom of Information Act (FOIA) by corporations bent on acquiring each other's secrets! A flurry of business magazine articles and subsequently a book-length study in the early 1980s (Casey *et al.* 1983) indicated that despite the explicit exemption of trade secrets from the Act's scope, both corporations and newly-established contract agencies were heavily involved in using the Act to acquire apparently general information which would none the less be highly revealing to someone in the business 'know'. In the years 1979–81 three agencies frequently probed – the Food and Drug Administration, the Consumer Product Safety Commission, the Environmental Protection Agency – received less than 5 per cent of their inquiries from media and public interest groups combined. Use of the Act rose 27 per cent each year from 1974 to 1981.

The main conclusion to be drawn from these instances of state/corporate secrecy interaction is that the former acts very carefully to promote certain types of information diffusion within corporate circles (for example, via the SEC) while valiantly defending their secrecy at other points (for example, the NSA secure-phones proposal, the Reagan team's blockage of corporate information accountability). The curious FOIA case may issue in the Act's emasculation, an outcome devoutly desired by many conservative interests.

In so far as the secrecy battleground is a key dimension of the battle for power over social development, the sometimes complex interaction between state power and corporate power should always be kept clearly in view. Too often, the government alone is in focus.

Secrecy or selective communication?

At the same time, the concept of secrecy is often too clumsy to capture the nature of the problem. Secrecy in both nations is not used as in impermeable shield blotting out all communication, but as a device to allow the pinnacle of the power-structure to communicate how and when it prefers. It is a mechanism of control over all the other echelons of government – or of attempted control, at least. Concretely speaking, this means there are two types of 'leak': those favoured by the executive branch leadership, and those infuriating to it (see Toinet 1983). The first type, together with official pronouncements, constitutes the selective communication which secrecy rules are designed to promote.

In Britain this system is formalized in ways different from the USA. The classic case is the lobby system in Parliament (Tunstall 1970), where journalists are accredited as a bloc to hear off-the-record briefings by senior ministers on a regular basis. Thus this elite corps is flattered to be privy to government confidences, but is bound by the rules of the game to censor itself when communicating many specific aspects of what it hears. Even this understates the muffling effect of the institution, for parliamentary correspondents are rarely adept at handling the specifics of the military or the economy, for instance, and thus can easily be fed comfortable generalities.

In Washington, DC, the comparable nerve-centre of US government despite the diffusion of the federal bureaucracy over the country, and despite the weighty roles of a number of state and metropolitan governments, the operation of selective communication is more complex. A frequent British image is one of tough, insistent reporters, fed with great meaty chunks of delicious, hot information by civic-minded civil servants anxious to ensure open government. The FOIA is seen as the investigative journalist's charter, and a large proportion of journalists as 'investigative'. This image is so strongly entrenched that I shall spend some time indicating its varied flaws in actual practice.

Firstly, the leaks – selective communication – in the federal capital mostly derive from quite different dynamics. The influential layer of the federal bureaucracy – not all of it present in the capital, admittedly – was 50 times larger in 1968 than the then 'administrative class' in the British Civil Service (Sigal 1973: 133). There exists no formal communication mechanism between all these people, divided into very different departments and sub-departments, and frequently warring against each other. The media – notably the *New York Times* and the *Washington Post*, but also weekly and monthly news magazines – are therefore the mechanisms by which civil servants will often try to communicate to each other. This communication is frequently adversarial, perhaps representing an attempt to prolong a battle by extending it outside the department in which one side has lost, or perhaps an endeavour to stifle a new initiative by disclosing it before the necessary coalition has formed to launch it successfully. Or an attempt to record that an upcoming policy disaster was vigorously contested before its implementation through *force majeure*.

Thus leaks are not normally whistle-blowing to the general public in the USA. Indeed, there is a whole series of reasons why this is a misconception. Most important of these is the fact that journalists rely on official sources for their information just as much as in Britain (Sigal 1973: ch. 6; Wilson 1982). Secondly, few media have the resources to pay a sufficiently large staff to do the necessary ferreting: 'Capitol Hill [is] the dominant location of Washington newsgathering. . . . Washington news reflects the perspective of Congress' (Hess 1981: 48–9).

Thirdly, whilst US civil servant whistle-blowers may not face jail for leaks, this is far from the only effective sanction: 'In the Soviet Union, whistleblowers are sent directly to criminal psychiatric wards. In this country, we drive our whistleblowers to the borders of insanity and sometimes over the edge by humiliating them, taking their jobs, demoting them, or forcing them to do non-work; slander and character assassination are frequently used' (Ball 1984: 307–10). The British campaigns to abolish the Official Secrets Act often seem to forget that it is only the most provocative measure in a whole armoury of reprisals.

Fourthly, we must bear in mind that 'the press. . . . *is* public opinion in the eyes of officials' (Sigal 1973: 135). In this elitist assumption, the US public is perceived as an intangible construct, and so is conveniently redefined as the Washington press corps (despite the latter's *own* overwhelming recognition that its sense is minimal for how the public is thinking at any given time (Hess 1981: 13)). Thus communicating with this body is not populism run riot on civil servants' part.

At the time of writing there is an additional dimension, this time to do with the nature of journalists' ferreting. According to one sympathetic outsider, himself a former leading member of Common Cause, a major public interest pressure group: 'Thousands of reporters swarm over Washington . . . many more than but 20 years ago . . . our constant thirst for exposés of the *private lives* of our government officials is short-sighted and ultimately crippling. By personalizing public life, the news media drive people away from public service' (Adams 1984, my emphasis). This observation is important. It indicates that much of the ferreting is not policy related at all, but personality related: an assault on privacy, not a dismantling of government secrecy. It means that in nations with the absurdly puritanical public codes of both Britain and the USA, the easiest way to sink any public figure not backed by a Kennedy-type machine is to publicize a so-called sexual or personal irregularity. This malign influence of religion in political life is losing a little of its sting, but only a little.

Finally, the Freedom of Information Act, although a valuable legislative advance, is administered so as to create lengthy delays in obtaining the information sought. In turn, the journalist on a daily, weekly, or even monthly assignment will find it too cumbersome a mechanism for the normal tasks in hand. This no doubt helps to explain the rather small use of the Act noted above, by both journalists and public interest groups.

The relation between media and government secrecy in the USA becomes much clearer, once secrecy is defined as the condition for selective communication by the power-structure – and once the limitations of journalists are recognized. The operation of selective communication in the state/corporate relation has already been noted, and below we shall return to analysing the nature of journalistic institutions. We may conclude for the moment that while there is greater openness in government in the USA (and thus the *possibility* of greater public awareness) than in Britain, the situation is not as open as some British reformers would often suppose.

When information is not power

Why has the British state clung so tenaciously to its armoury of reprisals against the free flow of information? The Civil Service will not allow former government ministers access to papers dating from outside their tenure in office, will not allow ministers in an incoming government to see the policy advice prepared for their defeated rivals; gaol, on top of dismissal, is the reward for dissident leakers (see Michael 1982; May and Rowan 1982).

One explanation for this tenacity might be the inertia of tradition. For Shils, in his oft-quoted study of the rise of government secrecy in the USA after the Second World War (Shils 1956), this British tradition represented a mature, healthy balance among privacy, government secrecy and publicity that was signally lacking in Senator Joseph McCarthy's USA. Without actually questioning the First Amendment, Shils identified 'the specifically American disequilibrium [as] the preponderance of publicity', compared to which British secretiveness was a problem 'restricted in range' (*ibid.*: 57).

This account would be music to the ears of traditionalist civil servants in Britain, but it is not an explanation of the situation. With all due allowance for the impact on new entrants of induction into a highly elitist, cohesive and career-structured body already stamped with the ethos of secrecy, a supposed cultural chemistry is an insufficient basis for explaining either persistence or change in political structures. Just as reference to the First Amendment in the USA often represents more by way of a celebratory ritual invocation than a profound political conviction, so too British secrecy structures must be researched beyond their proponents' rhetoric.

I am going to suggest that a major reason for their persistence is the Labour Party. Over the twentieth century we see three related trends in many parliamentary democracies. One is the rise of parties with a working-class base and some sort of socialist platform. The second is the decline of parliaments as organs of state power. The third is the rise in power of civil services. There are other reasons for the second and third developments beyond the first, but it has arguably been a key stimulus to both.

In Britain, it was exactly around the period after the First World War, when the Labour Party was clearly on the rise and the Liberal party definitively on the wane, that the professionalization of the Civil Service began to take a marked form. Previously, links were very close between it and the vertices of the Liberal and Conservative Parties. Notwithstanding its unchanging non-Marxist and reformist character – somehow perfectly distilled in Michael Foot's refusal in the 1970s to challenge his own refusal of security clearance by the secret service, even though he was then the third ranking Cabinet minister – the Labour Party was none the less seen as immensely threatening, and not just as wrong-headed, by very many within the power-structure. It was, after all, a grassroots party with close links to the unions; it was a coalition, which meant there would be some far Left elements in the leadership; and it was obviously British, not recognizable – except to the politically hysterical – as a Soviet fifth column. Its legitimacy was considerable. A 'communist' party might have been much easier to isolate. The very British diffuseness of the situation made it harder to handle.

I would argue, therefore, that one major response was the growing concentration of power in the Civil Service, represented by its professionalization, and the effective disciplining and status-crystallization of the apparatus through the Official Secrets Act. The 1911 version (further amended in 1920) was apparently only a revision of its 1889 predecessor, and ostensibly all versions were designed to focus on spying. In reality, the circumstances in which they all originated, and the uses to which they have most often been put, make this simple view hard to sustain (Michael 1982: ch. 3). The Tisdall case is a much better guide to the Act's functions than the Philby, Burgess, Maclean and Blunt cases. Signing the Act upon entering and leaving even lowly Civil Service employment is a potent ritual, stimulating a degree of awe, and an instinct for self-censorship and secrecy among those subjected to it.

Thus it is far harder for parliamentary select committees in England – themselves an innovation of the open government reformer and Labour Cabinet minister Richard Crossman in the 1960s – to prise information out of Whitehall than it is for Senate or house committees and sub-committees in Washington. The most plausible key to the puzzle of why secrecy varies between the countries is *the capacity of the Labour Party to mobilize*. I say 'capacity', because perception of potential counts for much in politics. Hard-bitten Marxists may sneer at the Labour Party, but their cynicism is not necessarily reflected in ruling circles' estimation of its mobilizing power.

Thus information could become power in Britain (not the same as saying it necessarily would). In the USA there has never been a nationally organized party with the Labour Party's philosophy and numbers: at the height of the Socialist Party's influence, fuelled by anti-war isolationism supporting its abstentionist platform in 1917, it polled a mere million votes. This absence of a national mobilizing force has probably made open government a less unsettling process for the US power-structure. The take-up of information that existed was limited to single-issue politics or pork-barrel politics. Where secrecy was most entrenched, namely in military matters, there was usually a bipartisan consensus which shored up executive power still further. Leaks in this latter realm were generally designed to accentuate US aggressiveness, not to question it (for example, the notorious 'missile gap' leaks which helped to get Kennedy elected over Nixon) (see Sanders 1983: 125–33).

It is intriguing to ponder whether the sharp increase in government secrecy under the Reagan administration – on which there is more to be said below – is not at least in part attributable to the latter's reaction against the marked growth in public interest lobbies and pressure groups in Washington and elsewhere from the 1970s, as well as against the development of peace and anti-nuclear research. These bodies are all single-issue mobilizers, and it is certainly not the case that they are all Left-inclined, but none the less they collectively activate a greater volume of political organization than has previously been the case. Information can become power, and one recalls the almost notorious warning in the report of the Trilateral commission that democracies were becoming ungovernable.

The media: watchdogs and tracker dogs?

Media professionals' analysis of government secrecy usually celebrates their own constructively antagonistic relationship to the power-structure. The presumption is that a free press is public guarantor of the right to be informed, and constitutes one of the fundamental differences between Soviet and Western societies.

The formulation blurs over certain less palatable realities. A sarcastic verse sums up the problem, at least from one perspective:

> You cannot hope to bribe or twist
> – Thank God! – the British journalist.
> But seeing what the chap will do
> Unasked, there's no occasion to.

There is an entrenched pomposity in media self-congratulation on their contribution to public debate, which cries out to be punctured. The very designation of a journalist as 'investigative' already implies the nature of conventional journalism, which largely consists, as we have noted above, of relaying routine information from official sources. These may be congressional, travel-related, financial, or whatever, but the amount of serious probing that takes place could hardly be said to be threatening either to the government's or the public's composure. As noted already, much of the 'digging' that takes place is of personal scandals. US journalists have a well-deserved reputation in this regard, but British editors and journalists are no slouches either.

At this juncture, the hurt tones of the 'quality' media spokespeople in both countries can be heard disclaiming identification with such methods, and distancing themselves from the 'yellow' or 'gutter' press. Fine; but in terms of the overall argument it still remains true that consistently investigative media are the exception. In Britain, there is Granada's *World in Action* television weekly, the *Guardian*, the *Observer*, the *New Statesman*. Others, like the *Sunday Times* and the *Daily Mirror* appear to have lost their former zeal. In the USA there is the *Washington Post*, the *Los Angeles Times*, the *Wall Street Journal* and some of the local or minority productions such as public broadcasting, or New York's *Village Voice*, the *Philadelphia Inquirer*, the *St Louis Post-Dispatch*, *The Nation*.

Thus the evidence for the embattled heroes seems a little scanty. Indeed, it has been argued rather convincingly that government secrecy has its pay-offs for journalists and their editors. Leaks, individual or institutional (for example, the lobby system), give a journalist status. Without them, without being privy to special information, from where could the journalist derive the necessary elevation over the rest of us? Chapman Pincher, for decades the British *Daily Express* defence correspondent; Jack Anderson, the syndicated Washington 'insider'; Victor Louis, the Copenhagen-based Moscow 'source': these are only famous names to illustrate the point. Obliterate secrecy and you obliterate them.

Furthermore, major media are rarely if ever prone to support small media doing the kind of investigative work which the giants of journalism always claim to be pursuing. In the USA the *National Guardian*'s lonely, principled fight against McCarthy's witch-hunts never drew support from the supposed defenders of First amendment freedoms such as the *New York Times*, even when McCarthy's machine forced one of the *Guardian*'s two chief editors, a British citizen, out of the country *for no crime* (Belfrage and Aronson 1978).

In Britain, there is now a whole dossier of cases in which the major media have chosen for the most part to restrain or censor serious investigative journalism about Northern Ireland (see Curtis 1984; Schlesinger *et al.* 1983). The point has been made by many people on many occasions, but the glaring paradox is still worth restating that those six counties, if part of Britain, demand *more* investigation, not less, given the evident bankruptcy of successive governments' policies in the region during this century. Why should there have been only a single major newspaper, the *Daily Mirror*, to grasp the nettle and query British control?

Thus we may conclude that contemporary increases in government secrecy will not automatically be offset by skilful, courageous media professionals. Indeed, for many, open government would sharply alter the practice of their craft. Those that jib against these constraints are deserving of great respect, but still have a long road before them in order to win the day.

Does the public object to government secrecy?

A climactic moment in the weeks following the 1983 US invasion of Grenada came when a huge media chorus of outrage at journalists' exclusion from the island until four days later was in turn met by an avalanche of letters and phone-calls denouncing the media for their presumption. The American media authorities were extremely shaken, and – very foolishly – ceased for the most part to persist with their case. They had reason to be surprised, for even Thatcher had permitted 'dependable' reporters to accompany the Malvinas/Falklands fleet (see Bellando 1984). Reagan had trumped her ace. The results of their climb-down were seen in October 1984, when the Department of Defense announced an eleven-strong media pool which it would allow in future to cover the initial phase of surprise military operations. TV, radio, magazines and news agencies would be represented, but not – oddly – newspapers. The latter responded by challenging their own exclusion, but not the principle of DoD media control – and certainly not the alarming implication that more Grenadas were being contemplated (Halloran 1984b: 1). The bait of privileged access never seems to lose its seduction for media executives.

The public outcry must, none the less, be taken into account in any analysis of government secrecy and the media in the USA – and probably elsewhere as well. It was the then Prime Minister Harold Wilson, who just before the second general election of 1974 said in a London *Sunday Times* interview that people did not want to think about government, but to have governments which simply let them get on with living their lives. Was he right?

In the USA, it is fair to say that information levels concerning foreign policy are abysmally low. Presidents, not to mention the general public, do not know even the most elementary facts, as was evidenced by Nixon's public apology on a trip to Brazil that he spoke no Spanish! A 1982 survey revealed that despite much media attention – quantitatively – to Central America, very many people did not know which side the USA was supporting in El Salvador or Nicaragua. It is quite frightening in the nuclear era to reflect that the public in both the USA and the USSR is, for different reasons, so ignorant of the planet over which their respective regimes conduct their furious competition – and thus have not even the wherewithal *in principle* to begin to challenge this menacing rivalry from inside.

Where does this reluctance to know originate? Is it a given fact of human nature that, as T. S. Eliot once claimed, it 'cannot bear very much reality'? Or is it, like other aspects of culture, a human product and not simply the spontaneous legitimation of private government?

Citizen disinvolvement is a complex phenomenon. It can certainly be stimulated in the USA by consideration of the gigantic sums required to run a campaign for elective office, or by the fact that successive administrations never, for some reason, seem to be able to tackle organized crime. Apathy can be stimulated in both the USA and Britain by the pressures of daily survival, nowhere nearly as acute as in the Third World, but none the less fraying. And in Britain apathy can be stimulated by the recognition that access to political influence depends to a pronounced degree on having the right social class background (less so in the USA). The public perception of party-political life, of squabbles, intrigues, corruption, self-seeking, also plays its part in alienating people from political involvement.

Crucially, however, it is the nature of mass education and communication about politics and science which lies behind contemporary disinvolvement. Once politics is defined as occupying the discursive space between the major parties, and once 'it' is thereby removed from the schools to avoid partisanship, and once its expression in the media is overwhelmingly focused on that discursive space, then – all human life is *not there* and politics becomes merely another facet of the division of labour, this time between those who act and those acted upon.

Science is left out of this equation at great risk. A US commentator recently noted that nearly half of government policy decisions today were scientific or technical in nature (Holton 1981). Popular science education is perhaps the single most important communicative exercise in the present era to enable citizen involvement. Without this education, the practice of government secrecy could increasingly become of marginal political relevance. Lack of demand for information is inevitable if people do not know what to ask for, or the information is found incomprehensible. Banking, genetic engineering, nuclear issues: the list is constantly growing. Trust is forced to supplant awareness. But this is the result of a social and cultural process, not a winsomely bestowed accolade on its rulers from a gratefully ignorant public.

The situation described touches once more on the relation of information to mobilization. Information without mobilization is not power; yet mobilization without meaningful information is very hard. There is a necessary cumulative interaction between the two. The weakness of US media, even more than British media, in explaining the rest of the planet is a perfect case in point (see Aronson 1970; Chomsky and Herman 1979; Said 1981; Downing 1975). Only when the coffins and plastic bags came home from Vietnam to the little towns and communities that make up much of the USA was there aroused a widespread public desire to know. All other major communications had failed the American people. Thatcher, similarly, was quite correct according to her priorities in trying to prevent the Malvinas/Falklands wounded from joining in the London victory parade in 1982. In it, they would have translated the official image of heroism instilled in the public mind into one of horror; of self-sacrifice into senseless savagery; of triumph into tragedy. No such communication could be contemplated. In both nations we see a dismal commentary, then, on the quality of information available to develop people's thinking *before* tragedy struck.

National security and government secrecy: the sacred cow

The ultimate tragedy is generally and rightly accepted to be a nuclear war, despite the cheery cretinism of some like the Federal Emergency Management spokesman who said in December 1980 that 'with enough shovels' to put together dirt-shelters, nuclear war would be just another experience. In other contexts, the risk of nuclear war has been a linchpin argument by state authorities in Britain and the USA in favour of retaining secrecy about all nuclear matters, whether strategic or energy-related. The argument for government secrecy to protect national security against nuclear catastrophe appears unassailable: only an extremely naïve pacifist, it seems, could pursue the anti-secrecy case beyond this juncture.

Yet it is always when faced with such seamless, glittering unassailabilities that we need to be most on our guard. The fear of nuclear destruction can terrorize us into ceasing to think. I would contend that at this juncture, the 'national security' juncture, people have often switched off their minds. Ideologies are at their most penetrative when in part they ring true to a major reality. Let us examine some cases of government secrecy on nuclear topics to illustrate the argument.

The only two nuclear bombs so far to be dropped on a human target were those unleashed on Hiroshima and Nagasaki in August 1945. Argument about their use has mostly been based on the rightness or wrongness of terrorism against a civilian population. From this perspective, the main differences between their use and the almost equally murderous assaults on Tokyo in March 1945, and on Dresden and Hamburg, consist in the long-term genetic effects of nuclear weapons, and the fact that these have developed from kiloton to megaton level in the years since.

There has been little public argument as to why they were dropped. Yet there is a current among contemporary historians which would question whether, covertly, the purpose in dropping them was not primarily to intimidate the Soviet leadership, rather than to bring the war with Japan to a speedy end and so to save US lives (see Alperovitz 1965; Maddox 1973: 63–78). They would dispute that an effective surrender by Japan was unobtainable by other, less violent means. If this contention is accurate, its implications for the present argument are considerable. It means that *from the outset* the uses of nuclear power have been shrouded in secrecy and thus have been able to be other than they were claimed to be. The sacrificial victims of this strategic decision were at least those Japanese against whom the bombs were unleashed. And since the Western powers were in error when they assumed the Soviet Union was not already developing its own nuclear weapons (Holloway 1983: ch. 2), it seems clear that, far from frightening the world into a Pax Americana, these secret decisions actually triggered an arms race which could end by destroying the planet.

A further example, this time from the world of strategic nuclear war planning, is the secrecy of the Rand Corporation during the 1950s and 1960s (Kaplan 1983). Time and again the varied policies generated in this prototype think-tank can be seen to have been based on the most partial and empirically flawed assumptions. None the less, it took itself, and more particularly was taken by the USAF high command, with intense seriousness, as offering the last word in wisdom for nuclear war. Yet, crucially absent from Rand's war-games was the consideration that nuclear war was unwinnable because some counterstrike missiles would be sure to create unimaginable destruction for the 'victor'. Secrecy led to lack of self-criticism; such lack of scrutiny might have led to nuclear disaster.

The situation in Britain was little different. The War Cabinet never discussed the atomic bomb in the period leading up to 1945; the (Labour) Deputy Prime Minister was told nothing about it; and the Labour Cabinet as a whole, after the 1945 election, never discussed Britain's own bomb. From then until now, every effort has been made to discountenance public debate on the subject.

The seriousness of the secrecy clamp has not been limited to nuclear weapons. Nuclear energy – repeatedly touted as the peaceful opposite to missiles, but directly linked to them by technology and by menace to safety – has also been the subject of extraordinary government secrecy in both countries (Hilgartner *et al.* 1983). Information about nuclear accidents, about fall-out effects, about environmental contamination, about profitability, about safety for nuclear plant workers, about safety measures against meltdowns, has been fiercely guarded and managed. Despite the dramatization of the issue in films such as *The China Syndrome* and *Silkwood*, as well as in a small flood of independently produced anti-nuclear documentaries in the USA, the powers that be have not willingly relinquished one iota of control over information in this area. Slowly, however, popular scientific education on this topic, at least, is beginning to make headway through anti-nuclear media and through intermittent information in the major media. Peace researchers in and out of universities have succeeded in piecing together a large amount of information on nuclear topics, both strategic and energy related. Once again, secrecy is a battleground, not a given.

There are still other developments which have taken place under the heading of nuclear-secrecy-for-security which also threaten our real security. In Britain, a 1976 law set up an armed police force, practically immune from government control, in order to defend – nuclear installations! To US readers this development might seem of minor significance, a curious topic for anxiety, since they have learned to live with armed police and security guards. But then they have also learned to live with, at some cost, a murder-rate 35 times higher per head for New York alone than for Britain as a whole. The development by piecemeal methods of an armed, irresponsible police force in Britain has not been a simple 'coming into line': it has represented the disappearance of an alternative, more civilized method of policing from the debate about social self-defence. This has not enhanced citizen security.

Yet the insecurities into which nuclear secrecy has led us are deeper still than these. Tightly restricted scrutiny and oversight have permitted the covert diffusion of nuclear technology and therefore bomb-making capacity to South Africa, Brazil and Argentina via West German sources, themselves still banned from making nuclear weapons, though not from a say over their use (Jungk 1979: ch. 5). It has also enabled Israel to acquire stolen plutonium for its weapons in the USA (Jungk 1979: 124; Hilgartner 1983: 172) – plutonium losses are a problem the US nuclear industry does not submit to public scrutiny. Nuclear proliferation, given the very large number of unaccountable governments and militarized states in the world, is hardly a security measure.

It seems, then, that the argument for secrecy from national security is less unassailable than it at first appears. The history of nuclear activity is littered with tragedies, menace, waste, and has been stamped with secretiveness. It is very hard to maintain that this secrecy has been in the public interest. The argument from national security is seductive *only* because it touches a nerve of fear.

The secrecy tug-of-war

Throughout, it has been argued that government secrecy is not a fixed category. It may well be a permanent tendency in government, at least in the type of governments we currently enjoy, but it can be rolled back or it can be allowed to flourish. (The former is much harder work.)

The problem of rolling it back is that government secrecy only tends to become an issue in the course of some major symbolic crisis. In the USA, Watergate became such an issue, which could be exploited to reveal covert and illegal action by the FBI and the CIA, as well as by the President. The Freedom of Information Act 1974 was the high-water mark of this movement. Yet as Demac has demonstrated in detail, the Reagan administration has worked exceptionally hard to subvert that achievement. One key area in which media freedom was increasingly being threatened during 1984 was through stricter applications of the libel laws, long a familiar mechanism for muzzling the media in Britain through the crippling costs of an unsuccessful suit. The Burger Supreme Court – Burger was appointed Chief Justice by Nixon in 1969 – has never found in favour of the media in libel cases, and was taking active measures in 1984 to restrict appeal courts' capacity to find for the media in them. The $120 million suit brought against CBS by ex-General Westmoreland for their portrayal of his role in Vietnam was the most public instance in 1984 of the attempt to use libel laws aganst the media (see Friedman 1984; Garbus 1984).

In Britain, the Thatcher administration's first attempt to tighten the reins of secrecy still further (the Protection of Government Information Bill 1980) foundered in the exceptional publicity suddenly given to Sir Anthony Blunt, the protected fourth mole in the Philby spy case of the 1950s. The bill would have kept Blunt protected, and so Thatcher had to retreat – a nice irony. However, when 'video-nasties' came up for agitated public discussion in the early 1980s, the Thatcher administration was able to recoup some of its ground by stimulating a wave of revulsion against these loathsome but practically unavailable and unseen products, to push a censorship law through Parliament (Barker 1984).

Conclusions

We have examined the connections between state and corporate secrecy, the nature of selective communication, the relation between civil servants and the media, the conditions under which information can become power and the mythology of 'national security' as a rationale for government and corporate secrecy in the nuclear age. We have seen that for both Britain and the United States, the notion that the more economically advanced the country the more liberal and open its government is a nineteenth-century nonsense. We are faced with a persistent attempt to reduce the free flow of information and to buttress government and corporate secrecy, in the interests of business rights and supposed national security. How public commentators can simultaneously speak of the coming of the information society is difficult to grasp, unless we are to assume that life is completely reducible to bytes, that one unit of information is as useful to democracy as another.

Yet both Britain and the United States have deeply rooted cultural traditions in favour of political liberties. The question for the 1980s and to the end of the century is how many people in each country have forgotten their value, and what experiences will be lived through to revive and enact a fundamental commitment to open government. It is possible that small-scale alternative media, of the kind already referred to, will find themselves bearing a particularly large brunt of this on-going battle (see Downing 1984).

At the same time, there is a key legitimacy problem for both regimes to handle. If they are to continue to preen themselves in public on the comparison of their secrecy records with the Soviet bloc's, then their strategy for information control must diverge from that model. The art in their strategy must be exercised in picking precise areas for secrecy, delicate mechanisms for controlling the media, reserve powers 'for emergencies only', a whole tactical array for ensuring the acceptable longevity of so-called 'Centre-Right' administrations. Yet, like tax laws, the more complex the apparatus, often the greater is its potential disarray. The campaign against the secrecy of power and for media responsive to the majority is in no respect already foreclosed.

9
Gatekeeper versus Propaganda Models: A Critical American Perspective

Edward S. Herman

*C*onservatives in the United States have maintained a steady barrage of claims that the mass media are hostile to business and tend to side with enemies of the state in foreign encounters. Secretary of State Shultz, for example, explained the exclusion of US journalists during the invasion of Grenada on the grounds that in an age of 'advocacy journalism' it seems as though 'reporters are always against us' (Massing 1984: 15). Liberal and Left analysts, by contrast, find the mass media system-supportive, but even they differ sharply among themselves in perceptions of the level and effectiveness of critical news and opinion and the volume and expansibility of 'space'.

Differences persist in part because of the absence of any clear standard for judging newsworthiness and bias. Thus the conservatives can show that the businessman is often displayed on TV as a villain and that government-sponsored murders in El Salvador are featured often in the press (see Theberge 1981; McColm 1982); and they claim that the media practically singled-handedly drove a president (Nixon) out of office. These attacks are easily shown to rest on hidden premises and lack of context (Herman 1983), but they are not directly refutable by any generally accepted criteria of bias. The ambiguities in the use of evidence are suggested by the fact that liberal analysts also cite the absolute volume and quality of mass media criticism of government action on El Salvador as proof of a new media critical capacity and the great import-ance of conflict between government and media (Hallin 1983). At the same time, liberal analysts also acknowledge a great deal of co-operation between government and media in disseminating information and opinion pushed by government officials. The balance between conflict and co-operation is left uncertain, the outcome depending on the personal choice of stress of the analyst.

Newsroom gatekeeper models

The most prominent analyses of the bases of mass media choices in the United States are the liberal newsroom and 'gatekeeper' studies, as exemplified by the works of Leon Sigal (1973), Edward J. Epstein (1973), Gaye Tuchman (1978), and Herbert Gans (1979). While there are substantial differences between them, they share certain methodological characteristics and other important properties. They focus mainly on the journalists and media organizations rather than on the system at large or outside actors like government and advertisers, who enter the picture as sources, pressure groups, regulators and those just doing business with the media organizations. Their methodology involves watching and interviewing media personnel to see how they choose and decide, with much less emphasis on examining and comparing actual outputs and their consequences. They stress the organizational demands of the news media as shaping their choices directly or indirectly.

News organizations seek efficient sources of authoritative and credible news on a regular basis. These are interconnected: the more authoritative and credible the source the easier it is to accept statements without checking, and the less expensive is news-making. Furthermore, assertions of high authority are newsworthy in and of themselves; hence the paradox that even if untrue, such statements may be disseminated without qualification as 'objective' news. The source that best meets these standards is, of course, the government. An oft-cited statistic, based on the examination of 2,850 stories in the *New York Times* and *Washington Post*, shows that 46 per cent originated with US federal government officials or agencies and 78 per cent with all government officials, domestic and foreign (Sigal 1973: 124). Second only to the government as a news source is the business community, which also showers the media with a vast array of press releases from both individual firms and associated trade and public relations offshoots.

The values of the powerful also tend to dominate news choices because they make their presence felt through channels other than directly as news sources. The government is the legislator, licensor of TV and radio stations, and the executive enforcing the laws through its agencies, courts, police and army. Advertisers are the prime source of media revenues, and must be persuaded to do business with particular companies and advertise through individual programmes. On TV, network affiliates must be induced to carry particular programmes, both entertainment and news. Well-organized groups in the community can impose costs on the media organization through direct and indirect boycotts, pressures on advertisers, regulators and legislators, and other forms of harassment. The messages of the powerful are thus favoured not only by the efficiency of their offerings, but also by the costs and risks of the critical, tendentious and unfamiliar. The top leaders and owners of media enterprises, usually wealthy and conservative members of the business elite, also help set the tone of the organization by selection of managerial personnel and occasionally the imposition of policy rules.

Bureaucratic rules and professional codes help prevent a great deal of direct intervention in large media organizations on the part of powerful outsiders and top insiders (board members, large owners). For the most part, values are internalized and reproduce the choices of the powerful by a process of self-censorship. For those at the lower rungs of the news ladder, a sensitivity to the criteria of choice at the top is necessary to the production of acceptable copy. At the top of the news ladder, it is decided what news is 'the' news and what story line will be applied to the newsworthy news.

Within this framework of control, negotiation and struggle take place among media personnel and between them and outsiders anxious to get their messages across. Whatever the advantages of the powerful, however, the struggle goes on, space exists and dissident light breaks through in unexpected ways. The mass media are no monolith.

These are the main themes of the newsroom-gatekeeper studies, which have added a great deal to the understanding of media processes. But they have their limitations. With a focus on the newsroom and media organization, and without any larger frame of analysis, there has been a strong tendency in gatekeeper analyses towards the taxonomic, enumerating and discussing each of a laundry list of factors affecting choices. Considerable energy is expended in locating and evaluating cases of explicit suppression, although the consensus is that value-loading will find expression primarily in self-censorship that is itself a product of mainly internalized values. Nevertheless, the heavy focus on journalist-media criteria of choice, often illustrated by struggles within the media as recounted by media personnel, and the lack of theory and quantification, yield a bias towards a stress on the possibilities of dissent, openings and 'space'. These methodological characteristics also lend themselves to refuting the 'extremes' while leaving the main drift, the net social outcome, in a state of neglect.

Gatekeeper analyses usually do not provide any extended treatment of actual media performance and impact on ideology and opinion. They also offer little in the way of dynamics that would show how the media mobilize public opinion, or are manipulated (or co-operate) in mobilization by others. Gans, for example, notes that the sources used by the media are not merely passive, but on the contrary try to use the media for their own ends. 'More often than not, sources do the leading', says Gans (1979: 116) and he points out that the media co-operated with the government in exceptionally unprofessional ways during the Cold War. The Cold War lasted a long time, however, and could even be said to have been a central feature of US political life in the post Second World War era. The arms race and weapons 'gaps' have also been integral elements of the American polity. But Gans provides no systematic analysis of government management of the media and joint ventures by media and government, or by media and other power groups like business and its various components.

Tying together the government and other power groups and the media in some systematic way presupposes a hypothesis or theory that would allow an exploration of linkages and a testing of consequences. The liberal media analysts have no such hypotheses or theories; they employ instead a kind of *ad hoc* empiricism that limits the scope of their investigations and conclusions. Their generalizations about the tendency of the media to support the status quo are often well argued and supported, but they tend to get lost in pluralistic conflict. As an illustration, Gans eventually addresses the 'functions' of the media, noting that his work had 'largely ignored the intriguing possibility that journalists and their firms were pawns of larger and more basic social processes to which they unwittingly respond' (Gans 1979: 290). What follows is another laundry list, this time of 'functions', that include some that the media ought to be performing and others that they do perhaps perform. Gans states that these are 'speculative', but of one of them he feels 'somewhat more certain', namely 'that one of the journalists' prime functions is to manage, with others, the symbolic arena, the public stage on which national, societal, and other messages are made available to everyone who can become an audience member (*ibid.*: 298). Is it managed to a purpose? How? With what effects? Gans notes that Marcuse on the left maintains that the mass media control by depoliticizing and diverting, and that Ellul on the right proposes that the mass media supply propaganda that victimizes poorly-educated audiences. While admitting some truth in these claims, Gans says that 'the charge attributes too much power to journalists and too little common sense to the audience' (*ibid*.: 296). But if the journalists 'manage' the symbolic arena 'with others' their conjoint powers may be great, and the common sense of audiences as an adequate offset demands an analysis and data that Gans fails to provide. He leaves his excursion into the broad picture contradictory and undeveloped.

A propaganda model

An alternative way of looking at the workings of the mass media which the present writer has found fruitful is based on the media's sharply dichotomous treatment of similar events which differ primarily in their political implications. I will call this a 'propaganda model', as it lends itself well to analysing the numerous and important cases where the mass media serve as instruments in campaigns of ideological mobilization. The term 'model' is used because it is possible to stipulate a set of behavioural actions and reactions of the media that is systematic although not as yet formalized and quantified. A propaganda model rests on certain structural and power assumptions and observations which constitute a background to analysing the mechanics, behaviour and performance of the mass media. It identifies the main power foci within the media and those in the larger community that are able, with and through the mass media, to mobilize bias. The stress, however, is on the management of the symbolic arena by this power collective.

The US mass media are highly concentrated, with about a dozen entities capable of establishing newsworthiness by their own decisions. The top dozen would include the three TV networks (CBS, ABC and NBC), four major newspapers (the *New York Times, Washington Post, Los Angeles Times* and *Wall Street Journal*) and five magazines (*Time, Newsweek, U.S. News and World Report, T.V. Guide* and *Readers Digest*). This list is somewhat arbitrary and could be expanded modestly (prominent candidates would be AP, UPI and Reuters) or contracted, but the list with agenda-setting powers does not run much over a dozen. They are all large business enterprises, heavily dependent on advertising for revenue and linked to other large firms by business and personal ties. A number of these entities have been owned and dominated by strongly conservative individuals and families who have pushed an aggressively ideological line in their controlled firms. The best-known have been *Readers Digest*, wholly owned by the very conservative Wallace family, the Luce Empire, including *Time* and *Life* magazines, and the Hearst empire, comprising mainly daily newspapers. Others are owned by corporate conglomerate parents. Some are controlled by the corporate managers themselves, although their domination is constrained by many market-oriented forces that keep them focused on the bottom line and stock prices (see Herman 1981: 85–113). All are direct members or subsidiaries of important constituents of the corporate community. When a large proportion of that community is agitated about an issue or trend, such as heightened labour aggressiveness, the encroachments of the welfare state, or revolutionary nationalism in the Third World, we would expect the large corporate media to reflect these attitudes and to respond accordingly.

The government is also a major factor in a centralized news production and dissemination system as legislator, regulator, fiscal manager, director of foreign policy and primary media news source. In foreign policy especially the government's unique position as a source, and its ability to rely on media loyalty in the face of conflict, give it tremendous manipulative powers. The collective power of the government and a normally co-operative mass media is very great. In tandem, they are able to use an effective monopoly over the symbolic arena in an area where nationalism and ignorance also make their work easy. They have the capacity not only to virtually suppress inconvenient facts and analyses, but also to orchestrate the dissemination of more serviceable new ones. A propaganda model assumes that this concentrated power to manage the public will be used; that the mass media will be periodically mobilized to serve the 'national interest' when this is needed and/or when national or international events present useful opportunities. It focuses on the numerous and important cases where the public is effectively managed and major ideological points are scored. In short, it addresses the main drift in the building of consensus and ideology rather than the individual episodes of struggle over a particular story and the exceptions at the margins.

The structure of the mass media and its relation to government and the corporate community suggest that joint propaganda service and ideology-building by this power collective should be normal and effective, with profound implications for news choices. Thus, even a cursory examinination of media behaviour reveals a systematic selectivity of coverage based on a division between the nation and its allies versus its foreign enemies. The US mass media, for example, tend to focus often and indignantly on the trials and tribulations of dissidents in enemy states while ignoring equally or more severe victimization in the 'colonies'. This dichotomous treatment extends not merely to isolated news items; there is also an observable tendency for enemy victims to be subject to intense coverage, virtual campaigns of day in/day out attention, which are almost never applied to victims in friendly states. An earlier tabulation by this writer showed that between 1 January 1976 and 30 June 1981 Andrei Sakharov was not only mentioned in 228 separate news articles in the *New York Times*, he was subject to intensive coverage on eight different occasions in that period (see Herman 1982: 197). During 1984, an even larger campaign was under way featuring Sakharov. No victim within the Free World has had remotely comparable coverage. A distinguished mathematician and former member of the Uruguayan parliament, José Luis Massera, was treated far more severely than Sakharov during the 1976–84 years (he was tortured as well as imprisoned), but he has been barely mentioned in the US media. This contrast is the rule, not the exception, and can be demonstrated across the board (Herman 1982: ch. 4).

The same treatment is applicable to any international events that might put the enemy or ourselves and allies in a bad light. For example, the alleged Bulgarian and KGB plot to assassinate Pope John Paul II in May 1981 generated enormous publicity in the United States, as did the crisis and installation of martial law in Poland. By contrast, the revelation (United States Senate 1975: 67–131) that the United States had participated in at least eight assassination attempts against Fidel Castro received quite muted attention. Further, the installation of martial law and severe repression in Turkey, which occurred in the same period as the events in Poland, received only passing mention in the United States (Herman 1982: 208–9).

These dichotomies have great ideological significance. The real and alleged misdeeds of the enemy, attended to according to opportunity and on a massive scale, serve to convince the public of a serious external threat and the need to arm according to plans conveniently already well under way. The playing down and rationalization of 'own' crimes and repression in friendly client states allows maintenance of the image of national beneficence, in contrast with the enemy proclivity to assassinate leaders and repress labour and democratic movements. It is a useful working hypothesis that massive publicity campaigns will be well timed to provide the ideological mobilization sought by important domestic power groups. The Red Scare of 1919-20 in the United States, for example, occurred at a time of threatening labour organization strongly opposed by the business community and it helped quash this threat (Herman 1982: 38–41). Senator Joseph McCarthy and the Red Scare associated with his name in the late 1940s and early 1950s served well to weaken the old New Deal reform coalition and replace it with a Cold War-arms race-growth alignment. The Bulgarian Connection was discovered and transformed into a major publicity campaign coincidentally with the heightened tension between the United States (and its allies, including Italy) and the Soviet Union over the placement of advanced new missiles in Western Europe (see Brodhead and Herman 1983).

Built on the hypothesis that news dichotomies and campaigns have a purpose and role, a propaganda framework lends itself to looking at the dynamics of media campaigns and identifying the sources, the conditions in which campaigns thrive and the mechanisms for originating claims, getting them disseminated widely and deflecting or neutralizing counterfacts and analyses. It also lends itself to close examination of the mechanics of media campaigns and the characteristics of news coverage during these periods. Briefly, the mass media and government can make an event 'newsworthy' merely by giving it their attention. By the same token, they can make another event that on the face of it would appear newsworthy by normal criteria, a non-happening for the bulk of the population. The government and mass media having decided that a particular story is worthy, and giving it publicity, public interest is aroused and the lesser media must follow to meet the demand for more of the same. Thus the 'news' is spread further through the community and its importance reinforced. The United States is so important and powerful as a leader of the Free World that when its government and news media decide that something is really newsworthy, the 'fraternal' media of its allies tend to follow in their wake, just as the lesser media at home do with respect to their national leaders.

When a news story becomes the subject of a durable campaign, publicity is not only intensive, it quickly goes beyond hard news to opinion, speculation and trivia. The rules of evidence are suspended and the media display little restraint in passing on implausible claims of fact and speculation without critical evaluation. Incompatible fact and opinion are brushed aside in a tidal wave of predetermined line and story. Another feature of such campaigns is that moral indignation is great in describing the depths to which the enemy has descended. A further characteristic is that as accumulating evidence is assembled showing the propaganda claims were exaggerated or untrue, the mass media will give it a minor attention at best and will not engage in retrospectives or apologies to the accused of earlier stories or to the audiences receiving their messages. These characteristics of propaganda campaigns will be illustrated below in a case study of media treatment of the 1983 Soviet shooting down of a Korean airliner.

I would hardly claim that this approach to investigating the mass media is the only fruitful one or applicable on every topic. The elephant is a large one and analysis that provides insight on a hind leg or, better, the general shape of the animal would be meritorious. This approach has been especially useful in looking at foreign policy issues, where propaganda campaigns and systematic dichotomization between us and them have been conspicuous and important. These may be explored with a great deal of profit without specifying the precise lines of causation and mechanisms whereby economic and political power are translated into media behaviour. Obviously the underlying causes and mechanisms are worthy of continuing investigation and may well yield a deeper understanding of the issues – but relating complex economic, political and media structures to media behaviour has not provided us with predictive models as yet. If media behaviour can be related to more global political and economic factors with suggestive hypotheses and insights, this would seem a useful basis for investigation pending the emergence of a more detailed structurally based explanatory model.

This approach has the merit of simplicity. It stresses dichotomization and pairing, thus providing a basis for the evaluation of objectivity and bias without resort to the explanations and rationalizations of the participants. It provides a way of looking at the media and asking questions within a larger framework of analysis than the gatekeeper models. The latter look at the news today, that is, discrete episodes, rather than parts of a larger news fabric, such as the handling of the Soviet threat or the Cold War. As noted, Gans states that the media 'cooperated' with the government during the Cold War. 'Perhaps no one thought twice because the Cold War itself was taken for granted and supported; in addition, cooperation did not interfere with getting the news' (Gans 1979: 271). If he had treated the Cold War as more than a fleeting episode a different model of news formation, ideology and objectivity would have been required.

By taking a larger unit of analysis, one necessarily raises the question of purpose in media choices as seen by all the actors who participate in supplying and disseminating information. The government may be the active manager of an information campaign trying to achieve some public relations objectives, not a passive source. If this is the case, it may be useful to examine carefully how the government formulates issues, manipulates symbols, elicits co-operation from the media and counters dissonant facts and claims.

This writer found a propaganda framework very helpful in trying to understand the mass media's handling of the elections in El Salvador in

1982 and 1984 (Herman and Brodhead 1984: ch. 5; Herman 1984). Those elections were staged by the US government for a distinctly propagandistic purpose, namely, to try to counter the opposition to intervention and the negative image of the Salvadoran regime at home by demonstrating to the American public, Congress and the world that the United States supported democracy, that the rebels in El Salvador opposed it and that the election outcome showed popular approval of the existing regime and US plans. The government used a powerful and effective symbolic format and had a definite agenda of relevant facts (closely similar to those employed in a US-sponsored election in South Vietnam in September 1967). It strove first to identify elections with democracy and to associate the Salvadoran government and army with these positive symbols. It stressed also the rebel unwillingness to participate and their alleged threats to disrupt the elections, interpreted as a rejection of 'democracy'. Finally, it identified voter 'turn-out' with popular Salvadoran rejection of the rebels and approval of the military regime.

Successful implementation of this symbolic framework required that the media use it and follow a related agenda of suitable and unsuitable facts. It was necessary to play down the fact that the rebels couldn't and weren't intended to run, and to avoid discussion of basic electoral conditions that might explain turn-out in terms other than popular support of the army. During the 1982 election, no mention whatsoever was made in the US mass media of the fact that voting was legally obligatory, that transparent voting urns were used, that the ballots were numbered and that the head of the army had announced in the Salvadoran newspapers that non-voting was an act of treason. The basic parameters that make an election meaningful or meaningless in advance – freedom of speech and the press, the rights of groups to organize and survive, and the ability of candidates to qualify and campaign without fear of murder – were almost entirely ignored in both 1982 and 1984. The background facts of a state of siege and over 500 civilian murders per *month* from 1980 onwards were deemed not relevant to evaluating electoral conditions or turn-out.

This treatment of the Salvadoran elections is in dramatic contrast with the media's handling of enemy-sponsored elections, where we can observe a complete reversal of symbolism and agenda of relevant facts. There the focus is on the basic parameters of an election that must be met in advance. Coercion by the government is pushed front and centre, and turn-out becomes a measure of coercion instead of approval of the government and its agenda. In connection with an election staged in January 1947 in a Soviet client state, Poland, the very *presence* of large numbers of security forces was found by the US media to compromise the electoral process and render the election a farce in advance (Herman and Brodhead 1984: 179). Only the security forces of client states 'protect elections'; those of enemy states interfere with the freedom of its citizens to vote without constraint.

The same dichotomization and bias was evident in press treatment of the Nicaraguan election of November 1984. The US media focused unremittingly on the limits on the press and rights of candidates to run and campaign in Nicaragua. The US government, desiring to discredit this election, called attention to constraints on freedom of the press and, particularly, the unwillingness of Arturo José Cruz to run. The media focused incessantly on Cruz, his charges and refusal to compete, and their implications for fairness. In connection with the Salvadoran election, where the rebel Democratic Front was off the ballot from the beginning by necessity and plan, this more decisive exclusion of the 'main opposition' from the election was entirely ignored by the US media and was not deemed relevant to fairness or meaning. A detailed comparison of the *New York Times*'s coverage of the 1984 Salvadoran elections and plans for the one in Nicaragua showed, for example, that of 28 articles on the Salvadoran election not a single one discussed freedom of the press, whereas of eight articles on the Nicaraguan election six treated freedom of the press, usually in some detail (Herman 1984: 10–11). This is not because freedom of the press is greater in El Salvador; the press has been less free (*ibid.*: 120–1). Nor is the dichotomous treatment confined to this one topic – the duality of treatment according to a patriotic agenda is systematic.

In these cases of markedly dichotomous treatment of elections, it seems clear that a propaganda model provides an insight that is lost in the gatekeeper laundry list. It is true that the gatekeeper analyses recognize that powerful sources like the government and the internalized values of journalists help to shape media choices. But these hardly prepare us for the depth of bias and the extent of asymmetrical treatment which is revealed by a politically based analysis and the pairing of similar events with different political implications.

The shooting down of the KAL 007: a case study

The utility of a propaganda model format is well illustrated by the history of the US mass media's handling of the 1983 Soviet shooting down of the Korean airliner KAL 007. The incident was extremely convenient to Reagan administration and New Cold War propaganda needs, and it occurred at a time when public fears and patriotic fervour had already been well prepared in advance. The Reagan administration and media took full advantage of an opportunity to score propaganda points. In the course of this triumph, the subordination of truth to propaganda needs was pronounced and of durable effect.

The basic facts of the case

Korean airliner KAL 007 was shot down by a Soviet fighter pilot during the night of 31 August 1983, with 269 passengers and crew members killed in the action. The huge Western outcry which immediately ensued was based not only on the act itself, but on the context of the incident as portrayed by the US government and mass media. The crucial claims were that: (1) the plane had flown over Soviet territory by error; (2) the plane had been identified by the Soviets as a civilian plane; and (3) that the Korean plane had not been properly warned, or had failed to respond to warnings because of technical malfunctioning. This combination of claims sustained a highly negative conclusion on Soviet international behaviour. The Soviets initially denied shooting down the plane, then claimed that it was on a spying mission. While expressing regret over the loss of life, the Soviet Union refused to apologize. Thus, to the other bases of recrimination, the Soviets were accused of lying and callousness.

Subsequent revelations and analyses have subsequently undermined the entire initial set of US accusations. On the alleged inadvertence of the overflight of Soviet territory, the evidence, still largely circumstantial, now suggests a strong probability that 007 was an integral part of a surveillance mission. Direct pilot observation of position (over land, not water), multiple and independent navigational aids, and advisories from perhaps a half-dozen US and allied tracking facilities that must have been watching the flight, should have given early and ample warning of a two-hour dangerously off-course flight if this had been unplanned (Pearson 1984). Furthermore, an RC-135 surveillance craft flew quite near 007 and could have communicated with it, and would have been in position to fly side-by-side with 007 in a radar-confusing pattern, as the Soviets claim it did. A Ferret surveillance satellite and the Shuttle flight which took off from Cape Canaveral on 30 August were in a position to co-ordinate with 007 at the exact time it flew over Soviet military installations. And not only was the 007 going over extremely sensitive Soviet facilities, the Soviets were scheduled to send aloft a new missile on the night of 31 August 1983.

182

There is other circumstantial evidence pointing in the same direction. Although the point had not been confirmed, a Japanese paper claims that Congressman Larry McDonald, killed on the flight, was warned beforehand not to take the flight. Thames Television programme *TV Eye*, in its July segment entitled *007 – Licensed to Spy?*, disclosed that an electrical maintenance worker at Anchorage air-traffic control was instructed to turn off a major radar feed an hour-and-a-half before the 007 take off. The Soviets claim that 007 had an additional complement of five crew members beyond the normal.

Thus, at this juncture, the most plausible hypothesis is that 007 was serving to activate Soviet radar and to test Soviet responses to radar confusion tactics. It is possible that 007 had surveillance or radar-jamming equipment on board. Both the 007 pilot and the KAL airline itself had long-standing relations with the Korean CIA, and the use of commercial airlines for spying purposes by US intelligence has a long history. A commercial airline may have been employed to reduce the probability that the Soviets would shoot the plane down. Whether this is so or not, if KAL 007 was part of a surveillance mission its 269 passengers and crew were hostages by US and South Korean official choice.

US officials and mass media claimed immediately and vociferously that the Soviets had deliberately shot down a recognizably civilian plane. *Newsweek* even quoted from alleged taped conversations of the Soviet pilot referring to a 'KAL airliner', but withdrew this later as unverified though the correction was not given as much prominence as the original allegation. The claim of Soviet recognition of 007's being a civilian craft was based mainly on the alleged uniqueness of the shape of a Boeing 747. In fact, a US airforce command and control plane, the E–4, has a size and shape identical to 007, a point not mentioned by the US media. Furthermore, that the silhouette of the plane would be visible to the Soviet pilot was simply assumed without discussion. Five weeks after the event, it was finally reported that the CIA was now of the opinion that the Soviets had *not* recognized that 007 was a civilian plane (see Shribman 1983). This was based on an analysis of the tapes of the Soviet pilot's exchanges with his ground command and other intelligence data. As these materials were surely available within a very few hours, it follows that the assertions of Reagan, Shultz and Kirkpatrick that the Soviets had knowingly shot down a civilian aircraft were deliberate lies. The Soviet lie dwelt on by the US media – the denial of having shot down the plane – was a lie of momentary confusion that would not fool anybody; the US lie was more devious and serious, based on suppressed information, and it fooled people on a worldwide basis (and continues to deceive them up to today despite an unpublicized retraction).

The Soviet failure to warn the airliner was another important claim and feature of the official media portrayal of a cold-blooded massacre. Mrs Kirkpatrick provided a carefully-edited and interpreted version of the taped interchange between the Soviet pilot and ground to prove the point, and the media followed uncritically. Her version, while presented to the UN as complete and unedited, omitted entirely the part of the tape showing that the pilot had fired warning shots six minutes before the attack. Former CIA chief Stanfield Turner found it 'difficult to divine' why the pilot of 007 failed to respond to the Soviet signals and took evasive action (quoted in Gervasi 1984), but the US line later changed to the contention that the pilot missed the Soviet signals – unproven and incompatible with evasive action.

The media response
The media response to the shooting down of 007 was extraordinary in volume and passion. The *New York Times* had 147 news items on the incident in September 1983 alone, covering 2,789 column inches of space. For ten consecutive days, a special section of the newspaper was devoted to the case. CBS Evening News attended to the event on 26 separate evenings from 31 August to 30 September. *Time* and *Newsweek* each had three long and emotional articles on the subject in September, occupying a remarkable total of 1,490 column inches between them.

Paralleling the volume was the passion. The titles of the opening articles by *Time* and *Newsweek* illustrate the general pattern – 'A Ruthless Ambush in the Sky' (*Newsweek*, 12 September 1983) and 'Atrocity in the Sky' (*Time*, 12 September). For the US media, this was a 'wanton slaughter' and 'deliberate cold-blooded murder'. Continuous attention was paid to the painful details of the sufferings of the relatives of the victims, the attempt to salvage the debris and the fury and denunciations of Western officials and personalities. The press spent a great deal of space describing the exchanges between the Soviet pilot and ground station (as edited by US officials) – 'The controller ordered him to fire. Pilot: "The target is destroyed. I am breaking off attack"' – which allowed them to convey the impression of cold-bloodedness. The extreme indignation came immediately, and served well to certify the truth and make it difficult as well as unnecessary to raise questions of fact.

The main source of fact and interpretation for the US mass media was

US government officials, who were invariably quoted as if disinterested parties. Soviet officials were the prime source of an alternative view, but they were not treated as objective. They were also usually cited in a sequence in which the official US view was vindicated. Almost never did the US mass media cite interpretations by domestic critics. As Soviet officials lack credibility in the United States, their predominant use as the opposition source is a form of 'straw man' citation and should be seen as a feature of biased reporting. This is a specific instance of a general media ploy of using weak or discredited individuals as the spokespersons for positions opposed by the media. A classic illustration is the *New York Times*'s choice for a long article following the Vietnamese defeat of the United States in April 1975. On the 18th they ran an item 'purportedly' written by Bernadine Dohrn, of the Weather Underground and on the FBI's ten-most-wanted list, entitled 'Of Defeat and Victory'.

The US government pressed relentlessly for an 'accounting', for a Soviet admission of guilt, for reparations, and the media did the same, a pressure strategy captured well in the title of one *Newsweek* article, 'Keeping the Heat on Moscow' (26 September 1983). When Moscow finally got round to a serious presentation of its position, while some segments of the media conveyed the Soviet claims, usually with great brevity and automatic US denials, the media felt no obligation to examine them closely or check them out. In the midst of the initial propaganda onslaught a number of questions had already arisen, including, for example, certain peculiarities of the flight (delayed take-off, extra gallonage of fuel), and the proximity of the RC-135 which the Soviets say ran alongside 007 for a while and which two former RC-135 pilots claimed would have been monitoring 007 closely (see Pearson 1984). Despite all of these controversial issues and the real possibility that the media may have been gulled into transmitting lies, the mass media did not rush into investigative action. Following the initial vast outpouring, silence prevailed, except for occasional reiterations of the established view.

New developments came entirely from investigators unconnected with the mass media. In May 1984 *Evergreen Review* carried a long, factual article by Tom Gervasi, 'Reckless Endangerment: the Attack on Korean Airlines Flight 7 and America's Response', which analysed a wide range of contradictions in the conventional account and misstatements by US leaders. In June 1984 *Defence Attaché* magazine in England published an article by P. Q. Mann (a pseudonym), 'Reassessing the Sakhalin Incident', which made a persuasive case that 007 was part of a spying mission tied in with both an overflight of a Ferret satellite and the Space Shuttle, launched from Cape Canaveral on the day before the 007 episode. The article showed that both the Ferret and Shuttle would have been in surveillance positions coincident with the 007 overflight and it suggested co-ordination with the RC-135 which met 007 and 'pursued a coincident path for some nine or ten minutes – the "dummy selling tactics"'. A more elaborate analysis of the contradictions in the US case was presented by David Pearson in *The Nation* 18–25 August 1984: 'K.A.L. 007: What the U.S. Knew and When we Knew It'. Pearson did not stress the co-ordination of 007, the Shuttle, Ferret and RC-135; instead he made a powerful case that the 007 equipment, radar, radio and the large number of US and Japanese monitoring facilities make it extremely improbable that the 007 course was not planned.

The media response to the new data and arguments fits the propaganda model extremely well. The US government has, of course, ridiculed the claims of a non-innocent flight, appealing to the findings of the International Civil Aviation Organization (ICAO) that there is no evidence that 007 was spying, and suggesting that the new claims are Soviet propaganda. The media followed closely in the government's wake. Gervasi's article was ignored entirely. The *Defence Attaché* article, published in a magazine catering to the defence establishment and providing considerable historical background and technical detail on US spying activities involving satellites, was harder to ignore. It was mentioned in a number of papers, getting a fair summary in the *Washington Post* and less satisfactory accounts in a number of other papers. Many papers, including the *New York Times*, ignored it altogether, and so did the major TV networks and news magazines. The Nation article was given very minor attention in the Press. The author Pearson did appear on CBS's *Today* show and was given one minute of time on ABC, but TV coverage was otherwise absent. At the time of the first anniversary of the event, the US mass media found that nothing had changed but a new Soviet propaganda campaign.

Table 9.1 US media coverage of the KAL 007 incident

Period of assessment:	*Month of September 1983*		*1 April–30 September 1984*			
	(1)	*(2)*	*(3)*	*(4)*	*(5)*	*(6)*
	# of articles	*Col. inches*	*# of articles*	*Col. inches*	*(3) as % of (1)*	*(4) as % of (2)*
New York Times	147	2,789	9	202	6	7
Time and Newsweek	6	1,490	1	30	17	2

Table 9.1 compares the news coverage of September 1983 alone in the *New York Times, Newsweek* and *Time* magazine with the volume offered by these media for the six-month period ending 30 September 1984. The latter period may be regarded as one of reassessment, when new facts and interpretations were being put forward and questions were being raised by non-official sources. It may be seen that these three leading media enterprises, which had passed on the official line in phenomenal volume and with almost complete patriotic credulity, felt no obligation to participate in the reassessment. And a closer examination of their performance shows that they were still playing the role of conduit for an official line.

Time magazine's single article in the period of reassessment, 'Fallout From Flight 007' (10 September), featured 'the inevitable conspiracy theories that are attracting worldwide, and often uncritical, attention'. *Time* disposes of these by quoting a US intelligence expert that there is 'a massive, overt disinformation campaign' by the Soviet Union (no details given); and by citing a whole series of US officials denying charges. *Time* dismisses the *Defence Attaché* article as 'unusually speculative' (no details given), while Pearson is dismissed as a 'graduate student' writing up a 'more elaborate theory' in a 'leftist magazine'. Actually, Pearson's effort was untheoretical, confined almost entirely to empirical evidence. Pearson was important enough for *Time* to feel obligated to use *two* official denials to repudiate. *Time* also resorts to what it calls 'the only authoritative investigation into the disaster', that conducted by the ICAO, which found no evidence of a spy mission. *Time* failed to mention that ICAO acknowledged its inability to get important data from the United States and Soviet Union, and its own technical arm, the Air Navigation Commission, took issue with the findings of the original report.

The *New York Times* did run a front-page story on 7 October 1983 which featured the CIA's admission that the Soviets had not known the 007 was a civilian aircraft. This was highly significant, not only upsetting an important leg of the deliberate civilian murder theme but also showing that US officials had knowingly lied in order to score political points. The *Times* did not draw this conclusion or discuss the implications of the admission, nor did it apologize for its editorial rhetoric grounded on an official fabrication. Thereafter, furthermore, the *New York Times* regressed into a combination of suppression and occasional parroting of the disintegrating official line. Its investigative resources appear never to have been applied to this subject, despite the enormous lacunae and opportunities. The articles by Gervasi, *Defence Attaché* and Pearson were unreported in its news columns, except for a few down-putting asides. The first mention of the *Defence Attaché* article appeared in a small back-page item on 8 July 1984, which featured Soviet refusals to pay compensation for the KAL losses. The source is an unnamed Washington official, who refers to *Defence Attaché* as 'supposedly a reputable magazine'. The article closes with the official suggesting a Soviet propaganda plot. The content of the article in *Defence Attaché* was not summarized even briefly. The first mention of the Pearson article was in a 31 August 1984 article datelined Moscow, by the *Time*'s Moscow correspondent Serge Schmemann entitled 'Soviet Is Pressing Its Case on KAL 007'. Again, the criticisms in the West are tied in with an alleged Soviet propaganda campaign. This is the core of an Op Ed column, also on 31 August 1984, by Richard Burt, a public information official of the State Department, who was assigned by the *New York Times* to summarize the state of the case one year later.

In sum, following the initial flood of US- sponsored claims, the media showed no inclination during the next year to investigate the many unsettled questions and were reluctant to report and discuss new facts and alternative interpretations put forward by others. With their government stonewalling and claiming that these new ideas were part of a Soviet propaganda campaign, the media did the same. There was a small quantum of seepage into the mass media, The Pearon article's findings found their way into the *New York Times* by means of two columns by Tom Wicker, plus a full-page ad taken by *The Nation* magazine to convey the message and win interest in the magazine. But it was not enough to cause the vast majority of the population to have any reason to doubt the original version of the case.

The dichotomies

A propaganda model suggests that the volume and character of coverage of an incident like the downing of 007 will be a function of political serviceability. The shooting down of 007 was enormously useful to Reagan and his associates. The early news reports and comment on the case noted that the United States was scoring valuable political points, and in a year-later retrospective published on 31 August 1984 Bernard Gwertzman of the *New York Times* writes complacently that US officials 'assert that worldwide criticism of the Soviet handling of the crisis has strengthened the United States in its relations with Moscow'. At no point do Gwertzman or his colleagues ever suggest that these political benefits might *help to* explain the volume or tone of the campaign, or that it was less than a natural and just outcry of independent opinion.

Table 9.2 US mass media coverage of the KAL 007 incident and four cases involving the destruction of civilian aircraft of unfriendly powers[a]

	KAL 007 1983	Angola 1983	Cuba 1976	Libya– Israel 1973	Air India 1955
Number of deaths in incident	269	126	73	108	15
Number of articles in *New York Times*	147	3	25	25	26
Expected # of articles in *NYT*[b]	(147)	69	40	59	9
Number of column inches in *NYT*	2,789	10	270	488	323
Expected # of col. inches in *NYT*[b]	(2,789)	1,311	1,531	1,116	167
Number of articles in *Time* and *Newsweek*	6	0	2	2	4
Expected # of articles in *Time* and *Newsweek*[b]	(6)	3	2	2	1
Column inches in *Time* and *Newsweek*	1,490	0	46	130	18
Expected # of col. inches in *Time* and *Newsweek*[b]	(1,490)	700	402	596	89

[a] The four cases, Angolan, a Cuban, a Libyan and an Air India aircraft, are described in the text. Air India was not a carrier of an unfriendly power, but in this particular case its plane was chartered to carry passengers of an unfriendly power (China).

[b] The expected number of articles and column inches is based on the deaths/number of articles (or column inches) ratio for the *New York Times*, and for *Time* and *Newsweek* together, in their coverage of the KAL 007 incident. This is then applied to the number of deaths in the other four cases to yield a proportionate level of coverage, which is the expected number.

On 8 November 1983, in the midst of the KAL 007 furore, Savimbi's UNITA successfully shot down an Angolan airliner, killing all 126 passengers. Table 9.2 shows that *Newsweek* and *Time* magazines never mentioned the incident; the *New York Times* had three tiny wire service notices aggregating ten inches of space. On the basis of purely humanistic concerns for passenger victims, that is, proportionality, based on 007 numbers we would have forecast for the *New York Times* 1,311 column inches on the Angolan event (126/269 × 2,789) and 700 column inches in *Time* and *Newsweek*. The heavily-political basis of the large shortfall is suggested by a headline placed over one of the tiny *New York Times* articles of 11 November 1983: 'Pro-West Angolan Rebels Say They Downed Plane'. Savimbi is an ally of South Africa and the rest of the Free World. Of course the victims also included no Americans, only unknown black people. But the American press is capable of deep emotion and devoted attention to distant peoples, for example, Cambodians and Miskito Indians in Nicaragua.

Table 9.2 also refers to three other cases where commercial airlines were shot down or blown up by planted bombs, but where 'enemy' airlines or passengers were victimized. It can be seen that US media attention was relatively modest in volume in these cases, with the exception of the 1955 Air India incident, the reasons for which are discussed below. Even more interesting than the relative volume is the objective tone and complete absence of indignation in these cases. In the 1955 incident, an Air India plane carrying 11 high Chinese officials from Hong Kong to Bandung was blown up, with 15 casualties. The *New York Times* headline of 12 April 1955 describing the incident stated '11 Reds in Air Crash on Way to Parley'. Chinese Premier Chou En-Lai had been scheduled to fly on that plane, but plans were changed causing him to miss that flight. The Chinese accused the United States of sabotage, which the United States denied. The media coverage of the incident was relatively extensive in terms of number of casualties, accounted for by the fact that the plane was carrying a large number of diplomats of a great power in an era of great international tension. But while voluminous, the coverage was quite matter-of-fact and completely lacking in expressions of outrage. The British Foreign Office found the incident 'unfortunate'. Given the severe criticism by Western commentators of the fact that the Soviet leaders would not apologize for 007 but would only express 'regret' at the loss of life, it is interesting to note that US officials in 1955 wouldn't even go so far as to express *regret* for the loss of Chinese Communist life: 'The officials say that the United States had nothing to do with the crash of the airliner [possibly untrue] and they see no useful purpose in a *deploring* [emphasis added] statement' (Abel 1955).

The Chinese claim of US complicity was 'vicious nonsense' and 'without a shred of evidence' according to a *New York Times* editorial of 15 April 1955. Drew Middleton referred to the 'supposed sabotage' of the Air India plane, and elsewhere the *New York Times* puts sabotage in quotation marks, suggesting doubts. United Press also refers to Peiping's 'propaganda broadcasts' suggesting sabotage. Even after an Indonesian Commission which had recovered the plane found the case to be one of sabotage by a planted bomb, A. M. Rosenthal on 31 May 1955 still referred to the 'alleged sabotage'. The Hong Kong police called the incident a case of 'carefully planned mass murder', language never duplicated in the US press. In November 1967 an American defector in Moscow, John Discoe Smith, charged that the CIA was involved in the Air India bombing, and that he himself had delivered a suitcase containing the explosive mechanism to a Chinese Nationalist in Hong Kong (Urquart 1972: 121–2) This statement was not mentioned in the five articles in the *New York Times* which discussed Smith.

The sabotage bombing of a Cuban airliner in 1976 caused only the slightest ripple in the US press, although this was a deliberate terrorist act in an era when the United States was very agitated about terrorism. The news coverage was again very matter-of-fact, totally lacking in regrets, in the use of strong language, or appeals for anti-terrorist action. Although the perpetrators of the act were Cuban refugee terrorists trained by the CIA, this point was mentioned in passing and led to no suggestions of 'surrogates' or other reflections on responsibility. When the principals in the bombing were eventually released by the Venezuelans (see Herman 1982: 68–9), this was not a *cause célèbre* in the US media. *Newsweek* noted that Bosch had been out of a US jail on parole, which he violated and jumped in 1974, and that a year previously 'Venezula offered to send Bosch back to the US, but Washington refused to take him on the grounds that he was an undesirable alien'. Although he had violated parole and should have been returned to prison, and was a world-class terrorist to boot, *Newsweek* raised no further questions and exhibited not a whit of surprise or indignation at the USA's behaviour.

The most interesting case concerns the Israeli shooting down of a Libyan airliner in 1973 with 108 lives lost. This incident offers a number of parallels with 007: it was Israeli military aircraft that shot the plane down; there was tense political conflict and Israeli security was brought into the picture as an explanation and an excuse for the Israeli action; and the Israelis, like the Soviets, while expressing regret at the loss of life refused to apologize or take blame for the act. The Israeli view, expressed initially by Minister of Defence Moshe Dayan, was that 'the blame lay with the pilot because he ignored repeated instructions to land' (see T. Smith 1973). An important difference in the two cases is that there was never any doubt that the Israelis knew they were shooting down a civilian plane. Despite this, the US government and media never suggested that this was 'deliberate murder' and the Israeli knowledge that its victim was a civilian aircraft was never considered a point of special interest. As noted, the US government suppressed the fact that the Soviets *didn't* know 007 was a civilian plane, and it and the mass media played furiously on the fact that the Soviets had killed civilians.

The 007 flight went over very sensitive Soviet installations in a context of active US surveillance activity. The Libyan airliner did not overfly analogous installations and there was definite and uncontested

Table 9.3 Differential language used by *Newsweek* and *Time* in describing the Soviet and Israeli destruction of a civilian airliner

Strong words applied to Soviet action	Strong words applied to Israeli action
ambush	aggression
angry (2)[a]	assault
assassination	blunder
atrocity	disaster (3)[a]
barbaric (2)	disheartening
callous	error
chilling	fury[b]
cold-blooded (2)	ill-fated
crime (3)	incident (2)
deliberate (2)	outrage[b]
evil (2)	over-reacted
heinous	shocked (3)
horrible	siege mentality
inexcusable	tragedy
liars (2)	unpardonable breach
murder-murderous (2)	of international
outrage (5)	decency
reprehensible	
revulsion	
slaughter	
terrorist	
tragedy	
wanton	

Source: A compilation of strong words used in *Newsweek* and *Time* in their first articles following each incident: 5 March 1973 and 12 September 1983.

[a] Number in parentheses is number of times the word was used.
[b] Words attributed to Arab sources but quoted in the US journals.

evidence that it was lost in a sandstorm. In both cases warnings were given and were either ignored or misunderstood. The Soviet act elicited a frenzied and sustained outcry of recrimination. The Israeli act was greeted in the West with understanding, forbearance and a complete absence of recrimination or threat. There was never a suggestion that the Israelis were proving their low regard for human life. The variation in word usage is illuminating. In Table 9.3, all the strong and invidious words used in the articles immediately following each episode are reproduced from *Time* and *Newsweek*. It is strikingly evident that invidious words are not used in reference to Israeli actions, while there are no holds barred in using extreme language in denigrating the Soviets. US allies 'blunder'; only the enemy deliberately 'murders'. Given the facts of the respective cases, this can only reflect political bias. The bias is thrown into sharper focus by the fact that the same violent language freely employed against the Soviets in the US media was regularly applied to Israel by the Arabs. In a front-page story the *New York Times* on 22 February quoted a Libyan official as describing the Israeli action as a 'criminal act'. The quick resort to such harsh language by the Arab states is frequently regarded in the West as a manifestation of authoritarianism and its propaganda. The symmetry of usage between the *New York Times* (and its associates) and the Arab states, with mere reversal in identification of the villain, is therefore of special interest in assessing the objectivity of the Western media.

The political basis for the dichotomous treatment of 007 and the Libyan airliner incidents was stated explicitly by the *New York Times* in editorializing on the Israeli action (1 March 1973): 'No useful purpose is served by an acrimonious debate over the assignment of blame for the downing of a Libyan airliner in the Sinai peninsula last week'. In other words, outrage and moral approbrium depend on utility. In the Libyan airliner case, the Nixon administration 'was saddened' by the incident and sent condolences, but it refused to criticize the Israelis, 'though a well-placed official said that State Department officials had expressed their unhappiness about the incident to Israeli embassy officials' (Gwertzman 1973: 9). When the Assembly of the International Civil Aviation Organization voted on 28 February 1973 to condemn the Israeli act, the United States voted 'reluctantly', on the grounds that this was prejudging Israeli actions before the investigation had been undertaken (Alden 1973: 7). No retaliatory action was carried out for this 'blunder', and Mrs Meier was welcomed in Washington within a week of the incident without the intrusion of any painful questions. The Soviets' 'criminal act', on the other hand, was prejudged before any investigation, and apart from massive and hysterical denunciations, there was significant retaliatory actions, including the organization of a boycott of Soviet air flights by at least 16 countries, the US harassment of Soviet officials desirous of attending UN meetings and a sharp cooling of relations between the United States and its allies and the Soviet Union.

While no 'useful purpose' was served by vilifying the Israelis, valuable political gains could be achieved by taking a high moral stance vis-à-vis the Soviets. The *New York Times* editorial which followed the 007 incident accuses the Soviets of 'cold-blooded mass murder' and asks 'whether the Kremlin accepts its responsibility for a minimally-decent international order'. This rhetoric and focus, applied with such blatancy and discrimination, strongly suggests a media role of serving the 'national interest' in its representation of 'news'. A propaganda model explains the rhetoric, the selectivity in fact and framework, the dichotomization and the propaganda role of the mass media in this important case.

Concluding note

The behaviour and performance of the media gatekeepers of the United States frequently conform to the characteristics of a propaganda system and can be fruitfully analysed in terms of a propaganda model. When the national elite and government are reasonably unified on an issue, the 'gatekeepers' can successfully institutionalize a suitable perception of reality independently of its truth or falsehood. This can be observed in the frequent dichotomous treatment of similar events that have different political consequences. An illustration discussed here is the contrast in media treatment of the shooting down of a South Korean commercial airliner by the Soviet Union in 1983 and the shooting down of a Libyan commercial airliner by Israel in 1973. In the former case, a worldwide campaign of denunciation was organized and orchestrated by the United States, and the Soviet Union was unable to prevent severe public relations losses. In the Israeli case, similar facts led to no significant outcry in the West although the Israelis knew they were shooting down a civilian plane, whereas the Soviet Union did not. Invidious words applied to the Soviets in 1983 were almost completely absent in the Western media in addressing the Israeli action, unless they were quoting from Arab sources.

The KAL campaign also had other propaganda charasteristics. Most important, the US government and media were able to tell deliberate lies and maintain them in the mass consciousness even after the government had quietly withdrawn them or the weight of independent evidence showed them to be false. This resulted from the fact that the media disseminated the initial fabrications with great fervour and assurance, whereas the subsequent repudiations and challenges were either suppressed, given muted and episodic notice and/or rejected by continuous resort to the government's indignant denials. Both the uncritical dissemination and subsequent aversion of the eyes from contradicting facts are in accord with the political demands of the national establishment. A repudiation of establishment (and mass media) fabrications and myths does not serve those demands, and there is no other social machinery for correcting such lies or for countervailing their ideological impact.

The KAL 007 case also illustrates the huge world imbalance in propaganda power. The United States was able to convert the incident into a major public relations success even while it built the case around a series of fabrications. Its allies were willing, or obligated in varying degrees, to go along with the United States in the chorus of condemnation and acts of harassment. The unravelling of the underlying fabrications has had no symmetrical effect in rehabilitating the Soviet Union and causing serious criticism of the United States. The United States wins in lying and does not have to absorb any losses in the exposure of lies. It may organize a huge campaign critical of the imposition of martial law in Poland, while at the same time quite openly supporting martial law and a violent crackdown on organized labour in Turkey, and derive a great deal of prestige for its fight for free labour. It can invade Grenada and organize armies to invade and ravage Nicaragua without any international campaign of condemnation or boycott emerging. This is largely a result of differential economic and political power. The Soviet Union also suffers from the disability that its propaganda system is crude and overt; that of the United States works by a system of voluntarism among the dominant elite gatekeepers. In the United States, the 'samizdats' may be freely produced, with the market left to assure their marginalization.

10
Armageddon, the Pentagon and the Press

David L. Paletz and John Zaven Ayanian

*F*or *three* minutes and twelve seconds on 3 June 1980 electronic monitoring devices at the Strategic Air Command (SAC) in Omaha, Nebraska, and the National Military Command Center (NMCC) at the Pentagon in Washington, DC, indicated that numerous Soviet sea-launched ballistic missiles (SLBMs) and inter-continental ballistic missiles (ICBMs) were headed towards the continental United States. Immediately, the SAC duty officer ordered SAC bomber crews to man their aircraft, start their engines and prepare for take off.

The North American Air Defense Command (NORAD) command post in Colorado Springs, Colorado, processes missiles warning information from radar stations and satellites for use by SAC and NMCC. However, these latter two commands also receive unprocessed information directly from the radar and satellite sensors. This double routing of information, known as 'redundancy' in systems terminology, serves as an internal check on the system. Thus, on 3 June, while the information from the NORAD command to SAC and NMCC apparently warned of a major missile attack, the sensors themselves registered no missile launches or flights. This anomaly suggested to officers at the SAC and NMCC posts that the information emanating from NORAD was erroneous. After the first warning of a missile attack, SAC personnel phoned the NORAD command and learned that officers there had no knowledge of any attack.

The NMCC duty officer convened by telephone a 'missile display conference' among the duty officers at NORAD, SAC, NMCC and the alternate NMCC. They compared warning information being received or not by the various commands. This conference is a preliminary action for evaluating sensor data. During the first six months of 1980 there were 2,159 routine conferences, and 69 conferences to evaluate possible threats.

As the sensor data were being evaluated, the NMCC duty officer convened by telephone a 'threat assessment conference'. This involves more senior figures than the command post duty officers; its purposes are to evaluate the nature of the perceived threat and to direct actions that will enhance the survivability of American forces. There were four such conferences during 1979 and 1980.

The 'threat assessment conference' did not involve the President or any Cabinet-level official. Had the threat been confirmed, however, the President and his senior advisers would have determined America's response through a 'missile attack conference'. The convening of such a conference has never been publicly acknowledged by the American government.

As part of the 3 June threat assessment conference, the airborne command post of the Pacific Command went into the air from its base in Hawaii. The NMCC duty officer terminated the conference when the NORAD commander confirmed that there was no threat. The SAC alert was cancelled one minute later. SAC bomber crews took about 20 minutes to turn off their engines and return to a normal state of readiness.

The cause of the false warning was thought by military officials to be a malfunctioning NORAD computer. So NORAD personnel applied monitoring equipment to their computers and deliberately left the suspect on-line. The NORAD commanders hoped that the specific cause of the malfunction could be determined if it recurred. On 6 June it did. The 3 June sequence was largely reproduced with SAC bombers going on alert for three minutes. But no aircraft were launched and it appears there was no threat assessment conference.

Subsequently, the offending computer was taken off-line and a back-up computer system substituted. The malfunctions were attributed to a faulty 46-cent computer chip.

The Pentagon perspective

Pentagon officials are not likely to inform press or public voluntarily of nuclear alerts. Word of the 3 June alarm leaked, however, to a local reporter in Norfolk, Virginia, from the headquarters there of the Atlantic Command. After checking with military bases around the country and receiving a chorus of no comments and refusals to confirm or deny, the reporter obtained official Defense Department confirmation. His paper, the *Virginia-Pilot*, a morning newspaper with a daily circulation of 126,165, published its scoop on 5 June under the headline 'Computer Goofs: Military Alerted'. This internationally important story appeared on page 3.

For the Pentagon spokesmen the problem now was not how to conceal the alert, but what to say about it. Their function, as they saw it, was to reassure press and thereby the public at home and abroad that nuclear war was far from imminent during the false alerts. Indeed, the events would be portrayed as a success because the safeguards in the American early-warning system had worked and prevented an accidental nuclear war. The severity of the alert would be downplayed.

The Pentagon argument consisted, therefore, of three main parts. First, a computerized early-warning system to detect missiles is necessary for the national defence because of the short flight time of missiles from launch. Secondly, when a missile threat is perceived, America must place its nuclear forces on alert to enhance their chances of survival. Thirdly and most importantly from the Pentagon point of view, computers could not launch America's nuclear weapons; only humans have the power to make that decision.

This is a plausible framework in which to place the nuclear alerts, and Pentagon officials did their best to ensure that the press would accept and propagate it. Their tactics included such oft-used weapons as secrecy, obfuscation and invoking technical expertise. But the Pentagon's most immediate technique was to funnel its favourable version of events to a preferred, because sympathetic, reporter.

So at approximately 10.00 a.m. on 5 June public affairs officials released a calm, reassuring and superficially detailed statement to the Associated Press (AP) Pentagon correspondent Fred Hoffman.

> Early Tuesday morning, June 3, 1980, a technical problem in a computer at the North American Air Defense Command caused erroneous data to be transmitted. Some displays at the National Military Command Center and Strategic Air Command Headquarters indicated multiple missile launches against the United States; however, other systems available directly from the warning sensor system continued to confirm that no missiles had been launched. As a precaution and in accordance with standard procedures, certain Strategic Air Command aircraft were brought to a higher state of readiness. These aircraft were manned and engines started. One Command and Control aircraft in the Pacific took off. There was no change in overall US defense posture and, after an evaluation, all systems were returned to normal. The computer technical problems are now being assessed to determine corrective action.

At 11.18 a.m. on 5 June Hoffman's story on the false alert was flashed across the country over the AP wire.

Eleven minutes later the Pentagon press corps gathered in the Pentagon briefing room. Assistant Secretary of Defense Thomas Ross opened the conference with the inquiry, 'Any questions?' Hilary Brown of the National Broadcasting Company (NBC) asked: 'Could you describe the circumstances that led to this false alarm early Tuesday morning?'

Ross responded to the question with a brief prepared statement which was a verbatim repetition of the statement that had been released to Fred Hoffman at 10.00 a.m. Ross's statement was followed by 52 questions on the false alert. Most of the Pentagon correspondents first learned of the alert at this briefing. Their impromptu questions dealt with such aspects as the specific actions taken, the time involved, the cause of the false information, the Soviet response and the nature of the early-warning system. When a reporter finally stated, 'I have a question on another subject', Ross replied, with a mixture of levity and relief, 'Thank God'.

The second alert, that of 6 June, was announced on Saturday, 7 June. Unable to prevent a leak after the first alert, Pentagon officials hoped to curtail public speculation by quietly announcing the second. No briefing was held; Thomas Ross simply prepared a brief statement that was telephoned to the major news organizations during the afternoon of 7 June.

> Friday afternoon, June 6, 1980, the same computer which gave the false indications June 3rd again gave erroneous signals. The computer had been deliberately left on-line with special equipment applied to it in an effort to determine the cause of the June 3rd malfunction. When the second malfunction occurred Friday we believe we detected the cause. The computer has now been taken off the line to absolutely pin-point the cause and correct it. Within three minutes, on Friday, it was positively determined that the cause was again a computer malfunction and that there was no threat to the U.S. As a precautionary measure the engines of some SAC Alert force planes were started but no planes *of any kind* took off. There was no change in the overall defense posture of the United States. The computer involved has been taken off the line until the problem can be determined.

The coverage

As Philip Elliott and Peter Golding observed: 'News is not simply a collection of raw facts about the world, reflecting events with debatable but empirically determinable accuracy. Rather is it an important part of the cultural system of modern society, particularly concerned with providing, in a preliminary fashion, frameworks for handling new and recurring problems for society.' And they noted that one way the news media do the handling is 'by elaborating continuing perspectives and images on particular topics so that each new event is incorporated into an on-going plot' (Elliott and Golding 1974: 230).

The nuclear attack alerts thus provide us with a fascinating opportunity empirically to pursue some of the important issues that concerned – that rightly obsessed – Philip Elliott. What types of news did reporters produce out of the events? Operating in the Pentagon, were they (unduly) subject to institutional and political constraints? Were they affected by the knowledge that their coverage could make the United States government and its nuclear strategy appear sane and restrained or rash and bellicose not just to Americans but, perhaps more significantly, to allies, neutrals and adversaries abroad. Above all, did reporters employ similar frameworks for handling the alerts? If not, how can we explain the differences?

In fact, American media coverage was not all of a piece. Indeed, it varied widely: from no stories at all in some publications, to docile acceptance of the Pentagon's perspective, through fragmentation, to consideration of the alerts' implications (what we call 'implicational' coverage); and, ultimately, to various forms of sensationalism.

Three sets of factors help to explain this spectrum of media coverage. Naturally, the time and competition constraints the reporters faced are important. So are the reporters' beliefs about the (different) missions of their organizations and, relatedly, the interests of their audiences. But above all are the reporters themselves, especially in their experiences, ambition and energy (or lack thereof), understanding of the technical issues involved in the alerts and their standing and relations both at the Pentagon and with the editors and media executives above them.

We shall briefly illustrate each type of coverage and suggest some of the reasons behind it.

None

Donald Sider has been the national security correspondent for *Time* since September 1978. He described his beat as 'geopolitics beyond diplomacy', incorporating issues from the Pentagon, CIA, White House, State Department and Congress. On the average, he visits the Pentagon three times a week (personal interview, 10 December 1980).

The mechanism for assigning stories at *Time* usually begins with a reporter submitting a brief sketch of a potential article to his editors. If the editors believe it will make a worthwhile story, they will assign it to the reporter. After Sider learned of the false alerts, he 'suggested a story or essay on the whole premise of accidental war', but his editors did not assign the story.

Conduit

The Associated Press essentially served as conduit for the Pentagon perspective. Its correspondent Fred Hoffman had a close relationship with Pentagon Public Affairs officials. Through five presidential administrations, as political appointees and military officers and members of the press corps came and went, he remained, a Pentagon fixture. An official described him as one of the chosen few reporters who have gained the respect of Public Affairs officials for their responsible (as defined by the official) coverage of Pentagon stories. Such respect made Hoffman a likely reporter to receive tips from officials, and simultaneously jeopardized his ability to question the accuracy, assumptions and implications of that information. No wonder Hoffman was the first Pentagon correspondent to be told about and report the false alerts. Moreover, when he received the official statement, Hoffman was under considerable time pressure to file his story before the news briefing and thus ahead of every other news organization. He had no time to approach different sources or much ponder the implications of the alerts.

Even though the time pressures subsequently diminished, Hoffman's coverage remained a conduit for the Pentagon. He accepted the Pentagon's explanation. As he said of the alert: 'It was the opposite of being on the brink of war. It proved the system works.' Moreover, he did not delve into the technical issues of the implications of the alerts because, as he put it, 'they say they are taking care of it, and if they explained it to me I probably wouldn't understand and my readers wouldn't read it' (all quotes from a personal interview, 21 August 1980). Complacent confidence in Pentagon officials, lack of the requisite understanding to tackle complex issues and prejudgement of readers' interest and intelligence – all combined with Hoffman's self-professed lack of vigour to ensure conduit reporting.

Fragmentation

The AP did not rely solely on its Pentagon correspondent; stories from other of its reporters contained passing mention of British Labour Party and Soviet comments on the alerts. But it was the AP's rival wire service, United Press International (UPI), that produced the more diverse range of coverage. These disparate reports were united, however, mainly by their common lack of analysis.

The one story from UPI's Pentagon correspondent was essentially a conduit in part because the time pressures prevented the reporter from contacting outside sources. But it and the reporter's failure to follow up were part of a more general philosophy about the purpose and function of the wire services. As the reporter said: 'We just reflect everything that happens, and when it's over, we just go on to the next day' (personal interview with Nicholas Daniloff, 19 August 1980).

The other UPI stories were reports of statements to the press: by the Pentagon, Union of Concerned Scientists, Senator John Tower (R-Texas), the Soviet news agency TASS and the Senate Armed Services Committee. Apparently UPI sought none of these statements, simply reporting what it was given without much probing. The result was fragmentation, a smorgasbord of reactions. Not provided was perspective, the kind of information that would explain the alerts and their implications.

Cursory

During the month of June 1980 the *Washington Post* published over 40 news stories related to the American military. So defense issues were clearly of interest to the *Post*'s editors. The newspaper's Pentagon correspondent, George Wilson, moreover, spoke of his role as one would expect of a reporter from an elite newspaper: 'I'm not here to try and duplicate the wires, I try and develop the stories. . . . What I'm here for is to get behind the façade and get them to open the kimono' (personal interview, 19 August 1980). Yet only one story on the alerts appeared by Wilson in the *Post*. Entitled 'Computer Errs, Warns of Soviet Attack on U.S.' (*Washington Post*, 6 June 1980), it was mainly a conduit for the official Pentagon statement of 5 June, and was relegated to page 5.

Three factors help to explain the *Post*'s cursory coverage. First, its Pentagon correspondent did not consider the false alarms particularly significant: as he said, 'the fact that it was nipped in the bud made it less of a story' (personal interview, 19 August 1980). Secondly, he apparently received no major pressure from his editors to pursue the story. Thirdly, since some rival media outlets were treating the issue as a major issue, Wilson and the *Post* would, in our opinion, have been confessing news judgement errors had they belatedly tried to catch up.

Implicational
The *New York Times* carried eight stories on the alerts. While these relied almost exclusively on US governmental sources, and none of them

appeared on the paper's front page, several of the sources used expressed anxiety and concern over the false alarms. The stories maintained questioning attitudes towards the Pentagon perspective and behaviour. And the two reporters who wrote the bulk of the stories took pains to probe the alerts' implications.

One reason for this implicational coverage was Richard Halloran. He began on the Pentagon beat for the *Times* in September 1979 and his limited experience there seemed to spur him to approach each new story as a learning experience. He thus sought more information than Pentagon officials were willing to reveal and raised questions in his coverage they preferred not to deal with publicly.

The *Times*'s coverage of the alerts was bolstered by stories from Richard Burt. Not bound by a specific institutional beat, Burt had the subject-oriented responsibilities of military-diplomatic and strategic military issues. In preparing his report, Burt found anonymous sources at the Pentagon and White House who diverged from the official line. Consequently, he wrote the most thorough discussion of the launch-on-warning strategy found in any mass media report. His special interest in nuclear strategy gave him the background to relate the false alerts to strategic questions, and the definition of his role at the *Times* encouraged him to do so.

So the combination of two reporters, one knowledgeable and operating at large, the other not bound to the shibboleths of the past; with neither beholden to Pentagon sources; and with both assuming that their newspaper's readers would be concerned and want to learn more about the alerts' causes and implications – this produced implicational coverage in the *Times*.

None the less, the *Times* never gave the alert articles page 1 prominence, printing them on the first national news page after page 1. According to Halloran, the editors believed these were 'good solid stories' but did not consider them weighty enough for the front page (personal interview, 5 January 1981). On 6 June, when Halloran's first story broke, the *Times* had two military stories on the front page dealing with the rescue mission to Iran and Secretary of State Cyrus Vance's call for an arms limitation treaty with the Soviet Union. The need for balance in front page subjects kept Halloran's piece off the front page. After 6 June the alerts were no longer breaking news. As evolving news, the false alert stories were relegated to the middle of the paper.

Confused–sensational

Hilary Brown became NBC's Pentagon correspondent in December 1979 with an admittedly limited knowledge of defence issues and operations. Commenting on her approach to the Pentagon, she said: 'It's your duty not to take what they tell you at face value. . . . Basically it's an adversary relationship' (personal interview, 6 August 1980).

Pentagon officials generally prefer a collegial to an adversarial relationship with reporters. To this end, they can be of great assistance to correspondents by suggesting sources and providing background information. The reporter need not be sycophantic, but only cordial personally and 'objective' professionally. Brown's somewhat strident attitude made her unlikely to receive the special support that would have rectified her unfamiliarity with the Pentagon. Compounding the situation, Brown's producers at NBC news were apparently uninterested in defence stories: she appeared just seven times on the evening news during the six or so months she worked at the Pentagon prior to the alerts.

Brown had wanted to do a report on the alerts but her producers were not interested. Then, two weeks later, they learned that ABC News was planning a two-part 'Special Assignment' series and promoting it in advance. They decided on 23 June to air their own investigative story beating ABC by one day. Brown had two days to compile her report. Consequently, time pressures generated by producer indecision, and misplaced perceptions caused by reporter inexperience, culminated in a confused and misleading and sensational news story.

Many of the visuals used in the story were taken from an air force film of a strategic military exercise. They were graphically edited to reinforce the frightening aspects of the story – this demonstrating that Defense Department file film can sometimes be used by the media to the detriment of the military.

Implicational–sensational

The American Broadcasting Company (ABC) in its evening news devoted the most air time of the three television networks to covering the false alerts. The first of its three stories primarily reported the official Pentagon announcement; but its second and third reports (a two-part series) used diverse sources of information and were extensive and complex. In part they were sensational: with exciting visuals (crews running to planes, small red flashing light, a missile launching as the camera looked down into the silo), quick editing, split screen and the constant reappearance of correspondent John McWethy as he guided us to and at the various locations. ABC even showed its audience an aerial view of the Washington Monument, ominously reminiscent of a missile. But the ABC stories also raised, even if they did not fully explore, such implications of the alerts as poor management, inadequate maintenance, the use of obsolescent computers and the isolation of decision-makers because of their dependence on computers.

ABC Pentagon correspondent John McWethy began working for the network in December 1979 having previously served as the science and technology and then White House correspondent for *U.S. News and World Report*. Before that, he had worked for *Congressional Quarterly*, where he had written a book on congressional oversight of the Defense Department.

McWethy's prestige at ABC News, combined with his producers' interest in the false alert issue, resulted in a decision to prepare a two-part investigative series which McWethy was given two weeks to prepare. Of all the Pentagon correspondents, he was therefore able to utilize the widest range and greatest number of sources: three political and three technical, three in government and three out of it, four Americans and two foreigners (including Soviet commentator Vladimir Pozner). ABC, moreover, was the only news organization to employ co-ordinated teamwork. The *New York Times* and the wire services all had more than one correspondent writing articles, but no one reporter for these organizations co-ordinated the coverage as McWethy did for ABC.

McWethy raised several of the important implications of the alerts in his two-part series. None the less, he did not detail them fully. Among the reasons were lack of time to delve into complexity, and concern that the evening news audience would be bored by technical language. But the most important explanation stems from the dovetailing of ABC's interest in an action-packed, exciting news story and McWethy's determination 'to convey the scariness of the incident' (personal interview, 4 August 1980). Thus the numerous freeze frames, editing of film into very brief cuts and emphasis on active images, all designed to create a mood of tension, tended to sensationalize the alerts.

What the news media missed

The debate in the United States about nuclear weapons has been traditionally quite limited. It is confined to a small community of military, strategic and technological experts who share many assumptions about the functions and purposes of nuclear weapons. The American public is minimally involved in the debate, partly out of ignorance, and also because nuclear war is a frightening topic. In reporting complex, secret military events such as the false alerts, the news media have the opportunity to ventilate issues which would otherwise receive little sustained public attention.

Certainly there were dramatic differences in the media's coverage of the false alerts. None the less, even the best coverage was incomplete and short-lived. Significant deficiencies occurred in stories of the 6 June alert, in the international, strategic, procedural and procurement implications of both alerts, and in the corrective measures subsequently taken in the early-warning system.

We briefly illustrate here with the international implications. For the consequences of a nuclear war would not be limited to any one country. An American attack on the Soviet Union could spur retaliation against America's allies. Radioactive fall-out would spread all over the globe. For these reasons, the false alerts cannot be a strictly American concern.

Most of the US news organizations gave only cursory consideration to the consequences of the alerts for the Soviet Union and for America's European allies. Although many of the news organizations presented the sensational Soviet condemnations of the Pentagon, only the *New York Times* discussed the possible military reasons for Soviet fear of American alerts. Some news organizations mentioned attacks on the Pentagon by British Labour Party members. ABC noted that many European leaders 'complained that the U.S. did not even tell them a major alert was underway in America' (*World News*, 26 June 1980). Only one report, by an AP correspondent in London, discussed why Europeans were concerned: plans to base cruise missiles in Western Europe could make these countries likely targets for Soviet missiles.

Why did most Pentagon correspondents neglect the international aspects of the false alerts? Reporters could have contacted foreign embassies in Washington, but embassies are not regular sources for military writers. Obtaining overseas information would have required time-consuming co-ordination with other correspondents. Most news organizations covered the false alerts for less than two weeks. Above all, the stories were written by Americans for Americans: ethnocentrism triumphed.

Conclusion

As discrete events with large implications, the false nuclear alerts of June 1980 afford a special opportunity to evaluate news coverage of the Pentagon. The alerts were typical of much Pentagon news: globally significant, potentially detrimental to the public image of the Pentagon and difficult to dissect because of their secrecy and technology.

News from the Pentagon passes through two filters, the government's and the media's. Traditional critiques of this newsmaking process, such as *The Pentagon Propaganda Machine* by J. W. Fulbright (1970) and *Minimum Disclosure* by Juergen Arthur Heise (1979), have focused on the Pentagon's power to impress its perspective on the media and the public. These books have depicted the array of tools used by the Defense Department to dominate the presentation of military news. We agree that the Pentagon withholds information, plays favourites with reporters and attempts to place a positive interpretation on disconcerting military events. But we go beyond the traditional view to demonstrate ways in which the media mould (and manipulate) military news. Definitions of newsworthiness, reporter inadequacies and organizational constraints within the media profoundly influence news from the Pentagon.

We saw in the news media a range of false alert coverage. The Pentagon presented its interpretation of the events, but could not uniformly enforce it on the press. Some reporters were unperturbed by the alerts, while others were very distressed; both conduit *and* sensational reports were evident. The primary press question became: 'How close were we to accidental nuclear war?' Obviously this was a necessary question to ask, but by dominating reporters' concerns, this inquiry concealed some very important, but less exciting, issues.

This distinction between exciting and important is essential to understanding the Pentagon press corps. Extraordinary events and dramatic policy changes will almost always be reported by Pentagon correspondents (if they are aware of them), but the opportunity to use these topics as newspegs for implicational discussions is rarely employed. Most Pentagon reporters pursue breaking news because these stories are most likely to be published or broadcast. Few incentives exist for reporters to follow issues over time.

Pentagon correspondents are understandably harried by the incessant demands of their beat. The quality of Pentagon news coverage would be likely to improve if news organizations also employed issue-oriented reporters less restricted by the beat. In addition, military news reports could contain more varied viewpoints if news organizations made a greater effort to co-ordinate their Pentagon correspondents with their other reporters. Although organizational influences weigh heavily on reporters, most newsmen perceive themselves as very individualistic and are not naturally inclined to seek assistance from their colleagues in other locales.

The relationship between the military and the media is complex. As was demonstrated after the false alerts, the traditional view of the Pentagon as the preponderant controller of military news is only partly true. Many problems in the false alert coverage resulted more from the inadequacies of the news media than from the overwhelming power of the Pentagon. Solutions to these problems require from news reporters and managers more questioning of the Pentagon, more initiative in developing stories and more reflection on the assumptions which guide their work than we found.

11
The Semantics of Political Violence

Peter Taylor

*A*bove *a photograph* of the fractured spine of the Grand Hotel, Brighton, the headline in *An Phoblacht/ Republican News* on 18 October 1984 proclaimed 'IRA Blitz Brits'. In an interview in the same issue a spokesman authorized by the General Headquarters of the Irish Republican Army (IRA) warned: 'Britain's occupation of Ireland is going to keep on costing her dearly until she quits.' 'Murder' was the verdict of the *Daily Mirror*. 'Unbowed', declared a defiant *Daily Express* headline the same day above a photograph of Mrs Thatcher; 'She flung defiance at terror with the words "Democracy will prevail".' The *Sun* demanded that those responsible 'must be hunted remorselessly and exterminated like rats'. Without doubt it was the most sensational attack the IRA had launched in its 15-year campaign, not to mention the most determined attempt to wipe out a British government since the Gunpowder Plot. The reaction of the media was akin to what Phillip Elliott described as 'the affirmatory ritual' which followed the assassination of Lord Mountbatten: in this ritual, according to Elliott (1980), press and broadcasting emphasized the integrity of the social order and represented terrorism as the inhuman and irrational embodiment of encroaching chaos. Thus in the aftermath of Brighton, Fleet Street declared that Britain would not be bombed out of Ulster and would emerge with renewed determination to defend democracy against the men of violence. The *Daily Mail* summed up the mood on 14 October as 'This outrage that unites the nation against terrorism'.

There is no doubt that the IRA poses a threat to the existence of the state because its campaign is directed at the severance of one part of it from the main body. Government has to counter the threat not only by taking direct measures againt those who seek to subvert it but by enlisting the support of the media in what it calls 'the battle against terrorism'. In its use of language and interpretation of events, the media helps to condition the way that 'battle' is perceived. This leads in turn to the synthesis of the political and public perception of the state's enemy. This is why words are so crucial in describing and defining the contemporary phenomenon of political violence not just in Northern Ireland but worldwide. These words can be an aid to understanding or a distortion of it. They not only reflect the journalist's perception of a particular situation but condition the way his report is received. The problem remains one of definition. As the BBC cautions on page 75 of the 1984 edition of its *News and Current Affairs Index*, 'some terrorist activity enjoys virtually no popular support and is totally reprehensible. But it is also true that sometimes yesterday's terrorists have become today's prime ministers, and that one man's terrorist may be another man's freedom fighter.' No doubt the deaths and injuries of 200 British officers and civilians in the bomb attack on Jerusalem's King David Hotel in 1946 provoked a reaction not dissimilar to Brighton. The fact that Menachem Begin, the leader of the Irgun, the Jewish resistance group responsible, went on to become the Prime Minister of Israel was not a consideration in the minds of British people who reacted with horror at the time.

So what is a terrorist? What is a guerrilla? What is a freedom fighter? The great dictionaries at least offer a starting-point. The *Concise Oxford English Dictionary* (1982) defines terrorist as 'one who favours or uses terror-inspiring methods ... of coercing government or community'; *Chambers* (1983) says a person involved in 'an organised system of intimidation, especially for political ends'; *Websters* (1983) has one who systematically uses 'terror especially as a means of coercion'. On this reading, the IRA and every other organization involved in political violence would fall into this category. What of guerrilla? According to the *OED*, he (or she) is a person taking part in 'irregular fighting by small independent acting groups'. *Chambers* says 'one who takes part in ... harassing an army by small bands: petty warfare'; and *Websters* has 'one who engages in irregular warfare especially as a member of an independent unit carrying out harassment and sabotage'. Under this definition, the IRA and most other groups around the world (with the exception of those like the Red Brigades, Baader Meinhof and the Red Army Fraction) would also fall into this category. And what of freedom fighter? The *OED* says 'one who takes part in resistance to an established political system'; *Chambers* 'one who fights in an armed movement for the liberation of a nation . . . from a government considered unjust (or) tyrannical'; *Websters* has no listing. All armed groups would see themselves in this category although none of their opponents and few of their recorders would grant their inclusion. But such dictionary definitions only tell us what the terms mean and do not offer a guide for their common usage. Each word now carries a particular nuance which cannot be divorced from the society in which it is used. It may depend on the circumstances of the particular event, whether the target is military or civilian (a distinction not specified in the dictionaries); or on the political circumstances surrounding it, for example, the political colour and nature of the regime under attack; or, perhaps most important of all, on the proximity of the events being reported. It remains a fact of life for journalists reporting the conflict in Ireland that the terminology used is not that which may be accorded to similar conflicts further from home. When I filmed the African National Congress training in the bush in a country outside South Africa, I was able to refer to them as 'guerrillas' – which is what I believed they were. Whilst in South Africa preparing the same report at the time of the Hunger Strike, I noted that Bobby Sands's status was defined in some of the South African press as an 'IRA guerrilla'. If I had been allowed to film a similar sequence with the IRA – which for legal and political reasons I would not – I doubt if I would have been able to refer to them as 'IRA guerrillas'. I have, on occasions, without problem, referred to the IRA as a 'guerrilla army' – which, of course, is what it is. Although logic demands that members of a guerrilla army are, *ipso facto*, guerrillas, political circumstances dictate that in Britain in print and word they are not. Certainly, at the time of the Hunger Strike, it would have been unthinkable to refer to Bobby Sands as an 'IRA guerrilla'. Significantly, much of the foreign press do refer to the IRA as guerrillas: Colin McIntyre, for example, writing in *The Advertiser* (Australia) on 15 August 1984 of the 15 years of conflict in Northern Ireland, referred to the 'increasingly well-trained and armed republican guerrillas fighting British rule in the province'. Although in theory, guerrilla is a neutral word between terrorist (the preferred political term where domestic conflict is involved) and freedom fighter, its interpretation by those who see or hear the word is, in present circumstances, unlikely to imply any neutrality. As for 'freedom fighter', it stays firmly within the covers of the dictionaries.

In collecting material for this essay, I contacted most of the national newspapers and broadcasting organizations to establish what words they used to describe various aspects of political violence and its practitioners, in particular with regard to the IRA. What follows is based on their replies in personal interviews or correspondence during the second half of 1984. Was there a policy? Were there guidelines? Were there political considerations? I found to my surprise that, with rare exceptions, there were few guidelines and not many had even given the subject much thought. Most relied on the experience and good sense of their reporters and a 'feeling' for the subject and their audience's response to it. Some responses were blunter than others. The editor of the *Daily Star* Lloyd Turner, told me that instructions to his journalists reporting violence in Northern Ireland were 'clear cut'. He said:

> Those fighting to overthrow the State – and the democratically elected representatives of the State – are terrorists. There are no freedom fighters in Northern Ireland. The people living in Northern Ireland have freedom of choice. They have democratic elections. They are not prevented from leaving Northern Ireland to live elsewhere. Those who want to change Northern Ireland are given the opportunity to do so at the ballot box. In fact they resort to bullets instead. That is terrorism.

The editor of the *Daily Express*, Sir Larry Lamb, was more judicious. He said the *Express* had no policy, just unwritten guidelines which 'every experienced reporter applies to the reporting of sensitive situations'. He concluded: 'As far as I am concerned there are no different rules for different conflicts and Belfast is no different from Beirut.' The *Daily Mail* replied:

> We do not issue any guidelines to our correspondents and reporters on the vocabulary to be used in reporting political violence. We leave it to their judgement on the spot in particular circumstances. I am afraid that the bustle of daily newspaper life does not always lend itself to neat academic pigeon-holing. ... But certainly, we would regard the IRA and others, catholic or protestant, who use violence to further their political ends in Northern Ireland as terrorists.

The editor of the *Morning Star*, Tony Chater, was more terse. 'We try to use words on violence that do not make the situation worse.' The editor of the *Sunday Telegraph*, William Deedes, was almost as brief: 'I am afraid we can offer very little guidance to assist you in these enquiries. We do not issue guidelines here but rely on the professionalism of our staff to gather and report the news as it comes.' The editor of the *Sunday Times*, Andrew Neil, was more forthcoming. He said:

> You raise a very difficult issue and I am afraid there are no clear guidelines laid down by the *Sunday Times* for distinguishing guerrillas, terrorists and freedom fighters. It is a thorny problem which appears to be addressed

through subjective convention rather than firm instructions from the editor. As a general guideline we believe a terrorist is an individual or member of a group that wishes to achieve political ends using violent means, often at the cost of casualties to innocent civilians and with little evidence of popular support among the people he claims to represent. On that basis we would describe the provisional IRA as a terrorist group and the PLO as a guerrilla group. However, the PFLP [the Popular Front for the Liberation of Palestine] we would describe as a terrorist organisation. These are naturally subjective interpretations but we feel they adequately reflect the situation.

The Times said: 'We have rules here which try to set out the circumstances in which somebody should be described either as a guerrilla or as a terrorist. Essentially, the difference should derive from the choice of target or the tactics of that particular violence. Terrorism, in our view, is any act of violence perpetrated willingly or inadvertently against non-military targets. Guerrillas may be guerrillas, but they are also terrorists when they attack buses full of civilians.' The editor of the *Observer*, Donald Trelford, made broader observations.

We do not have a 'policy' or 'guidelines' for writing about political violence. Each incident will dictate the choice of words – although we would never describe someone who throws a bomb into a busload of children as a 'guerrilla', still less a 'freedom fighter'. I rely on the feel for words of our writers and page editors, and their judgement. We prefer to avoid general words, and instead use phrases such as members of the IRA, etc. We would not hesitate to describe the perpetrators of the Brighton bombing as 'terrorists' but, to be specific, I find that in our issue after it, the word does not appear. (The leader has the expression 'cold-blooded IRA killer'.) In our follow-up to the storming of the Golden Temple in Amritsar the Sikh leader was described as 'the terrorist Bhindranwale'; the page editor deleted 'terrorist' in page-proof. In retrospect he has doubts about the deletion but stands by it on the grounds that Bhindranwale did not personally kill people. The November *Encounter*, writing about the Libyan People's Bureau incident this year, has the phrase 'Colonel Gaddaffi and other terrorists'. I would not have allowed that.

Mr Trelford also cited the experience of one of the *Observer*'s former American correspondents, Charles Foley. In the 1950s Mr Foley was editor of the *Times of Cyprus* and had been on the 'hit list' of the EOKA leader, Nikos Sampson. Many years later, Mr Foley was consulted by the *Observer* colour magazine which planned to refer to Mr Sampson as a 'terrorist'. Although he had been one of Sampson's 'targets', Foley dissented and, after discussions with the sub-editor of the magazine, the word 'terrorist' was replaced by a phrase like 'EOKA gunman'. Retrospectively, although he admitted there was room for doubt on the issue, Donald Trelford felt that Foley's instinct was right. The most detailed Fleet Street response came from Geoffrey Taylor, the chief leader-writer on Northern Irish affairs for the *Guardian*.

We have not made any rules about terminology because if we did we should find ourselves adjudicating on the exceptions. Obviously there is normally a case for using the least loaded and most objective word, but I doubt whether 'guerrilla' any more than 'terrorist' is now free of an ethical judgement by the writer or speaker. In the case of indiscriminate violence it seems unduly punctilious to use the word guerrilla if the immediate purpose of the operation was to spread terror, irrespective of what the ultimate textbook motive might be. Both words have emotional connotations: terrorist with the causing of random death or suffering and guerrilla with the nobility of a fight for liberation, as in France during the war. If we are forced into adopting definitions then 'guerrilla' will come to mean 'not in our opinion bad enough to be called a terrorist' and 'terrorist' will come to mean, 'not in our opinion worthy to be called a guerrilla'. In practice the choice does not often have to be made at all because the purely descriptive words 'gunman' or 'bomber' can be used. The only neutral word I can think of (and it would not be neutral for long) is 'insurgent' because the IRA is in a state of insurgency against the governments of the United Kingdom and the Irish Republic. But 'insurgent' is part of a highly sociological language and a paper which wrote about insurgents blowing up a pub in Birmingham would have parted company with its readers. We try to avoid impaling ourselves on definitions, and sometimes criticise other people for doing so. This makes us chary of forbidding what may seem the right word to use for the occasion. I agree that there is bound to be some subjectivity about that. One cannot entirely cease to identify with the society one lives in, and adopt an attitude of celestial superiority towards most of its other inhabitants. Half the time the word 'terrorist' is used in quoted speech, and a newspaper would not be entitled to force its own linguistic standards on people being interviewed or reported. Again, there must be occasions when the reporter's own experience of an event makes him regard a clinical word as inadequate. If so we can't haul him before a thought-court, deliver a lecture on the history of Ireland, and ask him in future kindly to guard his language. Should the reporter at, for example, the Darkley Pentecostal Church ring up the desk and ask for guidance about whether the attackers were terrorists or guerrillas? And if he did, and an editorial committee decided they were guerrillas, could not the victims of the attack object to being identified as legitimate targets in a struggle for civil or political rights? Hard cases make bad law, of course, but all the cases we are discussing are hard to those at the receiving end, and that is why it is better not to have a law at all. I am surpised to find myself arguing for the retention of the word 'terrorist' as one of the options open to a writer. (It is not a word I use much myself, simply because of its emotional overtones.) But I find it profitless to look for the precise demarcation line between terrorism and guerrilla activity. Where, for example, would the Red Brigades or the Red Army Faction fit into a precise set of definitions? Neither could claim to be under the heel of an authoritarian regime which could not be changed by non-violent methods.

I also conducted interviews with several senior television executives in Britain and Northern Ireland. The editor of Granada Television's *World in Action*, Ray Fitzwalter, said that in describing organizations like the IRA and the PLO and the ANC 'we prefer to avoid emotive descriptions, to avoid partisan expressions, to avoid descriptions which can change in their meaning according to the colour of the government or change through time. We usually use factual descriptions. Thus we would refer to the IRA, to IRA men, perhaps to gunmen, if it were appropriate, but we would not use phrases like terrorists, guerrillas or freedom fighters.'

The BBC, because of its unique position in broadcasting, shares the same problems as the other broadcasting organizations but perhaps feels them more acutely. As Philip Schlesinger, Graham Murdock and Philip Elliott observe in *Televising 'Terrorism'* (1983: 41), 'in Britain there is an important sense in which the BBC, in spite of its formal independence from the state is the national broadcasting organisation in a way in which the programme companies making up the ITV network are not'. The BBC does have guidelines which are updated from time to time by memorandum from senior executives. One such memo is referred to by Liz Curtis in her exhaustive study *Ireland: The Propaganda War* (1984). It concerns, however, not Ireland but the reporting of political violence in foreign parts. In 1974 a memo to BBC newsroom staff entitled 'Guerrillas and terrorists' said:

> 'Terrorist' is the appropriate description for people who engage in acts of terrorism, and in particular, in acts of violence against civilians, that is operations not directed at military targets or military personnel.
>
> 'Guerrilla' is acceptable for leaders and members of the various Palestine organisations of this kind, but they too become 'terrorist' when they engage in terrorist acts (unless 'raiders', 'hijackers', 'gunmen' is more accurate).

Liz Curtis also refers to the BBC's *News Guide*.

> Don't use 'commando' for terrorist or guerrilla. In the 1939–45 war, the word had heroic connotations, and it is still the name of units of the Royal Marines.
>
> Even so we still have problems with 'terrorist' or 'guerrilla'. The best general rule is to refer to 'guerrillas' when they have been in action against official security forces, and to use 'terrorist' when they have attacked civilians. Thus we should say 'Guerrillas have attacked an army patrol in the Rhodesian bush...', but 'Terrorists have killed six missionaries in Rhodesia...'. (Curtis 1984: 135–6)

The Head of BBC Television News, Peter Woon, and his Deputy, Robin Walsh, admitted that in days gone by Television News had 'transgressed on the Middle East' by allowing the expression 'PLO guerrillas' to creep in: the terminology was changed after vigorous representations from the Israelis; now less emotive words were substituted like 'fighters'. Would they ever call the IRA 'fighters'? No, they replied. They pointed out that there was a danger in sticking to the Oxford English Dictionary and said they had to be aware of the public perception of an act of political violence. 'If we know that the use of "terrorist" or "guerrilla" divides our audience, [and we use it] then we are not getting our story across as well as we should. Why use words which have such a subjective interpretation when others – like "gunmen" or "bombers" – will do?' Sometimes, they said, you need use no such descriptive word at all when the initials of the organization would suffice without adding colour to the report: if an excessively neutral word were required, then there was always 'paramilitaries'. Wasn't 'guerrilla' technically a neutral word, I asked. No, they said, at least not in the eyes of their audience. 'Guerrilla still carries connotations of the "good guys" because of Yugoslavia.' Would they ever call the IRA 'guerrillas'? They said they could never see it happening. But wasn't the IRA a guerrilla army? They thought a while and then acknowledged that it was true to say that it was but added that the term 'guerrilla army' wouldn't have the same connotation as describing its members, on air, as guerrillas. They admitted it might be a 'cowardly' way, but they tried to avoid labels – just as they tried to avoid the terms 'militant' and 'moderate'. There were no written rules. 'At the end of the day, you can't have a glossary. You have to rely on experience and common sense.' But there was one clear distinction; if the action was directed against the civilian population, it was an act of 'terrorism'. But what if an IRA man killed a British soldier? They admitted that, technically, it shouldn't be described as an act of a 'terrorist'. They said they avoid the problem by using another word. There *was* a difference, they agreed, between Belfast and Beirut. 'Beirut is a long way away.' With candour they admitted: 'we do work slightly differently when it affects us. Whether subconsciously or consciously we differentiate.' In conclusion I asked whether the security forces were 'fighting terrorism'. Again they paused for reflection before saying that they never reduced it to one phrase. 'Maybe it's a great criticism of our output that we've never grappled with that one. We've never felt the need to express a verdict.'

My own experience confirms that at the BBC there are no specific guidelines covering the words its correspondents use to describe the actions of the IRA and other paramilitaries. But, for understandable reasons, one does have to exercise care. I recall a line of commentary I had written for the opening sequence of a *Panorama* programme on extradition which examined the significance of the political offence exception. The film showed two men walking in Phoenix Park, Dublin, where a century earlier some forerunners of the IRA (called the Invincibles) had assassinated Lord Frederick Cavendish, the new Chief Secretary for Ireland. The point of comparison was that the men now seen in the Park were former members of the INLA which had 'assassinated' Airey Neave. Alan Protheroe, the Deputy Director General of the BBC, saw the film prior to transmission and said that the word should be 'murder' not 'assassination'. I said I had used the word deliberately to draw the parallel between that and the incident which had happened one hundred years before at the same spot. Mr Protheroe took the point but insisted that 'murder' was the 'more precise and accurate word'. So 'murder' was used. But there remains some difference of view at the BBC over the use of those particular words. Both Peter Woon and Robin Walsh said they would have said the 'assassination' of Airey Neave – as they would of Lord Mountbatten or of Mrs Thatcher had the Brighton bomb killed the Prime Minister. 'We had no hesitation in saying it of Mrs Ghandi.' But in the end they would be governed by any guidance given by the Director General's Office.

ITN operates on much the same principles although structurally it enjoys a greater degree of independence. David Nicholas, ITN's editor, explained that there are no written rules and that the use of these words had evolved over a period of time. 'We do refer to "terrorist explosions" in the UK', he said, 'but on the whole we prefer to say "bombers" or "gunmen". Occasionally we refer to the IRA as "terrorists". The IRA is outside the law – we have an anti-terrorist squad and anti-terrorist laws, so I wouldn't object to the use of the word. We never use the word "guerrilla", or "guerrilla army" – although that's what they might be. We try to find the most neutral word and that's not because we're impartial – we're not as far as the IRA is concerned.' Is there a difference between reporting political violence at home and overseas? 'I suppose there is a different standard when it applies in our own society', he admitted; 'we operate within the rules of a parliamentary democracy and we are observers of the laws passed by that democracy.'

I also spoke with those directly responsible for the local television output in Northern Ireland where every word is open to scrutiny by both communities and where the images and descriptions of political violence are redirected at the society from which it springs. Derek Murray, Ulster Television's Head of Local Programmes said: 'We have no policy, but it's probably true to say that we're less likely to use the word "terrorist" because they come from within our own society.

We're more inclined to talk about "paramilitaries" or use the recognised title of the organisations involved. We tend to use impersonal terms like "a terrorist bomb" or "support for terrorism" rather than the personal term "he is a terrorist". We recognise that "terrorist" is a term used by those who don't agree and that those who do agree would call them "freedom fighters" – but it's a term we would never use.' Would Ulster Television ever refer to IRA guerrillas? 'No, it's just not part of the language. Those terms are much more easily bandied about at a distance.' Would you refer to guerrilla warfare? 'Yes, to describe the nature of the operation.' So aren't they guerrillas? 'Yes', he smiled, 'I can see the logic but words spin off a typewriter without contemplating your navel.'

At Broadcasting House in Belfast, James Hawthorne, the BBC Controller Northern Ireland, said it was general policy to offend the least number of people. He used the Hunger Strike in the H-Blocks as an example of the great sensitivity of language. Every time a reporter spoke, he risked offending one section of the community as Protestants said 'Aitch-Blocks' and Catholics said 'Haitch-Blocks'. For grammatical reasons, the BBC decided that the Protestant version should prevail. I asked Mr Hawthorne about 'terrorist' and 'guerrilla'. He said that 'terrorist' was now seldom used as it was a word which faded in and out. But it was, he admitted, a word which was affected by political change, notably the rise of Sinn Fein. 'Guerrilla would jar', he said; 'it would get in the way of understanding. To introduce it now would produce 50 phone calls and cause an unnecessary additional obstacle to our credibility.' What about 'murder' and 'assassinate'? 'Assassination bestows rank on the victim but it also confers respectability on the part of the perpetrators. We've used both terms in relation to Airey Neave. Murder is not a neutral term. But we would use the words "shot dead" to describe the killing by the RUC of two suspected INLA men in Armagh. The SDLP and Sinn Fein would say "murder". We try to be neutral whilst trying to reflect something which society demands of us.'

But perhaps the most sensitive problem of all arises when the media have to report actions of the security forces which lead to the death of civilians. It is true that the popular perception of the civilian death-toll in Northern Ireland is often that responsibility for it lies with the IRA. The figures should be carefully analysed before any such judgement is made. By November 1984 a total of over 2,400 people had been killed in Northern Ireland. Over 1,300 of them were civilians. These figures are furnished by the Irish Information Partnership which provided much of the statistical evidence for the New Ireland Forum report. The Partnership's definition of 'civilians' is 'persons without manifest connection with paramilitaries, security forces, police or prison services'. It is worth noting that the RUC's definition of 'civilians' includes *all* those who are not members of the security forces. This means that any paramilitary who is killed is recorded as a 'civilian' death, following the logic of the policy followed by successive governments that the security forces are not fighting armed revolutionaries (or guerrillas) but common criminals. The breakdown of the agencies responsible for these *civilian* deaths show that the IRA is far from being entirely to blame. Since 1969 it is estimated that loyalist paramilitaries have been responsible for over 560 'civilian' deaths, republican paramilitaries for over 490 'civilian' deaths and the security forces (British Army, UDR and RUC) for 160 'civilian' deaths. (In all, according to a parliamentary answer given in June 1985, the security forces on duty have shot and killed 253 people since 1969.) The balance is made up of over 140 'unidentified and others'. The Irish Information Partnership concludes: 'it appears that well over half of those killed by the security forces over the past 15 years have been civilians. In three of the last four years, two thirds of those casualties were civilians.'

So how do the media describe the innocent victims of what some would call 'state violence' like John Boyle of Dunloy shot dead by the SAS in 1978 or Patrick McElhone of Pomeroy killed by a British soldier in 1974? Boyle was a 16-year-old Catholic who found an arms cache in a local graveyard and informed the police. When he returned out of curiosity, he was shot dead by two SAS men who had staked out the hiding-place. McElhone was a 22-year-old farmer's son who had been questioned by an army patrol which was searching the family farm. After he was told he could go on his way, a soldier was sent to fetch him back for further questioning. The soldier called on him to halt. When McElhone started to run away, the soldier shot him dead, thinking, as he told the court, he was a 'terrorist' trying to flee. In both cases, the judges acknowledged that both Boyle and McElhone were completely innocent. No doubt most journalists would refer to them being 'killed' or 'shot dead' by the security forces. But to anyone else reporting outside the political consensus, these shootings, like the shootings on Bloody Sunday, would be seen as murder pure and simple and recorded as such. The fact that I use 'shot dead' and 'killed' to describe the deaths of Boyle and McElhone indicates the difficult path one treads in working within a political framework which is itself under strain from the events one is reporting. Unlike the definitions in the dictionaries, the semantics of political violence are neither pure nor simple. The best one can hope for is to free the vocabulary from subjective political judgement and keep the words as far as possible consistent, accurate and honest.

221

Philip Elliott: A Bibliography

Books

Demonstrations and Communication: A Case Study. Harmondsworth: Penguin Books, 1970, 319pp. (with J. D. Halloran and G. Murdock).

The Sociology of the Professions. London: Macmillan, 1972, ix + 180pp. (Spanish edn 1975).

The Making of a Television Series: A Case Study in the Sociology of Culture. London: Constable, 1972, ix + 180pp.

Making the News. London: Longman, 1979, xi + 241pp. (with P. Golding).

Televising 'Terrorism': Political Violence in Popular Culture. London: Comedia, 1983, 181pp. (with P. Schlesinger and G. Murdock).

Research Reports

Peppermill 1969: Report on a Study of a Danish Television Series for Young People. Copenhagen. Danish Radio, 1970, 126pp.

Television For Children and Young People. Geneva. European Broadcasting Union, 1970, vii + 134pp. (with J. D. Halloran).

Contributions to books and conference proceedings

Television for children and young people: a summary of a survey carried out for the European Broadcasting Union, in *Television Research Committee: Second Progress Report and Recommendations*. Leicester: Leicester University Press, 1969, Appendix E, pp. 95–106 (with J.D. Halloran).

'The nature of prejudice', in *Sixth EBU Seminar on Teaching by Television: Adult Education*. Geneva: European Broadcasting Union, 1969.

'Selection and communication in a television production', in Tunstall, J. (ed.), *Media Sociology*. London: Constable, 1970, pp. 221–38.

'Some practical problems', in Halloran, J. D. and Gurevitch, M. (eds),

223

Broadcaster/Researcher Co-operation in Mass Communication Research. Leicester: Centre for Mass Communication Research, 1971, pp. 104–13.

'The process of television production', in Chaney, D., *Processes of Mass Communication*. London: Macmillan, 1972, pp. 97–114 (with D. Chaney).

'Mass communication: a contradiction in terms?', in McQuail, D. (ed.), *Sociology of Mass Communications*. Harmondsworth: Penguin Books, 1972, pp. 237–58.

'The news media and foreign affairs', in Boardman, R. and Groom, A. J. R. (eds), *The Management of Britain's External Relations*. London: Macmillan, 1973, pp. 305–32 (with P. Golding).

'Communication technologies and the future of the broadcasting professions', in Gerbner, G. *et al.* (eds), *Communications Technology and Social Policy*. New York: Wiley, 1973, pp. 505–19 (with Michael Gurevitch).

'Uses and gratifications research: a critique and a sociological alternative', in *Uses and Gratifications Studies: Theories and Methods*. Stockholm: Sveriges Radio Publik-Och Programforskning, SR/Pub, 1974, pp. 145–74. Reprinted in Blumer, J. and Katz, E. (eds), *The Uses of Mass Communications*. London: Sage Publications, 1974, pp. 149–68.

'Selection and communication in a television production', in Tuchman, G. (ed.), *The Television Establishment*. New York: Prentice-Hall, 1974, pp. 72–90.

'Mass communication and social change', in de Kadt, E. and Williams, G. (eds), *Sociology and Development*. London: Tavistock, 1974, pp. 229–54 (with P. Golding).

'Reporting Northern Ireland: a study of news in Britain, Ulster and the Irish Republic', in *Media and Ethnicity*. Paris: UNESCO, 1977, pp. 263–376.

'Media organisations and occupation: an overview', in Curran, J. *et al.* (eds), *Mass Communication and Society*. London: Edward Arnold, 1977, pp. 142–73.

'Professional ideology and organisational change: the journalist since 1800', in Boyce G. *et al.* (eds), *Newspaper History: From the 17th Century to the Present Day*. London: Constable, 1978, pp. 172–91.

'All the world's a stage or what's wrong with the national press', in Curran, J. (ed.), *The British Press: A Manifesto*. London: Macmillan, 1978, pp. 141–70.

'Production and the political content of broadcasting', in Clark, M. (ed.), *Politics and the Media*. Oxford: Pergamon, 1979, pp. 17–24.

'Information, propaganda and the British army', in *The British Media and Northern Ireland*. London: Information on Ireland, 1979, pp. 36–7.

'Eurocommunism: their word or ours?', in Childs, D. (ed.),*The Changing Face of Western Communism*. London: Croom Helm, 1980, pp. 37–73 (with P. Schlesinger).

'Press performance as political ritual', in Christian, H. (ed.), *The Sociology of Journalism and the Press*. University of Keele, Sociological Review Monograph no. 29, 1980, pp. 141–77. Reprinted in Whitney, D. C. *et al.* (eds), *Mass Communication Review Yearbook*, Vol. 3. London: Sage Publications, 1982, pp. 583–620.

Periodical, magazine and newspaper articles

'European broadcasters and children's television', *Television Quarterly*, 9 (3), 1969, pp. 65–75.

'A sociological framework for the study of television production', *Sociological Review, 17(3)*, 1969, pp. 355–75 (with D. Chaney).

'Professional ideology and social situation', *Sociological Review, 21*, 1973, pp. 211–28. Reprinted in Esland, G. *et al.* (eds), *People and Work.* London: Holmes McDougall, 1975, pp. 275–86.

'Misreporting Ulster: news as field–dressing', *New Society*, 25 November 1976, pp. 398–401.

'Misreporting Northern Ireland', *Irish Times*, 14 December 1976, p. 10.

'All the views fit to print', *New Internationalist, 47*, 1977, pp. 10–11.

'Vzytkowanie i Korzysci', *Przekazy i Opinie, 10 (4)*, 1977, pp. 49–64.

'Some aspects of communism as a cultural category', *Media, Culture and Society, 1 (2)*, 1979, pp. 195–210 (with P. Schlesinger).

'On the stratification of political knowledge: studying "Eurocommunism", an Unfolding Ideology', *Sociological Review, 27 (1)*, 1979, pp. 55–81 (with P. Schlesinger).

'The mass media and the manipulation of culture', *Massa Communicatie, IX (3)*, 1981, pp. 114–24.

'The state and "terrorism" on British television', *L'Immagine Dell'Uomo*, Spring 1982, pp. 77–130 (with P. Schlesinger and G. Murdock). Translated into Italian in Ferrarotti, F. (ed.), *Terrorismo e TV*, Vol. 2. Rome: Radiotelevisione Italiana, 1981, pp. 1–123. Abbreviated version published as 'Terrorism and the state: a case study of the discourses of television', *Media, Culture and Society, 5 (2)*, 1983, pp. 155–77. Reprinted in Collins, R. *et al.* (eds), *Media, Culture and Society: A Reader.* London: Sage Publications (forthcoming).

'Intellectuals, the "information society" and the disappearance of the public sphere', *Media, Culture and Society, 4*, 1982, pp. 243–53. Reprinted in Wartella *et al.* (eds), *Mass Communication Review Yearbook*, Vol. 4. London: Sage Publications, 1983, pp. 569–79 and in Collins, R. *et al.* (eds), *Media, Culture and Society: A Reader.* London: Sage Publications (forthcoming).

Contributors

John Zaven Ayanian graduated Summa cum Laude from Duke University with distinction in history and political science. His research interests have included: terrorism and the media, racism in health care and medical anthropology. He has also worked as a science reporter for the Portland *Oregonian*. Currently he is a student at Harvard Medical School.

Jay G. Blumler is Director of the Centre for Television Research at the University of Leeds, where he also holds a personal chair in the Social and Political Aspects of Broadcasting. In addition, he serves as Associate Director of the Center for Research in Public Communication at the University of Maryland. His extensive writings on political communication topics include: *Television in Politics: Its Uses and Influence* (1968); *The Challenge of Election Broadcasting* (1978); *Communicating to Voters: Television in the First European Parliamentary Elections* (1983).

Roger Bolton is Head of the BBC's Network Production Centre in Manchester, which includes in its journalistic output *Brass Tacks* on BBC 2 and *File on 4* on Radio 4. He joined the BBC in 1967, and was Editor of *Panorama*, *Nationwide* and *Tonight* before moving to Manchester in October 1983. During his editorship of *Panorama* he was involved in a number of controversies over programmes about the security services and Ireland (transmitted and untransmitted) and was libelled by the *Daily Telegraph*. He also edited the series of *Nationwide* Election programmes in 1983.

David Chaney is a Senior Lecturer in Sociology, University of Durham. He has worked in the field of mass communication studies as part of a more general concern with the sociology of culture for a number of years now, and was a colleague of Philip Elliott in the early years of the Leicester Centre for Mass Communication Research. His recent research has been into forms of spectacular imagery and social ceremonialization in different cultural contexts. He is the author of two books: *Processes of Mass Communication* (1972) and *Fictions and Ceremonies* (1979), and a number of papers in scholarly journals and collections.

John Downing holds the chair of the Communications Department, Hunter College, City University of New York. He was previously Head of the Sociology Division, Thames Polytechnic, London. His publications include: *The Media Machine* (1980) and *Radical Media* (1984). He is currently preparing a book on *Film and Politics in the Third World* (Praeger, NY) and researching Soviet international satellite communication, and Spanish-language media in greater New York.

Nicholas Garnham has been Head of the School of Media Studies at the Polytechnic of Central London since 1973. After studying English Literature at Cambridge he worked in television from 1962 to 1972 as a film editor and as a producer and director of arts programmes and documentaries for both the BBC and ITV. He is a founding editor of the quarterly review *Media, Culture and Society* of whose editorial board Philip Elliott was a member. He is the author of *The New Priesthood* (with Joan Bakewell), *The Structure of Television* and *Samuel Fuller*.

Peter Golding is Research Fellow at the University of Leicester Centre for Mass Communication Research. He worked for several years with Philip Elliott on comparative research into broadcast journalism. His current research is on various aspects of the links between the media and social policy. He is the author of *The Mass Media; Making The News* (with Philip Elliott); and *Images of Welfare* (with Sue Middleton).

Michael Gurevitch is a Professor and Director of the Center for Research in Public Communication at the College of Journalism, University of Maryland, USA. Prior to that he was on the staff of the Open University in Britain. He worked with Philip Elliott on aspects of broadcasting professionalism. His current research is concerned with the relationship between the media and political institutions and with media portrayals of social issues and political events. He is co-author of *The Secularization of Leisure* and *The Challenge of Election Broadcasting* and co-editor of *Mass Communication and Society; Culture, Society and the Media* and *Mass Communication Review Yearbook*, Vols 5 and 6.

Edward S. Herman is Professor of Finance at the Wharton School, University of Pennsylvania, specializing in financial and corporate structure and power. He also teaches a course on the Political Economy of the Mass Media in the Annenberg School of Communications at the University of Pennsylvania. His major recent writings include: *The Political Economy of Human Rights* (1979) (with Noam Chomsky); *Corporate Control, Corporate Power* (1981); *The Real Terror Network: Terrorism in Fact and Propaganda* (1982); *Demonstration Elections: US-Staged Elections in the Dominican Republic, Vietnam and El Salvador* (1984) (with Frank Brodhead).

Stuart Hood has had a distinguished career in broadcasting. In addition to writing and producing a wide range of programmes he has been: Editor, Television News BBC; Controller of Programmes BBC and Controller of Programmes Rediffusion TV. He has also held a number of academic positions including: Professor of Film and Television, Royal College of Arts; Lecturer in Communication Studies, Goldsmiths' College, University of London; Lecturer in Film and

Television, London College of Printing; Lecturer in Film Studies, State University of New York. His publications include: *The Mass Media* (1972); *Radio and Television* (1975); *On Television* (1982).

Denis McQuail is Professor of Mass Communications at the University of Amsterdam. Prior to that he taught in the Sociology Department of Southampton University. His main research interests have been in political communication, audience research and media evaluation research for policy. In this connection, he worked as academic adviser to the British Royal Commission on the Press, 1974–7 and as adviser to the Scientific Council for Government Policy in the Netherlands, 1981–2. He is currently engaged in a cross-national study of policies towards the new electronic media in Europe. His publications include: *Television and the Political Image* (with J. Trenaman) (1961); *Television in Politics* (with J. Blumler) (1968); *Towards a Sociology of Mass Communication* (1969); *Communication* (1975); *Communication Models* (with S. Windahl) (1982); *Mass Communication Theory* (1983).

Graham Murdock is Research Fellow at the University of Leicester Centre for Mass Communication Research and has been Visiting Professor at the Free University of Brussels and the University of California, San Diego. He worked with Philip Elliott on studies of the media coverage of political demonstrations and of terrorism. His current research is concerned with the impact of new communications media and with the political economy of the communications industries. His publications include: *Mass Media and the Secondary School* (1973) (with Guy Phelps); *Demonstrations and Communication* (1970) (with James Halloran and Philip Elliott); *Televising 'Terrorism'* (1984) (with Philip Elliott and Philip Schlesinger).

David L. Paletz is a Professor of Political Science at Duke University (Durham, North Carolina) where he teaches many courses including Politics and the Media, Political Participation and the American Presidency. In 1984 he received the Duke University's Alumni Distinguished Undergraduate Teaching Award. He is the co-author of *Media Power Politics* (1981) and *Politics in Public Service Advertising on Television* (1977), and editor of *Political Communication Research: Approaches, Studies, Assessments* (1985).

Dan Schiller is Associate Professor of Communications at Temple University, Philadelphia. He previously worked with Philip Elliott on an international study of journalists at the Centre for Mass Communication Research. He is author of *Objectivity and the News* (1981), *Telematics and Government* (1982) and *The Information Commodity*, to be published by Oxford University Press.

Philip Schlesinger is currently Head of Sociology at Thames Polytechnic, London. He is an editor of the journal *Media, Culture and Society* and has been a Nuffield Social Science Research Fellow and a Jean Monnet Fellow at the European University Institute. He collaborated with Philip Elliott in work on the media coverage of Northern Ireland, Eurocommunism, the intellectuals and terrorism. He is the author of *Putting 'Reality' Together* (1978), co-author of *Televising 'Terrorism'* (1983) (with Philip Elliott and Graham Murdock) and has written numerous articles on the political sociology of communication.

229

Peter Taylor was educated at Cambridge University, 1962–7. He reported for Thames Television's *This Week* throughout the 1970s and for BBC TV's *Panorama* since 1980. He has covered domestic, social and political issues as well as Vietnam, the Middle East, the USA and Africa. He has written and reported widely on the Irish Question and has made over 40 documentaries on the subject. He is the author of *Beating the Terrorists?* which won the Cobden Trust Award for the greatest contribution to human rights in 1981 and of *Smoke Ring – The Politics of Tobacco* (1984).

References

ARONSON, J., 1970. *The Press and the Cold War*. Boston: Beacon Press.

ABEL, E., 1955. 'US to shape test of Red "peace" aim in capital talks', *New York Times*, 12 June.

ABRAMS, E., 1983. 'The new effort to control information', *New York Times Magazine*, 25 September.

ADAM SMITH INSTITUTE, 1984. *Omega Report: Communications Policy*. London: Adam Smith Institute.

ADAMS, B., 1984. 'The frustrations of government service', *Public Administration Review*, 44 (1).

ALDEN, R., 1973. 'U.N. aviation body condemns Israel', *New York Times*, 1 March.

ALEXANDER, J. C., 1981. 'The mass media in systemic, historical and comparative perspective', in Katz, E. and Szecsko, T. (eds), *Mass Media and Social Change*. Beverly Hills, Calif.; Sage Publications.

ALPEROVITZ, G, 1965. *Atomic Diplomacy*. New York: Simon and Schuster.

ANDERSON, B., 1983. *Imagined Communities: Reflections on the Origin and Spread of Nationalism*. London: Verso Books.

AUBREY, C. (ed.), 1982. *Nukespeak: The Media and the Bomb*. London: Comedia Publishing.

BAGDIKIAN, B., 1983. *The Media Monopoly*. Boston, Mass.: Beacon Press.

BALL, H. (ed.), 1984. *Federal Administrative Agencies: Essays on Power and Politics*. Englewood Cliffs, NJ: Prentice-Hall.

BARKER, M. (ed.), 1984. *The Video Nasties: Freedom and Censorship in the Media*. London: Pluto Press.

BARNOUW, E., 1966. *A History of Broadcasting in the United States*, Vol. 1: *A Tower in Babel*. New York: Oxford University Press.

BELFRAGE, C. and ARONSON, J., 1978. *Something to Guard*. New York: Columbia University Press.

BELLANDO, E., 1984. *War Coverage: The Case of the Falklands*. University of Missouri School of Journalism, Freedom of Information Centre Report 494.

BIRNBAUM, N., 1955. 'Monarchs and sociologists', *Sociological Review*, 3 (1).

BLUMLER, J. G., 1969. 'Producers' attitudes towards television coverage of an election campaign: a case study', in Halmos, P. (ed.), *The Sociology of Mass Media Communicators*. University of Keele, Sociological Review Monograph no. 13.

BLUMLER, J. G. (ed.), 1983. *Communicating to Voters: Television in the First European Parliamentary Elections*. Beverly Hills, Calif: Sage Publications.

BLUMLER, J. G., 1984. 'The sound of Parliament', *Parliamentary Affairs, 37 (3)*.

BLUMLER, J. G., and GUREVITCH, M., 1975. 'Toward a comparative framework for political communication research', in Chaffe, S. H. (ed.), *Political Communications*. Beverly Hills, Calif: Sage Publications.

BLUMLER, J. G. and GUREVITCH, M., 1981. 'Politicians and the press: an essay on role relationships', in Nimmo, D. D. and Sanders, K. R. (eds), *Handbook of Political Communication*. Beverly Hills, Calif.: Sage Publications.

BLUMLER, J. G., GUREVITCH, M. and IVES, J., 1978. *The Challenge of Election Broadcasting*. Leeds University Press.

BLUMLER, J. G. and MCQUAIL, D., 1968. *Television in Politics*. London: Faber.

BOGART, L., 1982. 'Newspapers in transition', *The Wilson Quarterly, 6 (5)*.

BOYCE, G. *et al.* (eds), 1978. *Newspaper History: From the 17th Century to the Present Day*. London: Constable.

BRIGGS, A., 1961. *The History of broadcasting in the United Kingdom*, Vol. 1: *The Birth of Broadcasting*. London: Oxford University Press.

BRODHEAD, F. and HERMAN, E. S., 1983. 'The KGB plot to assassinate the pope: a case study in free world disinformation', *Covert Action Information Bulletin, 19*.

BURNHAM, D., 1984a. 'Computer dossiers prompt concern', *New York Times*, 10 June.

BURNHAM, D., 1984b. 'Study says thousands sign censorship pacts', *New York Times*, 14 June.

BURNHAM, D., 1984c. 'U.S.I.A. plans satellite news parleys', *New York Times*, 3 February.

BURNHAM, D., 1984d. '500,000 more spy-proof phones proposed by top security agency', *New York Times*, 7 October.

BURNS, T., 1977. *The BBC: Public Institution and Private World*. London: Macmillan.

BURROWS, A., 1924. *The story of Broadcasting*. London: Cassell.

CANNADINE, D., 1983. 'The context, performance and meaning of ritual', in Hobsbawm, E. and Ranger, T. (eds), *op. cit.* below.

CARDIFF, D., 1980. 'The serious and the popular: aspects of the evolution of style in the radio talk, 1928–1939', *Media, Culture and Society, 12 (1)*.

CASEY, W. L. *et al.*, 1983. *Entrepreneurship, Productivity and the Freedom of Information Act*. Lexington, Mass.: D. C. Heath.

CHANEY, D., 1983. 'A symbolic mirror of ourselves: civic ritual in mass society', *Media, Culture and Society, 5 (2)*.

CHANEY, D. and PICKERING, M., 1986. 'Democracy and communication: mass observation 1937–45', *Journal of Communication*.

CHOMSKY, N. and HERMAN, E., 1979. *The Washington Connection*. Boston, Mass.: South End Press.

CLOSE, A. C. (ed.), 1983. *National Directory of Corporate Public Affairs 1983*. Washington, DC: Columbia Books.

COHEN, S. and YOUNG, J. (eds), 1973. *The Manufacture of News: Deviance, Social Problems and the Mass Media*. London: Constable.

CROSS, J. M., 1982. 'The sound broadcasting of Parliament', *Independent Broadcasting, 32.*

CURTIS, L., 1984. *Ireland: The Propaganda War.* London: Pluto Press.

DALTON, H., 1935. *Practical Socialism for Britain.* London: Routledge.

DEMAC, D., 1984. *Keeping America Uninformed.* New York: Pilgrim Press.

DOWNING, J., 1975. 'The (balanced) white view', in Husband, C. (ed.), *White Media, Black Britain.* London: Arrow Books.

DOWNING, J., 1984. *Radical Media: The Political Experience of Alternative Communication.* Boston, Mass.: South End Press.

DRUCKER, P. F., 1984. 'Beyond the bell breakup', *The Public Interest, 77.*

ELLIOTT, P., 1971. 'Some practical problems', in Halloran, J. D. and Gurevitch, M. (eds), *Broadcaster/Researcher Co-operation in Mass Communication Research.* Leicester: Centre for Mass Communication Research.

ELLIOTT, P., 1972. *The Making of a Television Series.* London: Constable.

ELLIOTT, P., 1974. 'Uses and gratifications research: a critique and a sociological alternative', in Blumler, J. and Katz, E. (eds), *The Uses of Mass Communication.* Beverly Hills, Calif.: Sage Publications.

ELLIOTT, P., 1977. 'Media organisations and occupations', in Curran, J., Gurevitch, M. and Wollocott, J. (eds), *Mass Communication and Society.* London: Arnold.

ELLIOTT, P., 1978. 'All the world's a stage: or what's wrong with the British Press', in Curran, J. (ed). *The British Press: A Manifesto.* London: Macmillan.

ELLIOTT, P., 1980. 'Press performance as political ritual', in Christian, H. (ed.), *The Sociology of Journalism and the Press.* University of Keele, Sociological Review Monograph no. 29.

ELLIOTT, P., 1982. 'Intellectuals, the "information society" and the disappearance of the public sphere', *Media, Culture and Society, 4 (3).*

ELLIOTT, P. and GOLDING, P., 1974. 'Mass communication and social change: the imagery of development and the development of imagery', in De Kadt, E. and Williams, G. (eds), *Sociology and Development.* London: Tavistock.

ELLIOTT, P., MURDOCK, G. and SCHLESINGER, P., 1983. '"Terrorism" and the state: a case study of the discourses of television', *Media, Culture and Society, 5 (2).*

ELLIOTT, P. and SCHLESINGER, P., 1979a. 'Analysing ideological production: the case of "Eurocommunism"'. Paper presented to the Social Science Research Council/British Sociological Association Methodology Conference.

ELLIOTT, P. and SCHLESINGER, P., 1979b. 'On the stratification of political knowledge: studying "Eurocommunism" , an unfolding ideology', *Sociological Review, 27 (1).*

ELLIOTT, P. and SCHLESINGER, P., 1979c. 'Some aspects of communism as a cultural category', *Media, Culture and Society, 1 (2).*

ELLIOTT, P. and SCHLESINGER, P., 1980. 'Eurocommunism: their world or ours?', in Childs, D. (ed.), *The Changing Face of Western Communism.* London: Croom Helm.

ENZENSBERGER, H. M., 1976. *Raids and Reconstructions: Essays in Politics, Crime and Culture.* London: Pluto Press.

EPSTEIN, E., 1973. *News from Nowhere: Television and the News.* New York: Vintage.

FARRELL, W. E., 1984. 'Reagan used U.S.I.A.'s global network,' *New York Times,* 17 January.

FEDER, B. J., 1984. 'Markets role aids growth at Reuters', *New York Times,* 28 May.

FRIEDMAN, R., 1984. 'All-out battle: Westmorland's suit against CBS raises unusual libel issues', *Wall Street Journal*, 1 October.

FRIENDLY, J., 1984 'Pentagon news panel hears testimony', *New York Times*, 9 February.

FUERBRINGER, J., 1984. 'Washington watch', *New York Times*, 28 May.

FULBRIGHT, J. W., 1970. *The Pentagon Propaganda Machine*. New York: Liveright Publishing Co.

GAMAREKIAN, B., 1984. 'Press corps and government, at later perspective,' *New York Times*, 20 February.

GANS, H., 1979. *Deciding What's News: A Study of CBS Evening News, NBC Nightly News, Newsweek and Time*, New York: Pantheon.

GARBUS, M., 1984. 'New challenge to press freedom,' *New York Times Magazine*, January 29.

GARNHAM, N., 1983. 'Public service versus the market,' *Screen, 24 (1)*.

GERBNER, G., GROSS, L. *et al.*, 1980. 'The "mainstreaming" of America; Violence Profile No. 11', *Journal of Communication, 30 (3)*.

GERVASI, T., 1984. 'Reckless endangerment; the attack on Korean Airlines Flight 7 and America's response', *Evergreen Review*, May.

GITLIN, T., 1980. *The Whole World is Watching: Mass Media in the Making and Unmaking of the New Left*. Berkeley, Calif.: University of California Press.

GLABERSON, W., 1984. 'Corporate secrecy versus the public's right to know', *Business Week*, 13 February.

GLASGOW UNIVERSITY MEDIA GROUP 1976. *Bad News*. London: Routledge and Kegan Paul.

GLASGOW UNIVERSITY MEDIA GROUP 1980. *More Bad News*. London: Routledge and Kegan Paul.

GOLDENBERG, E. N., 1975. *Making the Papers: The Access of Resource-Poor Groups to the Metropolitan Press*. Lexington, Mass.: D. C. Heath.

GOLDING, P. and ELLIOTT, P., 1979. *Making the News*. London: Longman.

GOLDING, P. and MIDDLETON, S., 1982. *Images of Welfare: Press and Public Attitudes to Poverty*. Oxford: Martin Robertson.

GOMERY, D., 1984. 'Economic change in the U.S. television industry', *Screen, 25 (2)*.

GORDON, L., 1938. *The Public Corporation in Great Britain*. London: Oxford University Press.

GOULDNER, A., 1976. *The Dialectic of Ideology and Technology*. New York: Seabury Press.

GOWING, M., 1978. *Reflections on Atomic Energy History*. Cambridge: Cambridge University Press.

GRABER, D., 1971. 'The press as opinion resource during the 1968 presidential election', *Public Opinion Quarterly, 35 (2)*.

GREENBERG, D. W., 1985. 'Staging media events to achieve legitimacy: a case study of Britain's friends of the Earth', *Political Communication and Persuasion, 2(4)*.

GROSSMAN, M. B. and ROURKE, F. E., 1976. 'The media and the presidency: an exchange analysis', *Political Science Quarterly, 91 (3)*.

GWERTZMAN, B., 1973. 'US still hopes for Arab-Israeli dialogue', *New York Times*, 23 February.

HABERMAS, J., 1979. 'The public sphere', in Matterlart, A. and Siegelaub, S.

(eds), *Communication and Class Struggle*, Vol. 1, New York: International General.

HABERMAS, J., 1982. 'A reply to my critics', in Thompson, J. B. and Held, D. (eds), *Habermas: Critical Debates*. London: Macmillan.

HACKETT, R. A., 1984. 'Decline of a paradigm? Bias and objectivity in news media studies', *Critical Studies in Mass Communications*, 1 (3).

HALL, S., 1980. 'Encoding and decoding the television discourse', in Hall, S. *et al*. (eds), *Culture, Media, Language*. London: Hutchinson.

HALL, S., 1982. 'The rediscovery of "Ideology"; return of the repressed in media studies', in Gurevitch, M., Bennet, T., Curran, J. and Woollacott, J. (eds), *Culture, Society and the Media*. London: Methuen.

HALL, S. *et al.*, 1978. *Policing the Crisis; Mugging, the State, and Law and Order*. London: Macmillan.

HALLIN, D., 1983. 'The media go to war – from Vietnam to Central America', *NACLA report on the Americas*, July–August.

HALLORAN, R., 1984a. 'A nose for news and pseudo-news', *New York Times*, 14 June.

HALLORAN, R., 1984b. 'Pentagon forms war press pool; newspaper reporters excluded', *New York Times*, 11 October.

HARTLEY, J., 1982. *Understanding the News*. London: Methuen.

HEAD, S. W., 1972. *Broadcasting in America: A Survey of Television and Radio*. Boston, Mass.: Houghton Mifflin.

HEISE, J. A., 1979. *Minimum Disclosure*. New York: Norton.

HELD, D., 1980. *Introduction to Critical Theory: Horkheimer to Habermas*. London: Hutchinson.

HERMAN, E. S., 1981. *Corporate Control, Corporate Power*. New York: Cambridge University Press.

HERMAN, E. S., 1982. *The Real Terror Network: Terrorism in Fact and Propaganda*. Boston, Mass.: South End Press.

HERMAN, E. S., 1983. 'Michael Novak's promised land: unfettered corporate capitalism', *Monthly Review, 35* (5).

HERMAN, E. S., 1984. 'Objective news as systematic propaganda: the *New York Times* on the 1984 Salvadoran and Nicaraguan Elections', *Covert Action Information Bulletin, 21*.

HERMAN, E. S. and BRODHEAD, F., 1984. *Demonstration Elections: US-Staged Elections in the Dominican Republic, Vietnam and El Salvador*. Boston, Mass.: South End Press.

HERTSGAARD, M., 1983. *Nuclear Inc*. New York: Pantheon Books.

HESS, S., 1981. *The Washington Reporters*. Washington, DC: The Brookings Institute.

HILGARTNER, S. *et al.*, 1983. *Nukespeak: The Selling of Nuclear Technology in America*. New York: Penguin Books.

HIMMELWEIT, H. *et al.*, 1985. *How Voters Decide*. London: Academic Press.

HOBSBAWM, E., 1983. 'Inventing traditions', in Hobsbawm, E. and Ranger, T. (eds), *op.cit.* below.

HOBSBAWM, E. and RANGER, T. (eds), 1983. *The Invention of Tradition*. Cambridge: Cambridge University Press.

HOLLOWAY, D., 1983. *The Soviet Union and the Arms Race*. New Haven, Conn.: Yale University Press.

HOLTON, G., 1981. *Where Is Science Taking Us?* Washington, DC, National Endowment for the Humanities, Jefferson Lecture.

HUNTER, M., 1984. 'The 2,615 reports proposal', *New York Times*, 20 March.

JAROSLAVSKY, R., 1984. 'Reagan offers peaceful diplomacy scenes to counter his bellicose European image', *Wall Street Journal*, 6 June.

JENNINGS, H. and MADGE, C., 1937. *May 12, Mass Observation Day Survey.* London: Faber.

JONES, A., 1984a. 'A media industry innovator', *New York Times*, 30 April.

JONES, A., 1984b. 'Reuters offer spans Atlantic', *New York Times*, 16 May.

JUNGK, R., 1979. *The Nuclear State.* London: Calder.

KAPLAN, F., 1983. *The Wizards of Armageddon.* New York: Simon and Schuster.

KOENIG, R., 1984. 'Bell telephone companies plan move into local computer-data transmission', *Wall Street Journal*, 5 June.

LANE, C., 1981. *The Rites of Rulers: Ritual in Industrial Society – The Soviet Case.* London: Cambridge University Press.

LAZARSFELD, P. F. and MERTON, R. K., 1957. 'Mass communication, popular taste and organised social action', in Rosenberg, B. and White, D. M. (eds), *Mass Culture: The Popular Arts in America.* Glencoe, Ill.: The Free Press.

LOFLAND, L. H.., 1983. 'Understanding urban life', *Urban Life, 1 (4).*

MCCOLM, B., 1982. *El Salvador: Peaceful Revolution or Armed Struggle?* Freedom House, Perspective on Freedom.

MCFADDEN, M., 1984. 'Sponsor-backed cable programs catch on', *New York Times*, 10 June.

MCQUAIL, D., 1983. *Mass Communication Theory.* London: Sage Publications.

MCQUAIL, D. and VAN CUILENBURG, J. J., 1983. 'Diversity as a media policy goal: evaluative research and a Netherlands case study', *Gazette, 31 (3).*

MADDOX, R. J., 1973. *The New Left and the Origins of the Cold War.* Princeton, NJ: Princeton University Press.

MADGE, C., 1937. 'Anthropology at home', *New Statesman and Nation*, 2 January.

MADGE, C. and HARRISON, T., 1937. *Mass Observation.* London: Muller.

MARSHALL, T. H., 1937. 'Is mass observation moonshine?', *The Highway, 30.*

MASSING, M., 1984. 'Grenada, we will never know', *Index on Censorship*, February.

MATTERLART, A. and SIEGELAUB, S. (eds), 1979. *Communication and Class Struggle, Vol. 1.* New York: International General.

MAY, A. and ROWAN, K. (eds), 1982. *Inside Information: British Government and the Media.* London: Constable.

MAYER, J., 1984a. 'Reagan, in China, focuses on TV', *Wall Street Journal*, 27 April.

MAYER, J., 1984b. 'Right-wing thinkers push ideas', *Wall Street Journal*, 7 December.

MICHAEL, J., 1982. *The Politics of Secrecy.* Harmondsworth: Penguin Books.

MILIBAND, R., 1969. *The State in Capitalist Society: An Analysis of the Western System of Power.* London: Weidenfeld and Nicolson.

MOORE, S. F. and MYERHOFF, B. G., 1977. 'Secular ritual: forms and meanings', in Moore, S. F. and Meyerhoff, B. G. (eds), *Secular Ritual.* Amsterdam: Van Gorcum.

MOSCO, V., 1982. *Pushbutton Fantasies.* Norwood, NJ: Ablex.

MURDOCK, G. and GOLDING, P., 1977. 'Capitalism, communication and class relations', in Curran, J., Gurevitch, M. and Woolacott, J. (eds), *Mass Communication and Society*. London: Edward Arnold.

NEGT, O. and KLUGE, A., 1979. 'The proletarian public sphere', in Mattelart, A. and Siegelaub, S. (eds), *op. cit.*

NEW YORK TIMES, 1984. 'Downing of jet a year ago said to lead to US gains', *New York Times*, 31 August.

NOELLE-NEUMANN, E., 1980. *The Spiral of Silence: Public Opinion – Our Social Skin.* Munich: R. Piper.

PALETZ, D. L. and ENTMAN, R. M., 1981. *Media, Power, Politics.* New York: The Free Press.

PEARSON, D., 1984. 'K.A.L. 007: What the U.S. knew and when we knew it', *The Nation*, 18–25 August.

POLLACK, A., 1984a. 'Electronic almanacs are there for the asking', *New York Times*, 18 March.

POLLACK, A., 1984b. 'Selling phone information', *New York Times*, 5 April.

PYKE, G., 1936. 'King and country', *New Statesman and Nation*, 12 December.

ROBSON, W. A. (ed.), 1937. *Public Enterprise: Developments in Social Ownership and Control in Great Britain.* London: New Fabian Research Bureau.

ROSCHO, B., 1975. *Newsmaking.* Chicago: University of Chicago Press.

SAID, E., 1981. *Covering Islam.* New York: Pantheon Books.

SANDERS, J., 1983. *Peddlers of Crisis.* Boston, Mass.: South End Press.

SANDMAN, D., BRENT, R. and SACHSMAN, D., 1982. *Media: An Introductory Analysis Of American Mass Communications.* 3rd edn, Englewood Cliffs, NJ: Prentice-Hall.

SCANNELL, P., 1980. 'Broadcasting and the politics of unemployment. 1930–1935', *Media, Culture and Society, 12 (1).*

SCHILLER, A. R. and SCHILLER, H. I., 1982. 'Making information private', *The Nation*, 17 April.

SCHILLER, H. I., 1981. *Who Knows: Information in the Age of the Fortune 500.* Norwood, NJ: Ablex.

SCHLESINGER, P., MURDOCK, G. and ELLIOTT, P., 1983. *Televising 'Terrorism': Political Violence in Popular Culture.* London: Comedia Publishing.

SCHMID, A. P. and DE GRAAF, J., 1982. *Violence as Communication: Insurgent Terrorism in the Western Media.* Beverly Hills, Calif.: Sage Publications.

SEIB, G. F., 1983. 'Fearing Soviet gains, U.S. counterattacks in the propaganda war', *Wall Street Journal*, 17 May.

SELIGMAN, J., 1982. *The Transformation of Wall Street: A History of the Securities and Exchange Commission and Modern Corporate Finance.* Boston, Mass.: Houghton Mifflin.

SEYMOUR-URE, C., 1974. *The Political Impact of Mass Media.* London: Constable.

SHILS, E., 1956. *The Torment of Secrecy.* Glencoe, Ill.: The Free Press.

SHILS, E. and YOUNG, M., 1953. 'The meaning of the Coronation', *Sociological Review, 1 (2).*

SHRIBMAN, D., 1983. 'US experts say Soviet didn't see jet was civilian', *New York Times*, 7 October.

SIEBERT, F. S., PETERSON, T. and SCHRAMM, W., 1956. *Four Theories of the Press.* Urbana, Ill.: University of Illinois Press.

SIGAL, L., 1973. *Reporters and Officials.* Lexington, Mass.: D. C. Heath.

SMITH, A. (ed.), 1979. *Television and Political Life: Studies in Six European Countries.* London: Macmillan.

SMITH, S. B., 1984a. 'CBS buys Nixon interviews', *New York Times*, 13 March.

SMITH, S. B., 1984b. 'Electronic press kits pervade TV newscasts', *New York Times*, 30 January.

SMITH, T., 1973. 'Dayan blames Libyan jet', *New York Times*, 23 February.

THEBERGE, L. J., 1981. *Crooks, Con Men and Clowns: Business in TV Entertainment*. Washington, DC: The Media Institute.

TOINET, M. F., 1983. 'L'Amérique de M Reagan part en croisade pour la democratie', *Le Monde Diplomatique*, July.

TRACEY, M., 1978. *The Production of Political Television*. London: Routledge and Kegan Paul.

TREXLER, R. C., 1980. *Public Life in Renaissance Florence*. New York: Academic Press.

TUCHMAN, G., 1978. *Making News*. New York: The Free Press.

TUCHMAN, G., KAPLAN, D. A. and BENET, J. (eds), 1978. *Hearth and Home: Images of Women in the Mass Media*. New York: Oxford University Press.

TULLY, S., 1983. 'The big news at Reuters is its money machine', *Fortune*, 8 August.

TUNSTALL, J., 1970. *The Westminster Lobby Correspondents: A Sociological Study of National Political Journalism*. London: Routledge and Kegan Paul.

TUNSTALL, J., 1971. *Journalists at Work: Specialist Correspondents; Their News Organisations, News Sources, and Competitor Colleagues*. London: Constable.

UNITED STATES GENERAL ACCOUNTING OFFICE, 1984. *Report by the Comptroller General of the United States*, 'Effects on users of commercializing landsat and the weather satellites', GAO/RCED–84–93, 24 February.

UNITED STATES SENATE, 1975. Alleged assassination plots involving foreign leaders, *Interim Report of the Select Committee to Study Governmental Operations*, Report no. 94–465, 94th Congress, 1st Session, 18 November.

URQUART, B., 1972. *Hammerskjold*. New York: Knopf.

WEINER, R., 1980. *The Professional's Guide To Public Relations*. 4th edn, New York: Richard Weiner.

WESTERGAARD, J., 1977. 'Power, class and the media', in Curran, J., Gurevitch, M. and Woolacott, J. (eds), *Mass Communication and Society*. London: Edward Arnold.

WILLCOCK, H. D., 1943. 'Mass observation', *American Journal of Sociology*, 48 (4).

WILLIAMS, R., 1980. *The Nuclear Power Decisions: British Policies 1953–78*. London: Croom Helm.

WILSON, A., 1982. 'The defence correspondent', in Aubrey, C. (ed.), *op. cit.*

WOLF, L., 1984. 'Accuracy in media rewrites the news and history', *Covert Action*, 21.

WYNDHAM GOLDIE, G., 1972. 'The sociology of television', *The Listener*, 19 October.

Index